THE BATTLE FOR THE PACIFIC

Donald Macintyre

SAPERE
BOOKS

THE BATTLE FOR THE PACIFIC

Published by Sapere Books.
24 Trafalgar Road, Ilkley, LS29 8HH
United Kingdom

saperebooks.com

ISBN: 978-0-85495-377-6.

TABLE OF CONTENTS

PREFACE

The war in the Pacific, 7 December 1941 to 15 August 1945, though only one part of the cataclysmic Second World War, was, taken as a whole, by itself a wider-ranging and more intensive amphibious struggle than the world had ever seen. The two aspects of it — naval and military — are, of course, closely interlocked. Indeed, the influence of sea-power on the land fighting, each campaign of which was initially an amphibious operation, needs less stressing than in accounts of most wars.

On the other hand, so vast is the subject that nothing less than a work composed of scores of massive tomes could do it full justice or cover it adequately for the serious student. Even the official *History of United States Naval Operations in World War II* by Samuel Eliot Morison devotes nine of its fourteen volumes entirely to the Pacific theatre.

This single volume on the course of the naval operations is aimed at the non-professional reader who cannot devote the time to a study so detailed or so comprehensive. The inevitable compression results in somewhat superficial accounts of the major sea battles — those long-distance assaults by naval aircraft upon the carrier-centred fleets of their opponents and the defensive aerial fighting above them. The greatest of these have been the subjects of individual books. The several surface actions fought between the naval forces supporting the armies contesting the occupation of the island chain forming the southern limits of the Japanese conquests — the Solomons and the Bismarck Archipelago — have had less attention paid to them. This is perhaps because, more often than not, it was the eventual losers in the war who showed themselves so superior in that form of fighting.

Yet they are of considerable interest in that they demonstrate the triumph of human qualities instilled by intensive training, patriotic fervour and fanatical courage in a maritime people over material advantages enjoyed by opponents with less warlike inspiration operating in an element to which they were strangers. They took place by night when the scenario covering an area hundreds of miles in diameter, reaching out to the limits of the range of carrier-borne aircraft, shrank to the little circle of sea within the scope of human night vision aided, at first, only by binoculars.

Japanese possession, unknown to the Allies, of a torpedo of unprecedented range gave them a vital advantage. This, however, was not the only reason why the Americans and the few Allied units serving with them seemed amateurs in the ring with professionals. The Japanese were trained to a high degree of efficiency in night fighting; the crews of their opponents reflected the hasty expansion of their navy which threw them into battle lacking any expertise, the ships themselves being organised into squadrons with strangers; they suffered accordingly.

Even when the Americans acquired an effective surface-warning radar at a time when the Japanese had none, it still required time and some catastrophic defeats for them to learn how to take advantage of it.

In the air, too, the Americans and their Allies were caught unaware of the efficiency of men and material of the Japanese naval air arm. The British, without such justification as the Americans were able to claim from the treacherous nature of the Pearl Harbour attack, suffered the destruction of the *Prince of Wales* and *Repulse* by naval shore-based torpedo planes operating at a range far outside any that they believed possible. The chief surprise to the Americans was the superiority of the Japanese carrier-borne fighters and torpedo-planes over their own.

Fortunately the American Navy had, unlike the British, been able to retain their own, independent naval air arm; thus, not only did they have an effective strike plane in the Douglas 'Dauntless' scout-dive-bomber from the beginning, but, in Grumman's they had a firm of manufacturers with experience in the design of aircraft specially for carrier operation which was soon able to provide replacement fighters and torpedo-planes superior to those of the enemy.

Nevertheless there was a perilous period during which the U.S. Pacific Fleet was faced by a carrier superiority in quantity and quality, a situation they were only able to cope with through the inestimable advantage of having the key to the enemy's naval codes, and hence, his intentions. This enabled the Commander-in-Chief to deploy sufficient force in the crucial area, first in the Coral Sea and then off Midway.

Even after the 'incredible' victory at Midway there was an uneasy balance of naval air power with the Japanese qualities of fanatical, even suicidal courage and devotion in battle coming near to tipping it decisively in their favour. But the losses in trained and experienced aircrew entailed by such methods were far beyond their capability to replace them. The quality of their pilots fell rapidly away. The Americans were able to hold on until their vast industrial capacity could build up an enormously superior carrier fleet, which their huge naval air training organisation was able to produce a steady flow of experienced pilot replacements.

The outcome was the aerial massacre of the Japanese in the Battle of the Philippine Sea, the last desperate effort to force an old-fashioned surface battle off Leyte Gulf and, finally, the take-over of the suicide complex with the massed 'Kamikaze' attacks by half-trained boy pilots.

That sea-power alone cannot win wars is a truism, But perhaps never more certainly did it open the way to decisive victory than in the Pacific in the years 1942 to 1945. Japan had been totally defeated, mainly by sea-power, before the first atomic bomb was detonated over Hiroshima.

Donald Macintyre

1. THE PRE-WAR SITUATION

However unforeseen by the United States was the treacherous attack on Pearl Harbour which began the war between the Japanese Empire and the Western Allies, the war itself was the not unexpected culmination of a chain of events which had begun as long ago as 8 July 1937. On that day Japan had taken the first irrevocable step on the path which could only lead eventually to head-on collision with America and Britain and a choice between humiliation and war.

Ever since Japan, emerging from her long self-imposed seclusion, had signalled her accession to the ranks of world powers by her victorious wars with China and Russia, she had been resentful at the refusal of those Powers to allow her to retain the territorial spoils. A population explosion amongst her hard-working and skilful people called for territorial expansion. The rise to power of a militarist party, revering the martial Samurai traditions and inspired by the patriotic religious cult of Bushido, had made the pursuit of it by aggressive military means certain. The immediate object of their ambitions had been Manchuria.

In 1932 provocative acts by the Chinese, contrary to treaty obligations, against Japanese citizens in Manchuria had been made an excuse for occupation of the whole province and the establishment of a puppet regime. The half-hearted protests of the Western Powers to Japan and their acceptance of assurances with regard to the principle of the 'open door' had betrayed for the first time their unwillingness and the League of Nations' impotence to go to the aid of a victim of aggression. During the next five years, though she had signed the Nine-Power Peace Treaty of 1922, agreeing 'to respect the sovereignty, the independence and administrative integrity of China', Japan infiltrated steadily into the provinces of North China, taking advantage of the political confusion in the country. By July 1937 she was ready for the next step in open aggression. A manufactured 'incident' provided the excuse.

In accordance with treaty rights held since the Boxer War, 7,000 Japanese troops were maintained in the Peking-Tientsin area. On the night of 7-8 July, in the course of night manoeuvres, they 'attacked' the Marco Polo Bridge at Lukouchiao, 20 miles west of Peking. The Chinese 29th Army stationed in the area, taking the attack seriously, reacted vigorously. Casualties were heavy on both sides. The Japanese Government demanded satisfaction and, when this was acceded after prolonged negotiations, made the further demand that all Chinese troops should be withdrawn from the province of Hopei. The Chinese Government naturally refused.

The war which now followed, and was to continue until it merged with the Second World War, was not officially declared. Neither side wished to be classified as 'belligerents' with all the inconveniences that this would have entailed. Similarly, the United States, along with other Western Governments, avoided declaring that a state of war existed; for this would have invoked the American Neutrality Acts and would have prevented U.S. aid to China without which Chinese resistance must soon have ceased. On the other hand, bound by commercial treaty, the U.S.A, had to permit huge Japanese purchases of petroleum oils, iron ore and scrap. The situation was consistently referred to euphemistically by the Japanese as the 'China Incident'. Nevertheless it was a full-scale war which, while it impoverished Japan and drained her resources, enormously expanded her armed forces and gave them all the experience necessary to bring them to a concert pitch of efficiency at a time when the Western Powers were still struggling to arm themselves after the lotus years of appeasement.

Up to 1937 Japan had accepted the 5-5-3 ratio of naval strength agreed to by the Washington Naval Conference of 1921. With the expiration of the Naval Limitation Treaty in 1937 she was unshackled. Expansion of her fleet went ahead at a furious pace and included the laying down of the two biggest battleships in the world, the *Yamato* and *Musashi*, each mounting eight 18.1-inch guns. The most significant access of Japanese naval power, however, was in the field of naval aviation.

Having grasped at an early date the revolutionary effect of the air arm on naval warfare, the Japanese Navy had resisted the formation of an independent Air Force and had retained the equipment and control of naval aviation in its own hands. Aircraft of first-rate performance, excelling anything in the British or American Navies, came from the Mitsubishi and Nakajima factories, fighters, dive-bombers and torpedo-planes for the carriers and twin-engined bombers for the shore-based naval air fleets.

Barred until 1937 by treaty limitations from construction of aircraft carriers, Japan had taken full advantage of the concession which permitted conversion of existing hulls to produce two such ships, the *Kaga* and *Akagi*, and a light carrier, the *Hosho*. From their decks and from airfields in Kyushu and Formosa, aerial attack on the superior Chinese forces surrounding a Japanese garrison in Shanghai in August 1937 marked the opening of a campaign of bombing in support of the advancing Japanese armies, spreading to cities far inland up the Yangtse River, which was to continue intermittently for the next four years. Much of it was indiscriminate destruction of towns and slaughter of civilians. It brought down execration upon the perpetrators and the protests of the liberal Great Powers, but no positive action on their part. Great Britain and France were girding themselves against the war they knew was coming and could spare nothing but sympathy. The United States Government offered mediation and showered protests when American missionaries and their families were killed or property damaged; but they knew their people would not fight on China's behalf and even when the gunboat U.S.S. *Panay*, on the Yangtse, was deliberately bombed and sunk by Japanese naval planes in December 1937 and the survivors machine-gunned, they accepted the subsequent apologies for an 'unfortunate mistake' and an indemnity.

By July 1939, the whole Chinese coast, including the strategically significant island of Hainan dominating the Gulf of Tonkin, was in Japanese hands, and President Chiang Kai-Shek's Government had been driven far inland to Chungking where it was kept under constant aerial bombardment. The only route whereby American aid could reach China was over the tenuous Burma Road. Japanese terms for a peace settlement, which were such as to reduce China virtually to a colony, revealed their boundless ambitions. The last slender hope of checking them lay in the imposition of economic sanctions. President Roosevelt decided on 26 July to give the six months' notice, required by its terms, to abrogate the 1911 Treaty of Commerce.

The treaty duly lapsed on 26 January 1940. By means of discriminatory licensing, exports to Japan of aircraft and aircraft parts, aviation fuel and lubricating oil, and finally all iron and steel scrap, were then successively banned. In the crucial matter of oil fuel, however, Mr Grew, American Ambassador in Tokyo, had warned that an embargo would force Japan to turn south to seize what she wanted from the Dutch East Indies. Action went no further, therefore, than 'moral' persuasion of American shipowners and still permitted vast quantities to be shipped in neutral or Japanese vessels.

Nevertheless, bogged down in their war with China and encouraged by the catastrophes overwhelming the Allies in Europe, the Japanese now finally resolved on the southward drive to bring about the long wished-for 'Great East Asia Co-Prosperity Sphere'. From the powerless Vichy French Government they secured the right in August 1940 to occupy northern Indo-China. In the Marshall and Caroline Islands, held under League of Nations Mandate, they set about secretly preparing fortified naval and air bases. In September 1940 Japan allied herself defensively to Germany and Italy by the Tripartite Pact, and in April 1941 concluded a non-aggression pact with Russia which released Japanese forces guarding Manchuria. Finally in July 1941 she announced that Vichy France had consented to a joint protectorate of the whole of Indo-China, and Japanese forces began to move into the southern half of the country.

No doubt now remained as to Japan's intentions. With the Philippines directly threatened, America could hold back no longer. On 26 July 1941 all Japanese assets in the United States were 'frozen', effectively drying-up, for want of cash, supplies of oil from America or the Dutch East Indies. Thus a term was set — the period for which Japan could exist on her stored stocks of fuel and other raw materials — after which she must either ignominiously abandon her conquest of China and all her ambitious plans for imperial expansion, or go to war. With the militarists in unfettered control of Japanese policy, the former alternative was out of the question.

For the next four-and-a-half months diplomatic efforts to resolve the deadlock were earnestly pursued, but with the conditions for settlement of each side so totally inadmissible by the other that agreement was never in sight. A faint flicker of hope for a peaceful outcome remained until the eleventh hour in the minds of the opposing negotiators — the Japanese Ambassador, Admiral Nomura, and Secretary of State, Mr Cordell Hull — in spite of the uncompromising nature of Nomura's briefs, which were available to the State Department through American success in breaking the Japanese diplomatic cipher.

There was little doubt, however, in the minds of the Japanese military leaders. A comprehensive war plan had been prepared by which a complex southward thrust would be made to grasp, at the outset, the vital oil supplies of the East Indies. Thailand would be overrun; an amphibious force would invade Malaya and strike south towards Singapore; air-strikes on the Philippine Islands, supported by the whole Japanese Fleet, would be followed by invasion; the U.S. Fleet hurrying to the rescue would be harried by air and submarine attacks launched from the Marshalls and Carolines, before being brought to action by the superior Japanese Fleet in the Philippine Sea.

Such was the straightforward plan devised by the Japanese Army and Navy General Staffs, the latter headed by Admiral Osami Nagano. Early in 1941, however, it came under the critical scrutiny of the Commander-in-Chief of the Combined Fleet, Admiral Isoroku Yamamoto. An early convert to the paramountcy of carrier-borne air-power in naval warfare, he had seen the carrier force under his command grow in the last few years to six large and four smaller carriers equipped with the most advanced fighting aircraft in the world, capable of delivering a knock-out blow to an enemy fleet. To allocate to it a role so strategically defensive as that laid down in Nagano's plan dismayed him. With a realistic grasp of the true meaning of sea-power, Yamamoto had no illusions that Japan, an island empire totally dependent for its existence upon oversea supply, could wage successful war against America with its vast industrial potential and inexhaustible sources of fuel and raw material. When the conclusion of the Tripartite Pact had brought the likelihood of such a war closer, he had frankly warned the Premier, Prince Konoye, that: 'If I am told to fight regardless of consequence I shall run wild considerably for the first six months or a year, but I have utterly no confidence for the second and third years.'

Holding such views, he felt that any postponement of the initial clash with the U.S. Fleet would operate solely to the enemy's advantage. Even if the U.S. Pacific Fleet conveniently conformed to the Japanese plan and offered itself a target to the massive air and submarine attacks awaiting it, he feared the possibility of his own fleet being caught off balance, supporting the army's operations, when the time for battle arrived.

As early as January 1941, therefore, Yamamoto had begun to ponder the idea of using his naval air strength to destroy the U.S. Pacific Fleet by a surprise blow at the outset. Centred round a hard core of eight battleships, this fleet included three of America's seven aircraft carriers and was to be found at most week-ends thronging the congested waters of Pearl Harbour in the Hawaiian island of Oahu. For expert advice Yamamoto turned to Rear-Admiral Takijiro Onishi, Chief of Staff of the shore-based 11th Air Fleet. Any blow against Pearl Harbour, however, could only be mounted from carriers and

Onishi in turn recruited the best-known hero of such operations in the China War, Commander Minoru Genda, who was serving as staff officer of the carrier-borne 1st Air Fleet.

By May 1941 Genda had completed his study and produced a report in which he promised success provided that all six Japanese fleet carriers were committed and complete secrecy imposed. It convinced Yamamoto, who ordered concrete plans to be drawn up while he put the idea before the Naval General Staff. It was met at first with an obstinate disapproval. The carriers were essential for the southwards drive. A thrust across 3,400 miles of ocean was too great a gamble. This was the view also of the man who would be called upon to command the striking force, Vice-Admiral Chuichi Nagumo, Commander-in-Chief of the 1st Air Fleet, who was to remain a prey to nervous doubts to the end.

Yamamoto remained adamant. Confident that he would be able to overcome Nagano's objections in time, he pressed on with preparations. His carrier-borne squadrons were launched on a special training programme, concentrating on torpedo and dive-bombing attacks on targets in enclosed stretches of water such as Kagoshima Bay in southern Kyushu, and on intensive high-level bombing practice. Except for a handful of staff officers engaged with Genda in preparing the detailed plan, no junior officers were given a hint of their ultimate objective.

One difficult technical problem had to be solved. Torpedoes dropped from aircraft had to be released from a low level if they were to enter the water nearly horizontal. Even then they made an initial dive before taking up their set depth. The stretch of water in Pearl Harbour along one shore of which the American battleships moored was both narrow and shallow. Torpedoes launched there would hit the bottom in their initial dive, or, if they avoided this, would not have recovered their set depth before reaching their targets. Japanese technicians got to work and designed special torpedoes with fins attached which could be dropped from a considerable height and at high speed and yet pick up their running depth immediately. Production began in the middle of September 1941 and was feverishly pressed ahead to meet a deadline in mid-November.

In October, in great secrecy, a scale model of Pearl Harbour was set up in a compartment in the *Akagi*, Nagumo's flagship of the carrier fleet. Officer-pilots of the carrier air groups were now called aboard the *Akagi* and under seal of secrecy were given the electrifying news of their objective by Yamamoto himself. Training continued at an even fiercer intensity and with added enthusiasm. On 1 November, with his air groups now trained to a peak of efficiency, the Commander-in-Chief issued the basic operation order, naming 8 December (Japanese time) as the day of destiny. Two days later, 3 November, the Chief of the Naval General Staff, Admiral Nagano, at last allowed his objections to be overridden and gave his consent.

So the die was cast. Between 10-18 November, singly, or in pairs, the ships of Vice-Admiral Nagumo's striking force slipped away from their anchorages and steered by devious routes for a secret, desolate rendezvous in Tankan Bay on Etorofu, the largest of the Kurile Islands. The four large and two smaller carriers were crowded with 450 planes. A cruiser and nine destroyers would form the carrier squadron's screen. In support would sail two battleships and two cruisers. Absolute radio silence was imposed on all from the moment of sailing for the rendezvous, while the remainder of the fleet at Kure kept up a flow of radio traffic for the benefit of American radio intelligence.

Next to sail was the 'Advanced Expeditionary Force' of 16 submarines, five of which carried two-man midget submarines charged with the task of penetrating Pearl Harbour simultaneously with the air attack. The remainder, in addition to scouting for the carrier force, were expected to have an opportunity to torpedo any American ships that escaped seawards.

Meanwhile in Washington the stately masquerade of diplomatic exchange had been proceeding. Time was all that either side could hope to gain from continuing the negotiations; for Japan a week or two in which to complete preparations for her long-decided plan; for America every day gained assisted the war machinery, which was slowly grinding into motion despite the difficulties attending democratic procedure. At the same time the necessity to avoid anything that could be construed as a provocative action tied the hands of those who might have taken warlike precautions. Thus, though cryptography had revealed to the American Government that the Japanese Ambassador had been given a deadline of 25 November, later extended to the 29th, by which agreement must be reached, or after which events would have to take their course, it was not until the 27th that the U.S. Chief of Naval Operations, Admiral Stark, sent a war warning message to Admirals Kimmel and Hart, at Pearl Harbour and Manila respectively, authorising 'appropriate defensive deployment preparatory to carrying out the task assigned in WPL46' (the current war plan known as 'Rainbow 5').

So far as Pearl Harbour was concerned, the cogency of this message was greatly reduced by a statement contained in it that 'the number and equipment of Japanese troops and the organisation of naval task forces indicates an amphibious expedition against either the Philippines, Thai or Kra Peninsula or possibly Borneo'. Though the imminence of some overt Japanese act of war was deducible from the many diplomatic telegrams read by American intelligence services, none gave any hint that Pearl Harbour could be an objective. U.S. naval opinion was unanimous that the southward expeditions would absorb all available Japanese resources: and on 25 November U.S. Army Intelligence had reported a Japanese fleet off Formosa, carrying five divisions of troops, heading in a southerly direction.

Admiral Kimmel did order a state of alert in his fleet whereby a proportion of the close-range armament was kept manned, though ammunition was not kept immediately available. But pressing forward the training of a fleet which was in process of rapid expansion and suffering constant personnel changes, appeared even more necessary than placing it on a constant full alert against a remote threat which would interfere with such training. Less excusable was the maintenance of peace-time training schedules which included every week-end in harbour for rest and recreation with all-night leave for many of the officers and men. Aerial reconnaissance of the sea approaches was ordered but only between north-west and south-west of Pearl Harbour and to a maximum range of no more than 200 miles. Here again, the Admiral was influenced by the need to avoid expending the flying hours of his exiguous force of patrol planes on continuous long-range patrol and perhaps consequently finding them all on maintenance overhaul when the real emergency arose. General Short, the Army Commander, was similarly handicapped. In addition he was influenced by the need to avoid sounding too urgent an alarm and so perhaps provoking precipitate Japanese action. His forces were alerted only against acts of sabotage by Japanese inhabitants. The crews of his long-range aircraft were occupied with ferrying to Manila the Flying Fortresses on which the defence of the Philippines largely depended.

Governing all American naval and military appreciations of impending events was the belief that the Japanese resources were insufficient for a simultaneous attack on Pearl Harbour and on the Philippines; and all available intelligence pointed confidently to the latter as impending. Only from their aircraft carriers could the Japanese launch an air attack on Pearl Harbour. Certainly American radio intelligence had lost touch with the Japanese carriers, but this had happened before and had been later found only to indicate their presence in their home ports: and in any case only from these same carriers, it was believed, could a weighty air attack on the Philippines be mounted. This estimate was based on a lack of appreciation of the strength and capability of Japanese shore-based naval air-power. It had been overlooked that from the outset of the 'China Incident' Japanese naval shore-based bombers were making round trips of 1,250 miles from Formosa and Kyushu to attack targets in the Shanghai area, far in excess of anything of which British or American equivalents were capable. Their naval fighters even then, prior to the development of the famous Zero, proved at least equal to the best British, American and Russian fighters used by the Chinese Air Force. Yet the belief was generally held that the Japanese made indifferent pilots and that their aircraft were only poor imitations of foreign types. This miscalculation was to have a fatal influence on American preparations.

That war was imminent was hardly doubted after 20 November. Admiral Nomura had been joined by Saburo Kurusu, a career diplomat, personally briefed by the bellicose General Tojo, who had succeeded Prince Konoye as Prime

Minister. They now presented an ultimatum demanding a free hand in China and Indo-China and the release of Japanese assets and resumption of oil supplies, terms which, in the words of Secretary of State Hull, represented 'an abject surrender of our position under intimidation'. Nevertheless, in the hope of gaining time, counter-proposals, hardly less acceptable from the Japanese standpoint, demanding evacuation of China and Indo-China and recognition of Chiang Kai-shek's Government, were made on the 26th.

But the time had passed, if indeed it had ever existed, when negotiations were anything but shadow-boxing. At Tankan Bay the final briefing had been completed of captains and air-squadron commanders gathered round the plaster model of Pearl Harbour in the *Akagi*. Boats had been hoisted and Nagumo's ships snugged down ready for the buffeting to be expected in the wintry North Pacific. Then, in every unit the ship's company had been mustered and the scope and destination of the great adventure revealed to them, evoking wild enthusiasm. At first light on 26 November the signal to weigh had flashed round the bleak, rain-swept anchorage. Punctually at 0900, the anchors of six carriers,[1] two battleships, three cruisers, nine destroyers and eight tankers and supply ships had thudded home in the hawsepipes and the fleet had headed out into storm and fog. The receipt of a final executive signal from the Commander-in-Chief confirming the date of the attack would be made as soon as the Japanese Cabinet had, in the presence of the Emperor, taken the irrevocable decision to go to war. Thereafter the final responsibility for launching the attack on Pearl Harbour would be Nagumo's and would depend upon whether his force had been discovered during its passage.

---

[1] *Akagi* (flagship), *Kaga*, *Sbokaku*, *Zuikaku*, *Hiryu*, *Soryu*.

2. THE STORM BREAKS: PEARL HARBOUR

To avoid encounter with any ships which might report its presence, Nagumo's Pearl Harbour Striking Force followed a northerly route remote from normal traffic lanes. Concealment was assisted by the foul weather, storms and thick fogs, through which at first the force wallowed eastwards along the 43rd Parallel at the pace dictated by the slow speed of the replenishment tankers. Anxiety in this respect, which plagued the far from confident Admiral, now transferred itself to the need for reasonable weather in which to refuel. On 1 December (Hawaiian time), the brief code phrase *Niitaka Yama Nobore* (Climb Mount Niitaka) was received — the executive order to proceed with the attack on 7 December. At last, on the 2nd, the weather moderated and the warships' fuel tanks were replenished. By the following evening the force had reached 178° west longitude, where it altered course for a position 500 miles due north of Pearl Harbour which it was planned to reach on the evening of the 6th.

In Washington during this first week of December 1941, the Japanese reply to the American proposals of 26 November was uneasily awaited. That it would be a rejection could hardly be doubted. The only question was whether some formula would be found whereby negotiations could be kept open. Ominous items were to be found amongst the spate of Japanese diplomatic messages decoded by the Americans. Japanese Embassies had been ordered to burn all ciphers but one — but this had happened before during a previous crisis. The Japanese consul at Honolulu had been ordered to send detailed daily reports of warships in Pearl Harbour — but consuls elsewhere had similar orders with regard to their own areas. From the bulky raw material of radio and other intelligence it was deducible that war was near: but the few grains of precious metal amongst it which pointed to Pearl Harbour as a Japanese objective were hard to pick out.

Soon after midnight 5-6 December Nagumo received the latest information from Tokyo on the state of affairs in Pearl Harbour, based on the messages from the Japanese consul at Honolulu. It reported all the heavy ships of the U.S. Pacific Fleet lying at their customary moorings — with two significant exceptions, the aircraft carriers. This was a serious set-back. Rich targets as the stately battleships represented, the carriers were the top-priority objective. Nagumo called his staff to confer with him. It was decided to carry on with the attack. The carriers might return to harbour during the 30 hours or so remaining until zero hour.

During Saturday, 6 December, Nagumo's force continued to steer south-east, excitement mounting hourly amongst the carrier crews. At 2100 that evening came the moment of dedication. All hands were piped to assemble on the flight decks. Patriotic speeches were made amidst scenes of great emotion. To the masthead of the *Akagi* rose a historic signal flag used by Admiral Togo before the Battle of Tsushima 36 years earlier. As the force swung round on to a southerly course to head for the flying-off position arranged for dawn on the morrow, the ships' companies dispersed. Everything was in readiness. Nothing remained to be done before, to the clanging of the elevator bells, the aircraft would begin to be sent up on deck from the hangars. Few would sleep that night, however. At about the time that cries of 'Banzai' were greeting the fervent speeches of air group commanders aboard Nagumo's carriers, at the U.S. Navy radio station on Bainbridge Island a

25

Japanese diplomatic message of the utmost importance was being intercepted. It was passed to the Navy Department's cryptographers and by 0600 on the 7th (Washington time), it was known that the Japanese Ambassador had been instructed to deliver to the U.S. Secretary of State at 1300 Washington time — 0730 Hawaiian time — a message finally breaking off negotiations.

Peace-time Sabbath calm still regulated the administrative pace at Washington. Not until 0915 did this vital message reach Admiral Stark, Chief of Naval Operations, by hand of his Director of Naval Intelligence, Rear-Admiral T. S. Wilkinson. Thirty-five minutes later it was seen by the Secretary of State, Mr Hull, and the Secretary of the Navy Department, Mr Knox. It was pointed out to them that 1300 would be about sunrise at Honolulu. A further 70 minutes of inactivity elapsed. Admiral Stark saw no reason for alerting naval authorities. This could be a false alarm as other significant deciphered Japanese messages had proved in the past. General Marshall, Chief of the U.S. General Staff, was out on his regular morning ride. He saw the message on his return at 1130 and at once proposed to Stark that a special war alert should be sent out jointly. When Stark disagreed, he drafted his own message to Army commanders. It concluded: 'Just what significance the hour set may have we do not know, but be on the alert accordingly.' It was handed in for coding and dispatch at 1200.

At that moment (0630 Hawaiian time), the first wave of Nagumo's striking aircraft had already been launched — 50 Type 97 bombers (soon to be nicknamed 'Kates') each armed with a 1,760-lb. armour-piercing bomb, 70 more 'Kates' each carrying a torpedo, 51 Type 99 dive-bombers ('Vals') each loaded with one 550-lb. bomb. Forty-three Zero fighters accompanied them to provide escort and to deliver ground attacks.

General Marshall's message could just have reached the Army Commander at Pearl Harbour in time for him to order a full alert and to warn Admiral Kimmel. Whether it would have had such a result in the sleepy calm of a sunny Sunday morning will never be known, for in fact, owing to transmission delays, it did not reach the General's headquarters until after the blow had fallen. The likelihood of swift action from the administrative machine at Honolulu may perhaps be gauged from the Navy's reactions to a different sort of warning.

At 0342 the destroyer U.S.S. *Ward*, on night patrol off Pearl Harbour, was called up by signal light from the auxiliary minesweeper *Condor* carrying out a routine sweep two miles off the harbour entrance buoy. A periscope had been sighted. For two hours the *Ward* searched without result. Periscope sightings were notoriously unreliable even when reported by experienced seamen and no doubt the *Condor*'s message was treated with cautious scepticism. Certainly no report to any shore authority was made by the destroyer until, after a Catalina flying boat had also sighted a periscope and marked it with smoke bombs, the *Ward* gained contact with a midget submarine and sank it with gunfire and depth-charges at 0645. Nine minutes later a coded radio message reporting the encounter was made from the *Ward* to the shore authority. At 0712 it reached the Port Admiral (Admiral C. C. Block, Commanding 14th Naval District) who ordered the ready-duty destroyer, *Monaghan*, to get under way and assist the *Ward*, and a stand-by destroyer to raise steam. By 0725 the warning had reached the duty officer on Admiral Kimmel's staff who was only able to get through to the Commander-in-Chief at his house after some delay, owing to congestion on the telephone system. At 0750 Kimmel was making his way to his office when an explosion on Ford Island, the Naval Air Station in the middle of the harbour, marked the opening of the attack by Nagumo's aircraft.

By this time at least one other midget submarine had passed through the gate in the boom defences, which had been carelessly left open since the entry of two minesweepers at 0458. It was not detected until it reached the area north of Ford Island where, during a lull in the air attacks, it was sighted from the seaplane tender U.S.S. *Curtiss* and engaged by gunfire. A torpedo from the midget sped past the tender and exploded against a jetty at Pearl City. The destroyer *Monaghan*, under way to go to the assistance of the *Ward*, joined the fray and, after dodging a second torpedo which exploded harmlessly against the shore, sank the submarine with two depth-charges. Of the other three midgets launched from their parent submarines, two were lost without trace; the third, after running on a reef and being fired at by the destroyer *Helm*, was finally beached and her crew taken prisoner. The parent submarines and the 11 other large boats, of which much had been hoped, achieved nothing.

Whatever view is taken of the inertia prevailing in the higher levels of command, the alertness of crews of sea-going ships must be considered admirable indeed to have ensured so complete a failure of one section of a treacherous attack delivered while peace still officially reigned. Within the limits imposed on them by the degree of alert ordered, their reaction to the totally unexpected assault from the air was equally swift.

Since 0615 the first wave of strike aircraft from the Japanese carriers had been flying southwards, led by Commander Mitsuo Fuchida, the air group commander, in the leading 'Kate' high-level bomber. They were watched, with mild curiosity, on the radar scan of a trainee army operator whiling away the time until the routine truck arrived at the mobile radar station to take him to breakfast. He assumed that they were a flight of U.S. bombers expected that morning from the States.

A second wave, led by Lieutenant-Commander Shimazaki, the senior flying officer of the carrier *Zuikaku*, had taken off an hour later. It comprised 54 'Kate' bombers armed with 550-lb. bombs with which they were to attack the several Army and Navy air bases on Oahu, 80 'Val' dive-bombers and 36 Zero fighters. It was just 0710 — ten minutes after the hour at which the Japanese ultimatum was to have been presented in Washington — when Fuchida led the first wave down through the overcast and sighted the surf-lined northern shore of Oahu ahead of him. By Japanese ethics treachery had thus been avoided; but even this hypocrisy had been nullified through delays in preparing a translation of the note in the Japanese Embassy, so that Admiral Nomura's meeting with Secretary of State Hull had been put off to 1400. Before that hour the message 'Air Raid, Pearl Harbour — This is no drill' had reached an incredulous Washington. It had been broadcast at 0758 (1328 Washington time) by orders of Rear-Admiral Patrick Bellinger, commanding the Naval Air Station on Ford Island.

The first wave of attacking aircraft had followed the western coastline of Oahu. But little interest stirred the many civilian and service families living along the shore. They were used to seeing large formations of friendly planes — though not as a rule on a Sunday. It crossed their minds that they might be the air groups from the carriers *Lexington* and *Enterprise* which were expected. By 0750 Fuchida was able to see across the central plain of the island to Pearl Harbour, lying bathed in early

29

morning sunlight. Through binoculars he was able to count the eight battleships moored two by two on the eastern side of Ford Island. Though no carriers were to be seen, this was enough to warrant the attack going ahead as planned. To the air fleet he radioed the executive order.

Already the dive-bombers, led by Lieutenant-Commander Kakuichi Takahashi of the *Shokaku*, had climbed to the attacking height from which they would plummet down like stooping hawks to drop their bombs. And now the torpedo 'Kates' of Lieutenant-Commander Shigehoru Murata put their noses down for the long shallow dive to their torpedo launching positions abreast the battleships. Not a gun had opened fire yet. Not one defending fighter had taken off. At 0753 Fuchida signalled back to the anxiously awaiting Nagumo that surprise was complete.

Almost simultaneously the dive-bomber force of the first wave, splitting up into sections just as they had practised again and again, swooped on the Army air base at Wheeler Field in the centre of Oahu, on Ford Island, on the Army's Hickam Field hard by Pearl Harbour, on the Navy Seaplane Base at Kaneohe Bay on Oahu's east coast, and on the Marine Corps Air Base at Ewa, a few miles west of Pearl Harbour. At the airfields, fighters and bombers were drawn up wing-tip to wing-tip in parade-ground regularity, making perfect targets. As the 'Val' dive-bombers roared away, leaving smoking ruin behind them, the Zero fighters, by now confident that there would be few opponents for them in the air, streaked down from the sky to add their contribution to the destruction.

With perfect timing, as the first bombs burst on Ford Island, Murata's 'Kates' came sweeping in from the south-east to launch their torpedoes at the seven battleships where they lay securely moored in 'Battleship Row', with many of their

30

officers and men ashore on week-end leave, the duty watch quietly preparing for the eight o'clock ceremony of hoisting the colours. Five of them — *West Virginia, Arizona, Nevada, Oklahoma* and *California* — were rent open by torpedo hits in the first few minutes. Only the *Maryland* and *Tennessee*, berthed along the inner side of the *Oklahoma* and *West Virginia*, and the *Pennsylvania*, flagship of the Pacific Fleet, in dry dock, escaped torpedo damage. Other torpedo-planes selected for their targets the smaller ships and the old target battleship *Utah* berthed to the north-west of Ford Island. The *Utah*, twice torpedoed, quickly capsized and sank. The light cruiser *Raleigh* took a torpedo hit amidships, as did the *Helena* berthed alongside the dockyard wall.

While the suddenness of the catastrophe still held everyone rooted in shocked immobility, the rising whine of diving 'Vals' was heard, as they plummeted down to drop their bombs on the stationary, defenceless targets in 'Battleship Row' and in the dockyard.

Nevertheless, amidst the shudder and shock of underwater explosions, the searing eruption of bombs followed by the ominous lurching list of the great ships and the roar and crackle of flames, the American crews, for the most part, recovered themselves with admirable speed. While some of the 'Kates' were still launching their torpedoes the anti-aircraft guns and machine-guns of the fleet were in effective action. Five torpedo-planes were shot down as well as a number of the dive-bombers, the latter meeting a particularly hot fire from the light cruisers, destroyers and auxiliaries to the north-west of Ford Island, as well as from the *Pennsylvania* and other ships in the dockyard. Damage control parties were working manfully to minimise the consequences of flooded compartments, counter-flooding to keep the foundering ships on an even keel, restoring electric and waterpower and communications, fighting the fires. One battleship, the *Nevada*, having the good fortune to be berthed alone at the northern end of 'Battleship Row', was got under way by Lieutenant-Commander F. J. Thomas, U.S.N.R., the senior officer on board at the time, and she headed for the harbour entrance.

Meanwhile, high up above the smoke and confusion, at 10,000 feet, the 'Kates' with armour-piercing bombs had begun their approach. Unhindered by any fighter defence and little inconvenienced by the sparse gunfire directed at them, they were able to aim with careful precision. Some groups, their aim obstructed by wisps of cloud, circled and repeated their approach runs two or three times before releasing their bombs with devastating accuracy; one plunging through five inches of armour to burst inside a turret of the *Tennessee*, another penetrating to the forward magazine of the *Arizona*, which blew up, another bursting below the forecastle of the *Maryland*, while two struck the *California*, setting off the ammunition in her anti-aircraft magazine and tearing her bow plates apart.

When a lull occurred at 0825 as the first wave of Japanese aircraft turned for home, their missions accomplished, 33 naval planes at Ford Island had been destroyed or badly damaged; hardly a single Catalina flying-boat, out of the 33 caught immobilised at Kaneohe, remained undamaged; at Ewa 33 Marine planes were destroyed; 18 aircraft and the principal installations at Hickam had been wiped out, while at Wheeler Field hardly a serviceable plane remained.

In 'Battleship Row', the *West Virginia* was sinking on an even keel and on fire; the *Tennessee* was badly on fire; the *Arizona* had settled on the bottom with more than a thousand of her crew fatally trapped below; the *Oklahoma* had rolled over on her side as she sank, settling on the bottom with her keel above water;

the *California* had received damage that was eventually to sink her in spite of all efforts of her crew. Elsewhere, all that was left visible of the *Utah* above water was her upturned keel. The *Raleigh*, deep in the water from flooding and counter-flooding, was being kept upright by her mooring wires.

The interval before the second wave of Japanese aircraft arrived over Oahu gave a breathing space during which ammunition supply for the guns was replenished and gun crews reorganised and reinforced. The 'Kate' high-level bombers were able once again to cross and recross their targets little inconvenienced by the inexperienced and disorganised high-angle gunfire; their bombs further damaged a number of ships. The dive-bombers which accompanied them, however, were met by a fierce concentration of fire and suffered losses. Nevertheless they scored a damaging hit on the *Pennsylvania* and wrecked the two destroyers *Cassin* and *Downes* which were sharing the dry-dock with the battleship. Another 'Val' put a bomb into the destroyer *Shaw* in the floating dock, detonating her forward magazine and blowing off her bow in a spectacular explosion. The *Nevada*, feeling her way towards the harbour entrance through the billowing clouds of black smoke from burning ships, was set upon by a section of 'Vals' and repeatedly hit, so that it was necessary to beach her to prevent her sinking in mid-channel and blocking it.

North-west of Ford Island, the many smaller ships moored there achieved a daunting volume of fire between them, and the 'Vals' which concentrated on the *Curtiss* lost several of their number for the satisfaction of damaging the seaplane tender and causing nearly 80 casualties. At the various airfields, also, the dive-bombers had a fierce reception and added little to the damage the initial attacks had caused.

Suddenly, at around 1000, it was all over. Having lost only nine Zeros, 15 'Vals' and five 'Kate' torpedo-planes out of the total of 354 planes engaged, the Japanese striking force was streaming back to Nagumo's carriers. The damage they left behind them, had it been inflicted in pitched battle, would have comprised a naval defeat ranking with Admiral Togo's decisive destruction of the Russian fleet at Tsushima. Altogether, 2,403 Americans had died, 1,176 more had been wounded. Four battleships had been sunk, one beached and three severely damaged, putting out of action the entire battleship force of the Pacific Fleet.

Such a material achievement in battle would have had a demoralising effect on the American Navy so profound as to impose a sense of inferiority that would have taken months to eradicate. But, in fact, the treacherous nature of the attack induced instead only a fierce flame of fury and a passion for revenge. When stock was taken and it was realised that the fleet carriers with their great power to strike back had escaped and that the naval base with its repair facilities and huge stocks of fuel and stores was virtually undamaged, the Japanese accomplishment came to be assessed as the indecisive blow it was.

It is not surprising, on the other hand, that the anxious Nagumo, when he received the report from Commander Fuchida, who had remained over Oahu, noting the results till the last moment, felt that enough had been achieved. The success seemed too miraculously complete and the price paid so small that it would be tempting fate to return to the attack as Fuchida and other air group leaders urged. Nagumo ordered his force to steer away to the north-westward to rendezvous with his replenishment tankers and thence on a course for Japan.

It was a fateful decision. Apart from the repair facilities of the naval dockyard and the oil tanks brimming with fuel, both intact and virtually defenceless, and without which Pearl Harbour would have been for many months useless as a naval base, a rich reward awaited a second sortie by Nagumo's exulting airmen. The large fleet carrier *Enterprise* was less than 200 miles west of Oahu, returning from a mission to deliver a Marine fighter squadron to Wake Island. She could hardly have survived a massed aerial torpedo attack. With the *Lexington*, which at the time of the Japanese attack had been approaching Midway Island on a similar mission to deliver a Marine scout-bomber squadron, and the *Saratoga*, about to come west from San Diego, California, the *Enterprise* comprised the core of a still formidable Pacific Fleet of which five cruisers and 29 destroyers had survived the disastrous 7 December, while a further 11 cruisers and 11 destroyers had been absent from Pearl Harbour. Not yet was it appreciated by either side that battleships with their large-calibre guns were no longer the arbiters of naval battle; that, indeed, with their limited speed and inadequate defence against massed air attack, they could be a liability rather than an asset in the exercise of sea-power.

At Pearl Harbour, the impressive but false facade of the battle line was torn down, revealing the air-borne torpedo and the dive-bomb rather than the big gun as the main striking power of the fleet, and the fighter aircraft as the primary means of defence. The U.S. Navy was thus projected, willy-nilly, into the carrier age of sea warfare. Far to the south-westward, across the wide Pacific, America and her allies were at the same time having painfully demonstrated to them the effectiveness of well-equipped and practised amphibious forces, when backed by a powerful naval air force operating from shore bases.

3. OPENING MOVES — JAVA SEA

The total surprise inflicted on the U.S. Naval and Army Commands at Pearl Harbour was the subject of painstaking examination and enquiry. The mass of evidence taken has since been exhaustively analysed.[2] Although the Commander-in-Chief Pacific Fleet, Admiral Kimmel, was inevitably selected as scapegoat, responsibility for the debacle was in fact spread so widely through governmental and service organisations that individual error other than excusable human fallibility was not pin-pointed. The facts were that no one imagined it possible for the Japanese to mount such an operation simultaneously with those known to be imminent in the South-West Pacific and that no specific warning had been deducible from the mass of inadequately digested intelligence material, including deciphered Japanese diplomatic messages, which had been flowing in during the final weeks of peace.

The thunder-clap of Pearl Harbour and the magnitude of the destruction and casualties inflicted in the space of a few hours stunned the imagination. Far less indignation was expressed at the manner in which the American air defences of the Philippines were caught equally by surprise and annihilated, although massive evidence of Japanese intention to begin the war by a southward thrust existed.

The Philippines had until quite recently been considered by the Army General Staff to be indefensible by the mixed forces of the United States and Philippine Armies, some 125,000 strong, backed by the small, heterogeneous Asiatic Fleet of

---

[2] Roberta Wohlsetter, *Pearl Harbor* (Stanford University Press).

largely obsolete war vessels commanded by Admiral Thomas C. Hart. During 1941, however, the acquisition by the U.S. Army Air Force of new and powerful bombers, the B-17s or Flying Fortresses, and the allocation of a number of them to the U.S. Army Forces Far East under Lieutenant-General Douglas MacArthur in the Philippines, led to a belief that a Japanese invasion of Luzon could be repulsed. Deployment of these B-17s from the U.S.A, to the airfields round Manila had been going on via Hawaii, Wake and Guam for some months and on 8 December 35 of them were available for duty. Fighter defence was provided by some 90 P-40s and P-35s. To both Japanese and Americans, this concentration of air-power round Manila was recognised as the key to the defence of the Philippines.

The 'war warning' message from Washington on 27 November had expressly mentioned the Philippines as one of the possible objectives of a Japanese amphibious expedition 'expected within the next few days'. Admiral Hart and the U.S. Army Air Force commander, General Brereton, co-operated in organising aerial reconnaissance of the seaward approaches, Flying Fortresses reconnoitring to the northward as far as Formosa, while naval flying boats searched the Indo-Chinese coast. Any serious threat of air attack, it was assumed, must come from aircraft carriers operating in the areas searched. Underestimation of the capabilities of Japanese shore-based air forces masked the danger of attacks on Manila being mounted from Formosa. Dispersal of American aircraft concentrated on Clark and Nicholls Fields near Manila had been ordered but not yet implemented. This was to prove a fatal mistake.

In late August 1941, with war against America and Britain clearly impending, the Japanese shore-based naval air forces comprising the 11th Air Fleet under Vice-Admiral Nishizo

Tsukahara, had been withdrawn to Formosa from the China war to prepare. There the twin-engined bombers, Mitsubishi Type 1 (nicknamed by the Americans 'Betty') and the Mitsubishi Type 96 ('Nell'), underwent intensive training particularly in their alternative role as torpedo-planes. In October, on the Japanese occupation of southern Indo-China, the headquarters of the 22nd Air Flotilla, commanded by Rear-Admiral Sadaichi Matsunaga, moved to Saigon. The 'Genzan' and 'Mihoro' Air Corps of which the Flotilla was composed, 48 'Nells' each, were deployed on two nearby airfields. Their task was initially to be the neutralisation of the British naval and air base at Singapore; but torpedoes were available should British warships threaten the projected amphibious expedition to be landed near the Siamese-Malayan border.

Meanwhile the 21st and 23rd Air Flotillas had been allotted the task of striking at the airfields near Manila as soon as possible after the Pearl Harbour attack (0230, 8 December, Philippine time). The distance between the Japanese naval air base at Takao in southern Formosa and the target area was some 500 nautical miles, the extreme operational range for the bombers — outside it, indeed, in the opinion of American and British Intelligence. As for fighter escort, this could only be provided if mounted from the decks of aircraft carriers operating off the coast of Luzon — or so it seemed at first — and, when all the fleet carriers were allocated to the Pearl Harbour operation, it was decided that the three small auxiliary carriers *Ryujo*, *Zuiho* and *Kasuga Maru* would embark as many Zeros as possible for this purpose.

Under this arrangement, however, problems of co-ordination were acute; the number of fighters would be reduced and the value of surprise would be jeopardised. Only by enormously increasing the endurance of the Zeros could these difficulties be overcome. The Japanese set about experimenting with methods of achieving this, flying the aircraft with the weakest possible fuel mixture and training their pilots to make longer and longer flights until they could remain in the air on simulated combat missions for as much as 12 hours continuously. Well in advance of the date for action, Admiral Tsukahara was able to report that the carriers would not be required and they were released for allocation to subsidiary operations.

So it was that when, at 0300 on 8 December, the American commanders in the Philippines received the startling news that Pearl Harbour was under air attack, an immediate threat to the Manila area did not seem too serious. An alarm at Clark Field, the principal Army Air Station, at 0830, sent the P-40s and P-35s streaming off into the air; but it proved false and by 1000 they had landed for refuelling. A reconnaissance towards Formosa was discussed but with little sense of urgency. The forenoon wore on uneventfully.

Unknown to anyone at Manila or Clark Field, small forces of Japanese Army Air Force bombers had struck at Baguio, the summer capital, and an airfield at Tugugarao in norther Luzon at 0930. At Takao, however, dawn had broken in thick fog. The naval air striking force had been unable to take off until 1015; but now, following an off-shore route, 108 bombers, escorted by 84 fighters, were approaching Manila undetected. As on the airfields of Oahu, U.S. Army Air Force planes waited unsuspectingly on the ground for the blow which befell them at 1245. The Japanese bombers made unopposed passes overhead and, following the bomb-bursts, the Zeros swooped down, their machine-guns completing the holocaust.

When silence settled down again and the rumble of the Japanese air armada faded away as they made off on their long journey back to base, more than half of the American bomber strength, on which defence of the Philippines mainly relied, had been destroyed, together with 30 P-40s. The elimination of American air-power was completed two days later when a second raid was made on the Manila airfields simultaneously with the devastation of the Navy Yard at Cavite, which deprived the U.S. Asiatic Fleet of its only base. The Japanese were then free to throw in their invasion forces at selected points on the coast of Luzon without effective opposition. Conquest of the Philippines became only a matter of time. Manila fell on Christmas Day after which only the Bataan Peninsula remained in American hands, holding out gallantly but hopelessly until 8 April, the island fortress of Corregidor not falling until 6 May.

The Philippine Islands, themselves, had little of value to offer the oil-hungry Japanese. Their occupation was important only to prevent the resurgence of an enemy naval and air base poised on the flank of the many-pronged southward thrusts which were to gain possession of the rubber plantations of Malaya and the oilfields of Sumatra and Borneo.

The first of these expeditions, comprising an amphibious invasion of Malaya, had been under way since the evening of 4 December, when a troop convoy including 19 transports sailed from Samah Bay in Hainan. Not until the 6th was it detected by a reconnoitring flying boat of the R.A.F. when it had already rounded the southern point of Indo-China and was steaming westwards as though headed for Bangkok. Out in the South China Sea hovered a supporting force under Vice-Admiral Kondo composed of the battleships *Kongo* and *Haruna*, three heavy cruisers and a destroyer screen. By this time reconnaissance by the Japanese naval air force based on Indo-China had discovered the arrival at Singapore of the battleship

Prince of Wales and the battlecruiser *Repulse*. The naval base was thereafter kept under regular surveillance and submarines were deployed to intercept the British ships should they sally forth. The 96 bombers of the 22nd Air Flotilla, reinforced by 27 further 'Betties' of the Kanoya Air Corps which joined them in the Saigon area from Formosa, prepared to attack Singapore in the opening moments of the war. After that they would concentrate on the two capital ships which must at all costs be prevented from intercepting the vulnerable troop convoy. If they remained in harbour the whole air force would carry bombs. If they came to sea, half the strike force would be armed with torpedoes.

As dusk fell on 7 December, the Japanese invasion force, in two sections, was approaching Singora in Siam, near the Malayan border, and Kota Bahru on the northern coast of Malaya. During the night, when Nagumo's carriers far to the eastward were manoeuvring in the early morning twilight and preparing to fly off the Pearl Harbour Striking Force, 54 bombers of the Japanese 22nd Air Flotilla took off from Saigon and headed for Singapore. Half of them met thunderstorms and, losing cohesion in blinding tropical rain, were recalled; but the remainder broke through to bomb Singapore town and airfields.

At about the time that the last of Nagumo's planes were leaving Pearl Harbour to return to their carriers, Japanese troops were pouring ashore, unopposed, at Singora. At Kota Bahru the troopships were at first repulsed by coastal defences, but succeeded in landing their troops later in the day.

The two British capital ships, under Admiral Sir Tom Phillips at Singapore, had been sent there in November at the insistence of the Prime Minister who, contrary to Admiralty opinion, considered they would act as a deterrent to Japanese aggressive intentions. By 1 December enough was known of Japanese preparations to make it clear that their presence had failed in its object and the Admiralty, alive to the exposed position of the squadron, began to urge Admiral Phillips to leave Singapore. By 3 December the Prime Minister had also come round to this view and on the 5th the *Repulse* sailed for Darwin in North Australia.

But it was too late. The next day the Japanese troop convoy was sighted. With Malaya now openly threatened, it was inconceivable that the Royal Navy should turn tail, no matter what the odds, and leave its comrades ashore to face the enemy alone, unless directed to do so by Government order. Although, as Winston Churchill has told,[3] by the evening of the 9th it was generally agreed in London that the ships 'must go to sea and vanish among the innumerable islands', no such order was given. The *Repulse* was recalled to Singapore, and there she lay in company with the flagship, *Prince of Wales* when, early on the 8th, the crump of bombs bursting on the town and airfields announced the opening of war with Japan. News of the assault landings in the north followed.

A few hours later the two capital ships with a screen of four destroyers sailed for the Gulf of Siam, where Admiral Phillips hoped to be able to fall upon the Japanese invasion forces on the 10th, with a reasonable chance of success if surprise could be achieved and if fighter cover could be provided by the R.A.F. It was a forlorn hope from the start. Not only was the Gulf of Siam being kept under constant watch by Japanese aircraft and submarines but the landing operations would have been completed and the transports started on their way back to base during the 9th. The R.A.F.'s exiguous force of outmoded

---

[3] W. S. Churchill, *The Second World War*, Vol. III (Cassell and Co. Ltd.).

fighter aircraft was totally committed to the land battle and none could be spared to cover the naval squadron. When, therefore, Japanese naval aircraft on reconnaissance were sighted during the afternoon of 9 December, Admiral Phillips reversed course to return to Singapore.

News of his whereabouts had meanwhile reached Admiral Matsunaga's headquarters at Saigon from the Japanese submarine *I-56*. At the Saigon airfields there was at once feverish activity to arm half the strike bombers of the 22nd Air Flotilla with torpedoes. Not until dusk was the task completed and it was into a dark, moonless tropical night that the 'Nells' and 'Betties' roared off, squadron by squadron. The airmen's enthusiasm had however, outrun their good sense. Without radar their chances of intercepting the enemy ships were very small and when they came near to attacking Admiral Kondo's squadron by mistake they were recalled.

The torpedo-bombers were now faced with landing in the darkness on blacked-out airfields with their dangerous, bulky weapons still slung beneath their bellies. Fortunately by this time the moon was rising and, by waiting in the air until the runways could be seen by its light, the pilots landed safely. At dawn they would set out again.

While it was still dark a small force of reconnaissance aircraft took off in search. Touch with the British squadron had been regained by the submarine *I-58*, which reported its position and course. By this time Admiral Phillips had received a message from Singapore reporting a fresh enemy landing at Kuantan halfway down the east coast of Malaya, and soon afterwards he altered course towards that position. Maintaining radio silence, he could neither inform Singapore of this nor could be request air cover to be provided at daybreak. If he hoped for this, he relied too much upon intelligent anticipation by those responsible, particularly as the fact was that the report of a landing at Kuantan had proved false. The risk of serious air attack must in any case have been judged to be small: for by daylight he would be more than 400 nautical miles from the nearest Japanese-held airfields, a distance thought to be beyond the operational range of naval bombers. Furthermore, it was generally believed by the British as well as the Americans that the Japanese were indifferent aviators — a belief which had possibly been nurtured by the Japanese themselves, just as they had hidden their latest aircraft from Western eyes and kept secret their remarkable qualities and performance. The stage was thus set for tragedy. Having found no shipping off Kuantan, Phillips had turned seawards and was investigating some small craft off shore when the rumble of numerous aircraft engines announced the raising of the curtain.

No fresh news of the whereabouts of the British squadron had reached the Japanese bomber squadrons when they took off — 52 torpedo-planes and 34 high-level bombers — early on that fateful morning, 10 December 1941. Conserving fuel to the utmost, the formations flew south from Cape Cambodia, picking up the ships' assumed route to Singapore while information was awaited from the reconnaissance planes.

An account of the events which followed, written at the time by Lieutenant Sadao Takai, leader of the 2nd Squadron of the Genzan Air Corps, appeared in *Zero!*[4], from which the quotations in this chapter are taken. After describing the abortive night sortie and the briefing and take-off of the weary air-crews the next morning, he goes on:

> As our planes carried torpedoes today, we had in our tanks about 30 per cent less fuel than normal. We flew in a very

---

[4] By M. Okumiya and J. Harikoshi (Cassell and Co. Ltd.).

large formation and for reasons of safety our radius of operation was fixed at a maximum of 400 nautical miles. However, should we find the enemy ships more than 400 nautical miles from Saigon, we would naturally press home the attack. All pilots were trying to use as little fuel as possible.

As the miles slipped beneath our wings and we flew further south, the weather constantly improved. Finally the sky was completely clear. We maintained a flight altitude of between 8,300 and 10,000 feet.

Nearly 1,000.[5] What is the matter with our reconnaissance planes...? We have passed the danger line of 400 nautical miles from Saigon. Still no report of the enemy ships. The pilots are becoming more and more anxious about their remaining fuel. We measured the rate of fuel consumption as carefully as possible and reduced it to the lowest possible level. It was not the best way to treat the engines, but we had little choice.

One of the squadrons armed with armour-piercing bombs evidently decided that it had reached its prudent limit of endurance, for it unloaded its bombs, ineffectively, on a small cargo ship sighted, and then headed for home.

Nine 1,100-lb. bombs were lost [commented Takai], dissipated without results, after all the trouble of carrying them for such a long time! We continued to fly southward. Far ahead and to our right we could make out the southern tip of the Malayan peninsula.

We were dangerously close to passing the 'point of no return' when we would lack the fuel to return to our base. Our only hope, in the event of our passing this point, was to make a forced landing at Kota Bahru, which our troops had already invaded.

---

[5] Tokyo time kept by the Japanese forces, two hours later than local time.

Then at 0945 (local time) the long-awaited message from a reconnaissance plane was received — two enemy battleships 70 miles south-east of Kuantan. The leader of Takai's wing, Lieutenant-Commander Nakanishi evidently failed to take in the message, and it was a further ten minutes before Takai could get it through to him, when the formation wheeled round on to a north-westerly course.

> Everybody was straining to look ahead of our bomber to sight the enemy fleet. Everybody wanted the honour of being first to see the British warships …… Low clouds were filling the sky ahead of us. Fully five hours had passed since we left Saigon that morning. The enemy fleet should become visible any moment. I became nervous and shaky and could not dismiss the sensation. I had the strongest urge to urinate. It was exactly like the sensation one feels before entering a contest in an athletic meeting.
>
> At exactly 1303 a black spot directly beneath the cloud ahead of us was sighted. It appeared to be the enemy about 25 miles away. Yes — it was the enemy... the long-awaited *Prince of Wales* and the *Repulse*.... Lieutenant-Commander Nakanishi ordered 'Form assault formation'. A little later, 'Go in.'...
>
> Without interference from enemy fighters we could make our attacks freely. Co-ordinating my movements with those of the 1st Squadron, I led my squadron to the attack so that the enemy ships would be torpedoed from both flanks. The 1st Squadron was circling about four miles to the left and forward of the enemy ships and was about ready to begin its torpedo run.

When the Genzan Air Corps, to which Takai's squadron belonged, thus reached the scene, the British ships had already been the target for the high-level bombers of a squadron of the Mihoro Air Corps. Though this form of attack was rarely effective on ships free to manoeuvre, as had been repeatedly demonstrated in the European theatre, on this occasion one hit had been scored on the *Repulse*, but without seriously injuring her. The torpedoes that followed were a different matter. Assaulted on both flanks, the *Prince of Wales* could not avoid them all and two hits crippled her. The next wave of torpedo-planes, attacking simultaneously with more high-level bombers, selected the *Repulse* as their target. Both bombs and torpedoes were avoided; but then, as more and more Japanese aircraft arrived on the scene, coming in from every quarter, the *Repulse* suffered her first torpedo hit, followed by another which jammed her steering gear and left her an easy target. The already crippled *Prince of Wales* was again hit four times. A few minutes later three more torpedoes tore open the *Repulse*'s hull. The old veteran of World War I could not withstand such blows and was clearly doomed. Her commanding officer, Captain W. G. Tennant[6] afterwards described how:

> When the ship had a list of 30 degrees to port I looked over the side of the bridge and saw the commander and two or three hundred men collecting on the starboard side. I never saw the slightest sign of panic or ill-discipline. I told them from the bridge how well they had fought the ship, and wished them luck. The ship hung (for several minutes) with a list of 60 or 70 degrees to port and then rolled over at 1233.

The *Prince of Wales*, a comparatively new ship, took longer to succumb to her many torpedo hits; but her end had been certain for some time when, at 1320, she too capsized and sank. Admiral Phillips and Captain Leach, the flag-captain, went down with her, but 1,285 her complement of 1,612 were rescued by the attendant destroyers, as were 796 of the 1,309 officers and men of the *Repulse*. As the work of rescue was in

---

[6] Later Admiral Sir William Tennant, K.C.B., C.B.E., M.V.O.

progress, British fighter aircraft arrived. They had been despatched on receipt of the *Repulse*'s signal reporting the opening of the attack, but the Japanese aircraft were already well on their way back to base, except for the reconnaissance plane flown by Ensign Hoashi which had made the first sighting and had remained, a jubilant spectator of the subsequent action.

Lieutenant Takai has described how, as the attack planes flew home:

> We happily listened to each of Ensign Hoashi's radio reports as he told how the burning and exploding enemy ships were sinking.... While he observed the sinking of the *Prince of Wales*, Hoashi sighted eight enemy fighters racing to the scene. Their belated appearance was of no avail, for the *Repulse* and the *Prince of Wales* had already disappeared beneath the waves...
>
> Not a single plane was forced to make an emergency landing at Kota Bahru, and all bombers were able to return to their respective bases in Indo-China. Furthermore, only the three planes which fell in flames during the sinking of the enemy warships failed to return! It was a great and glorious victory!

This, indeed, must be conceded. It was a staggering demonstration to the veterans of two years of warfare in the west, as well as to the newly belligerent Americans, of the dominant role that an air force properly equipped and trained for naval warfare could play. For two years and more, the Royal Navy had had to fight for sea supremacy in European waters supported by a shore-based maritime air force much smaller in numbers and far less well-equipped. Fortunately Britain's European enemies were similarly badly served in this respect, and the score in that theatre was thus equalised.

The Japanese Navy, with all opposition by capital ships eliminated and with its aircraft, shore-based and ship-borne, providing complete air superiority, was now free to bring forward the several troop convoys which comprised the many-pronged invasion of the East Indies. Like the waters of a bursting dam, Japanese forces poured southwards in two main streams divided by the land mass of Borneo. As the various key ports were reached the progress of the flood was checked as the surrounding land area was secured and air bases established from which the next advance could be covered. Before the end of January Sarawak, Brunei and Jesselton on the west coast of Borneo had been occupied, as had the oil ports of Tarakan and Balikpapan on the eastern shore, Menado, Kendari in Celebes, and Amboina Island. Far to the south-east an amphibious force had captured Rabaul in the Bismarck Archipelago whence Papua and the Solomon Islands and the Coral Sea could be brought under Japanese air domination. On 15 February the naval and air base of Singapore fell into Japanese hands.

The invasion forces were now poised for the conquest of the 'Malay Barrier,' the long chain of islands marking the western boundary of the South-West Pacific, from oil-rich Sumatra in the west to Timor in the east, facing the Australian Port Darwin across less than 300 miles of sea. Opposing them was a heterogeneous force of American, British and Dutch cruisers and destroyers under the tactical command of the Dutch Rear-Admiral Karel Doorman, flying his flag in the cruiser *De Ruyter*, based on Surabaya on the north coast of Java. Doorman first lunged north-eastwards towards the Makassar Strait, where a Japanese invasion force had been reported, only to be set upon by a large force of twin-engined naval bombers from the newly established air base at Kendari. When the U.S. cruiser

Marblehead had been severely damaged and put out of action and the U.S. cruiser *Houston* had had her after turret wrecked by a bomb, Doorman was forced to retreat south of Java and thence to Batavia.

On 12 February came news of an invasion force heading for the Sumatran oil port of Palembang. Once again Admiral Doorman sallied forth, leading five cruisers and ten destroyers to bar the way. Once again he was turned back by prolonged and heavy air attacks. Skilful manoeuvring saved his ship from any direct hits, though two of his American destroyers were put out of action by near misses; but Doorman, weighing the obvious risks against the possible gains, decided he must retire, this time to Tjilatjap on the south coast of Java and out of range of Japanese bombers. On the 16th the Japanese landed at Palembang.

During the next few days Doorman's Striking Force became dispersed as units were despatched on various missions. So that, when news of a Japanese landing on Bali reached him, his sortie to attack the transports in the Badung Strait during the night of 19-20 February was disjointed and unsuccessful, the Dutch destroyer *Piet Hein* being sunk and the cruiser *Tromp* roughly handled: two enemy destroyers were damaged. After this third unsuccessful lunge at the enemy's smaller expeditions, the Allied naval forces were deployed in preparation to meet the main thrusts at Java which were now imminent. A Western Striking Force, comprising the Australian cruiser *Hobart* and two old British light cruisers, *Dragon* and *Danae*, with two destroyers, *Scout* and *Tenedos*, was based for a few days on Batavia but after a fruitless sweep in search of the enemy towards the Banka Strait during 26 February it was withdrawn, first to Tjilatjap and then to Ceylon. Except for the *Hobart*, these ancient ships could have served no other purpose but to offer themselves as useless sacrifices in any encounter with the enemy.

The remainder of the Allied ships joined Admiral Doorman's flag at Surabaya where, by the 26th, he commanded a force of two heavy cruisers, H.M.S. *Exeter* and U.S.S. *Houston*, three light cruisers H.N.M.S. *De Ruyter* and *Java* and H.M.A.S. *Perth*, three British, two Dutch and four American destroyers. This Eastern Striking Force was, on paper, impressive, even when the *Houston*'s disabled after turret was taken into account. The reality was otherwise. Doorman would be operating blindly in waters dominated by the enemy's aircraft, his every move watched and countered. His ships had dissimilar armaments and capabilities; they had no joint system of manoeuvring signals; tactics would be governed by a choice between conflicting alternatives and subject to no common doctrine. Communications would be affected by difficulties of language and differing signal equipment. Ships and men had already nearly reached the limit of endurance.

Such was the naval squadron which stood sacrificially in the path of whatever strength the Japanese Navy considered adequate to shield the main invasion forces. The Japanese by no means over-estimated its fighting capabilities. Their two troop convoys, the Western Group of 56 transports approaching from the Anambas towards Batavia and an Eastern Group of 41 transports heading for Surabaya, were covered by cruisers and destroyers only. Neither their battleships nor the carrier striking force of Admiral Nagumo were called upon to brush aside the opposition.

On the day on which Admiral Doorman's heterogeneous squadron assembled, 26 February, the Eastern Attack Force was reported some 190 miles to the north-east of Surabaya. That evening, after a day of conferences to hammer out some workable system of command and control, Doorman led the way to sea. Lacking effective air scouting, he could only place himself in the enemy's expected path and await the outcome. When no contact resulted, Doorman returned to Surabaya during the afternoon of the 27th to allow his destroyers to top up their fuel tanks. As he was entering harbour there came the news for which he had been waiting, an enemy convoy 80 miles to the northward. This was the Eastern Invasion Force commanded by Rear-Admiral Nishimura, flying his flag in the light cruiser *Naka*, accompanied by six destroyers and supported by the heavy cruisers *Nachi*, flagship of Rear-Admiral Takagi, and *Haguro* and a force of seven more destroyers led by Rear-Admiral Tanaka in the light cruiser *Jintsu*.

Doorman reversed course at once and steered to intercept. His every move was watched by Japanese scouting seaplanes from the cruisers of Nishimura who ordered the convoy to keep clear and with his warships headed across Doorman's front. At once the limitations imposed on Doorman by the polyglot composition of his force began to be felt. Restricted to single line ahead, he was in danger of 'having his T crossed', bringing a concentration of 20 eight-inch guns on to his flagship in the van. If he turned his ships at once to a course parallel with the enemy's, only the eight-inch guns of the *Houston* and *Exeter* would be within range to reply.

Doorman at first compromised by turning 20 degrees to port, which continued to close the range while allowing the *Exeter* and *Houston* to engage. But the six-inch guns of the remainder were still out of range when a massive torpedo attack by the Japanese cruisers and destroyers, though ineffective through being delivered at too long a range, caused him to turn parallel to the enemy on a westerly course.

Up to this time the gun duel at the great range of more than 13 miles had achieved only a single hit, which failed to explode, on the Dutch flagship *De Ruyter* — though ships on both sides had been straddled and shaken by near misses again and again. The Japanese destroyers, moving out to make their attack, now gave the smaller Allied cruisers targets for their six-inch guns, and the *Perth* got one hit home on the *Asagumo*, which brought her, crippled, to a halt while the remainder retired again behind a smoke screen.

Meanwhile the Japanese cruisers, with their greater speed, had been drawing ahead of the Allied line and, when Admiral Doorman altered course to try again to close the gun range, they were once more slanting across his bow. The heavy cruisers on the horizon launched 16 torpedoes unobserved, while Tanaka in the *Jintsu* led his eight destroyers racing into a closer-range attack in which 52 further torpedoes were fired. These torpedoes, using liquid oxygen propellant, had been developed from a British design passed to the Japanese in the days of the Anglo-Japanese Alliance. It had been discarded by the Royal Navy on account of the dangers of using and storing so volatile a fuel; in the hands of the Japanese and quite unknown to the Allies, it had been improved to give a running range of 22,000 yards at 49 knots and as much as 44,000 yards at 36 knots. Compared with British and American air- and steam-driven torpedoes, they left very little track.

What results they might have achieved now, had the Allied ships continued on their steady course, cannot be known. For at this moment an eight-inch shell from the *Haguro*, falling almost vertically after its long flight of more than 12 miles, plunged down on the *Exeter*, second ship of the Allied cruiser line, penetrating to her boiler-room where it exploded. The British cruiser's speed fell away sharply and Captain Gordon steered her out of the line. The *De Ruyter* steamed on but the ships astern of the *Exeter*, thinking an alteration of course had been ordered, followed the British cruiser round. Suddenly the Allied line had broken up in confusion and in the midst of it the Dutch destroyer *Kortenaer* exploded and sank as a torpedo hit her amidships. The *Perth* steered to lay down a smoke screen between the *Exeter* and the enemy. Torpedoes were sighted again and again amongst the Allied ships, some of them surfacing and exploding as they completed their runs. Three enemy destroyers could be seen racing forward to finish off the crippled *Exeter*, limping away southwards at 15 knots.

Smoke billowing over the battle area was adding to the Dutch Admiral's difficulties in communicating with his ships but, as he steamed in a wide circle until he was heading eastward, collecting his cruisers astern of him as he went, he succeeded in getting an order through to the senior officer of the widely separated British destroyers, Commander C. W. May of the *Electra*, to cover the *Exeter* by counter-attacking. Into the thick smoke barrier to the north-west laid by the *Perth* plunged the *Electra*. As she broke through into clear air she found herself confronted by the three advancing Japanese destroyers. Guns flashed out on both sides, but before the British destroyer could get an effective shot home, she was herself hit in her after boiler-room, the shell bursting with shattering effect, bringing her to a stop and disrupting her gun control communications. Two of the Japanese destroyers pressed on into the smoke, leaving the third to hammer the crippled *Electra* to a wreck. One by one her guns were silenced and, as she heeled over and began to settle, the order was given to abandon ship. Overwhelmed by superior gunnery though they had been, her crew remained undaunted in defeat. Her gunner, Mr T. J. Cain, who was to be among the 54 survivors later picked up by the U.S. submarine *S-38*, described how, from the water, they cheered their captain as he waved farewell to them from the bridge, the last time he was seen alive. 'She was a grand ship,' Mr Cain wrote, 'and I am proud to have served in her with such a fine crowd of men.'

The other two British destroyers, *Jupiter* and *Encounter*, following the example of their senior officer, had also turned towards the smoke barrier to interpose themselves between the *Exeter* and the approaching threat. The *Encounter*, through gaps in the smoke, and the *Jupiter*, as the enemy appeared clear of it, engaged the Japanese destroyers and forced them to retire without delivering their attack on the *Exeter*.

Meanwhile, after ordering the *Exeter* to make for Surabaya escorted by the Dutch destroyer *Witte de With*, Doorman had reformed his remaining cruisers in line, the *Perth*, *Houston* and *Java* following the flagship in that order, with the four American destroyers bringing up the rear. Steering to the eastward, they ran clear of the smoke and were again in sight of the Japanese heavy cruisers on an opposite course on the northern horizon. The *Houston*'s eight-inch guns could reach them, but to bring her two serviceable (forward) turrets to bear she had to swing out of line at each salvo. Her forward magazines and shell-rooms were by now empty and ammunition for the forward guns was being laboriously manhandled from the after magazine. Under these conditions it was not surprising that she failed to hit the enemy. Her luck had not yet run out, however, as two Japanese shells that hit her failed to explode, and did only minor damage. At about the same time the light cruiser *Naka* with five destroyers came briefly out of the smoke to fire 24 torpedoes at the Allied cruisers — once again ineffectively.

Doorman's objective, which he never lost sight of throughout the long hours of battle and manoeuvre, was not unequal, sacrificial combat with the Japanese cruisers and destroyer flotillas, but to get at the troop convoy somewhere beyond them. To do that he must give the enemy the slip as soon as sunset brought the brief tropical twilight at 1821. Shortly before 1800, therefore, he led away to the southward to break contact, while the U.S. destroyers were told to counter-attack, an order soon cancelled and replaced by one to make smoke.

Commander Thomas H. Binford, U.S.N., senior officer of the division of four old 'four-stacker' destroyers, aboard the *John D. Edwards*, led the *Alden*, *Ford* and *Paul Jones* away in compliance, steering to screen the cruiser line. As soon as the smoke was effective, Doorman signalled to Binford to 'Cover my retirement' and led round on to an easterly and then north-easterly course, trying to circle round the rear of the Japanese force. The Admiral must have intended that the U.S. destroyers should continue to screen him from the enemy's view with smoke until darkness hid his encircling move; but Binford decided that the most effective way to cover the Allied fleet's retirement was by attacking with torpedoes. He proceeded to do so but at such a long range as to be ineffective, and then steered to rejoin the main body.

Night had now fallen. Under cover of it Doorman turned northward and then north-west, probing hopefully for the troop convoy he correctly guessed must be no distance away. But soon after 1930 he found his way barred by the *Jintsu* and her destroyers, dimly visible in the moonlight. Flashes betrayed the firing of torpedoes by the *Jintsu* and the Allied line swung away to avoid them. Frustrated for the time being, Doorman led his ships southwards towards the Javanese coast. Reaching shoal water a few miles off shore soon after 2100, he altered course to the westward to begin once again a circling manoeuvre to bypass the enemy cruiser force. It was a vain hope, for every move was being watched by Japanese seaplanes, every alteration of course reported to the Japanese Admiral.

Meanwhile the Allied force was further whittled away. The U.S. destroyers, their torpedoes expended and fuel running short, were ordered away to Surabaya. Then at 2125 an explosion tore asunder the *Jupiter* in the rear of the Allied line. The Admiral had led his force through a Dutch minefield laid, unknown to him, that very afternoon. Nevertheless he now put on a bold front and turned northwards again towards the enemy. His course took him by chance past the spot where the *Kortenaer* had sunk four-and-a-half hours earlier. Some 113 survivors, including her captain, Lieutenant-Commander A. Kroese, were rescued by the *Encounter* which took them to Batavia. The remainder of Doorman's ever-dwindling force pressed on.

Well informed of the Allies' movements, the Japanese were moving in for the kill. The *Nachi* and *Haguro* were first sighted steaming on an opposite track but Takagi at once reversed course and a gun duel developed, under cover of which 12 torpedoes were launched by the Japanese cruisers.

Up to now these remarkable weapons had proved surprisingly ineffective. No less than 139 had been fired, of which one only had hit and sunk the *Kortenaer*. But night action was the ideal setting for their use and they were now to justify themselves. Almost simultaneously the *De Ruyter* and the *Java* leapt under the shock of fearful explosions. Both were brought to a standstill. For a while they lay burning furiously, then their flames were suddenly extinguished as they slid beneath the waters of the Java Sea.

Captain Waller, R.A.N., of the *Perth* now became the senior Allied officer. A last message from his Admiral ordered him to retire to Batavia. He had little choice but to obey for, as he subsequently reported:

> I had now under my orders one undamaged six-inch cruiser, one eight-inch cruiser with very little ammunition and no guns aft. I had no destroyers. The force was subjected throughout the day and night operations to the most superbly organised air reconnaissance. I was opposed by six cruisers and 12 destroyers. By means of their air reconnaissance they had played cat and mouse with the main striking force and I saw no prospect of getting at the enemy … he had ample destroyers to interpose between the convoy and my approach — well advertised as I knew it would be.

So ended the Battle of the Java Sea, a victory, though hardly a very glorious one, for an integrated force enjoying a small degree of gun superiority, a clear margin of powerful, modern destroyers and complete domination of the air, opposed by a hastily gathered, mixed, multinational force of cruisers and old destroyers hampered by a lack of common signal systems. In the circumstances it could have had no other outcome. Even had Doorman's dogged efforts to get through to the troop convoy succeeded, it can hardly be imagined that his ships would have been able to inflict decisive damage before being themselves overwhelmed by the Japanese escorting force.

This in fact is what occurred the following night when the *Perth* and *Houston*, retreating from the Java Sea through the Sunda Strait, ran into the Japanese Western Invasion Force disembarking in Banten Bay. They managed to sink one transport and force three others to beach themselves before being set upon by the escorting warships. Hitting out valiantly at the enemy cruisers and destroyers surrounding them, the *Perth* and *Houston* between them damaged a cruiser and three destroyers, only to be overwhelmed and sunk by repeated torpedo hits after a wild melee lasting over an hour.

A few hours later the damaged *Exeter* and the destroyers H.M.S. *Encounter* and U.S.S. *Pope* accompanying her met a similar fate. Leaving Surabaya on the evening of the 28th and hoping to make the passage of the Sunda Strait under cover of darkness the next night, they were quickly detected by the ubiquitous Japanese reconnaissance planes and shepherded to their doom at the hands of four cruisers and three destroyers on the morning of 1 March. With their destruction the last obstacle to the unopposed landing of the Japanese forces in Java had gone.

4. THE BATTLE OF THE CORAL SEA

The Allied naval forces in East Indian waters had been vainly attempting to delay — they could not hope to halt — the long-prepared and meticulously organised Japanese amphibious expeditions. Thrusting southwards, like tentacles, to grasp the chain of islands which, stretching from the Andamans in the Indian Ocean to the Bismarcks in the South Pacific, constituted in the Japanese War Plan the defensive perimeter of the 'Southern Resources Area', they had been able, with contemptuous ease, to sweep aside the sparse and ill-prepared opposition. Americans and British had been forced to leave the small naval forces deployed in Asiatic waters to sacrifice themselves in hopeless rearguard action. It might have bought time for the Allies — in the event it caused the Japanese only negligible delay — but the inevitably heavy and tragic losses had been accepted as the price of preservation of such imponderables as honour and 'face'.

In the meantime the Allies had been gathering their resources further afield. The British, hard-pressed in European waters, had set about assembling an Eastern Fleet from what could be spared, principally a squadron of battleship veterans of First World War vintage and capabilities and two modern carriers equipped with outdated aircraft. With these they hoped to retain control of the Indian Ocean. The Americans had been forced willy-nilly by the holocaust of Pearl Harbour to depend upon their aircraft carriers, three of which had been available — *Enterprise*, *Lexington* and *Yorktown*. A fourth, the *Saratoga*, had been torpedoed by a Japanese submarine on n January and had limped back to the United States for repair and modernisation. Until the American war machine gathered momentum, a strategic defence had to suffice. This had not precluded tactical offensive moves, but the first duty had been the protection of the island chain stretching from Hawaii to Midway, and of the communications with Australia and New Zealand, by way of Palmyra, Samoa, Fiji and New Caledonia. On the way back from escorting a troop Convoy to Samoa, where U.S. Marines landed on 23 January, the two carrier groups centred on the *Enterprise*, flagship of Vice-Admiral William Halsey, and the *Yorktown*, flagship of Rear-Admiral Frank Fletcher, which had raided Japanese bases in the Marshalls and Gilberts. Their achievements were meagre and experience was bought at the cost of high casualties. On 20 February the *Lexington*'s carrier group under Vice-Admiral W. Brown, steering to deliver an air attack on Rabaul in New Britain where the Japanese had established a main sea and air base, had been attacked by shore-based naval bombers of the 25th Air Flotilla which had been sent out without fighter escort. The *Lexington*'s Wildcat fighters tore into them and worked great execution, few of the enemy bombers surviving, but the raid on Rabaul had had to be abandoned.

It was Admiral Nagumo's hard-hitting carrier force that, further west, had been setting the pattern for war in the Pacific. Since Pearl Harbour, its aircraft, swarming in without warning from over the seaward horizon, had hammered Wake, Rabaul and Amboina into surrender. On 19 February they had suddenly swooped on Darwin, devastating the town and harbour and sinking the numerous ships gathered there. In reply the Americans, forced to spread their limited forces thinly, had again sent a single carrier group to pound ineffectively Wake and Marcus Islands.

But now, at the end of February 1942, with the Malay Barrier falling so unexpectedly cheaply into their hands, the Japanese warlords, intoxicated by the heady draughts of easy victory, were being tempted to speed up the next phase of their war plan. From Rabaul the chain of the Solomon Islands, reaching away south-east towards the communicating route between Hawaii and Australia, and the south-eastern peninsula of Papua with its air base at Port Moresby whence Australia could be attacked, was luring them on to further easy conquests. As a start they occupied Lae and Salamaua on the northern coast of Papua on 7 March. The Americans who, profiting from the painful lessons of massed attack hammered home by Nagumo, had joined the *Yorktown*'s group to that of the *Lexington* in the South Pacific, sent the combined force against the two ports three days later. Flying over the lofty Owen Stanley mountains from the Gulf of Papua, the striking force of 103 naval planes achieved complete surprise and met little opposition. The airmen had much to learn yet, however, and they achieved only a minor success against the numerous ships of the Japanese expedition.

If the vaunted American sea-power seemed to be showing itself to be lacking teeth, the British Navy, so recently the teacher and exemplar of the Imperial Japanese Navy, was about to suffer a second ignominious reverse at the hands of its one-time pupil. Except for delivering another of its annihilating strikes on the port of Tjilatjap, Admiral Nagumo's carrier force had taken little part in the conquest of Java and had returned to Stareing Bay in Celebes, to refuel and prepare for a westward lunge to neutralise British sea-power in the Indian Ocean. On 26 March it sailed — the fast carriers *Akagi*, *Soryu*, *Hiryu*, *Shokaku* and *Zuikaku* accompanied by four fast and powerful battleships, two heavy cruisers, a numerous destroyer screen and a replenishment group of six tankers. On 4 April it was discovered by a British reconnaissance plane 360 miles south of Ceylon.

Admiral Sir James Somerville, commanding the recently assembled British Eastern Fleet, had received warning of the coming blow but had expected it on 1 April. For three days he had cruised and waited, ignorant of the vastly superior strength of the Japanese force, and then, disappointed, had been forced to retire to the fleet anchorage at Addu Atoll in the Maldives to refuel his low-endurance ships. He sailed at once on receipt of the report but was still more than 500 miles away when the familiar pattern of attack, first demonstrated at Pearl Harbour, descended on Colombo. This time, however, the enemy was expected and the harbour cleared and shipping dispersed. Damage was kept to a minimum; but Japanese disappointment was offset by the lucky discovery of the cruisers *Cornwall* and *Dorsetshire* hastening from Colombo to join Admiral Somerville. Dive-bombers back from raiding Colombo were re-armed and flown off, to gather like birds of prey over the luckless ships. Diving vertically, their accurately aimed 500-lb. bombs tore the cruisers asunder. Within a few minutes all that remained of the ships were the remnants of their crews floating in an expanse of oil-covered water.

Coming up from the west, Somerville sought to gain contact with the enemy fleet. Though by this time he knew that he was too weak to accept action with it by day, he hoped he might be able to send his slow, defenceless Albacore torpedo-planes to deliver an attack by night. But Nagumo had already departed eastwards to prepare for his next strike — against Trincomalee in the north-east of Ceylon; what must surely have been an appalling disaster for the Royal Navy was thus avoided. On 9 April Trincomalee shook under the attack of 54 of Nagumo's bombers. Once again the raid had been expected and the harbour cleared of shipping; but once again Nagumo's luck was in, as the small carrier *Hermes* was sighted by one of his planes, hugging the eastern shore of Ceylon. Dive-bombers made short work of her and of her escorting destroyer *Vampire*, the corvette *Hollyhock* and two tankers.

Though Nagumo's operation was only a hit-and-run raid and he now left the Indian Ocean to return home, it had effectively accomplished its objective of securing the western flank of the Japanese 'Southern Resources Area' and of the forces engaged in overrunning Burma. The homecoming of his carriers on 18 April was indeed a triumphant one. Since their aircraft had opened the war at Pearl Harbour, they had careered like a whirlwind across one third of the globe leaving a trail of destruction behind them — at Wake, Rabaul, Amboina, Darwin, Tjilatjap, Colombo and Trincomalee. Harbour installations, merchant ships, warships and enemy aircraft had gone down before the guns and bombs of their planes. The two most powerful navies in the world had been neutralised, leaving the Japanese free to pursue their ambitions unopposed. In all this time Nagumo's ships had suffered no loss or damage and, indeed, except for brief glimpses during the operations off Ceylon, they had not even been sighted.

The time had come, according to the original Japanese war plan, to implement Phase Two: the consolidation and strengthening against the inevitable counter-attack of the defensive perimeter — the great line circling from the Kuriles through Wake, the Marshall and Bismarck archipelagos, Timor, Java, Sumatra, Malaya and Burma. Only when this had been done and the vital supplies of oil from the Dutch oilfields assured, were further advances to be undertaken. Admiral Yamamoto accordingly re-disposed the various groups of the

64

Combined Fleet. Many of the Japanese leaders, however, particularly the Generals, who had control of strategy, forgetful or ignorant of Yamamoto's prophecy of early, easy triumphs, succumbed, in the words of Rear-Admiral Hara, one of Nagumo's subordinate squadron commanders, to a 'Victory disease'. Success had come with so unexpectedly few casualties that contempt for their enemies and a foolish underestimation of American strength in the Pacific had grown up in their minds. Nothing seemed to stand in the way of immediately expanding the perimeter to take in the Western Aleutians in the north; Midway in the east, whence Hawaii could be neutralised or the U.S. Pacific Fleet brought to decisive action; and in the south Samoa, Fiji, New Caledonia and Port Moresby from which Australia could be threatened. These were glittering prizes beckoning to the Japanese warlords flushed with early victory. They failed to understand that successful war in the Pacific depended upon an adequate sea-borne supply system, which would support the ever-multiplying military units scattered in defence of the perimeter, and upon superior sea-power with which to protect it.

The former had been uncertain from the start, owing to Japan's insufficiency of merchant tonnage and its inefficient organisation, by which a large proportion of it was allocated exclusively to the Army or the Navy, leaving an inadequate residue for the import of vital raw materials. It was further threatened by an almost total failure to organise any system of defence of merchant shipping against submarine attack. Sea-power itself had been clearly shown, largely by Nagumo's exploits, to depend principally upon carrier-borne air forces. In this, Japan had apparently displayed a clear superiority. But, in fact, the spectacular success was blinding eyes to the fatal wastage in aircraft and combat-skilled, experienced pilots that the continuous operations of the first four months of war had cost. Though the various individual successes had each been won at a low cost in casualties, by the end of April 1942 315 naval aircraft had been lost in combat, of which 244 were carrier types; a further 540, of which some 300 were carrier types, had been lost 'operationally'. Such numbers were not yet irreplaceable but they boded ill for the Japanese, with their limited industrial capacity and man-power, compared to those of America and her Allies. The quality of air-crew replacements was already perceptibly lower, and they needed operational training. So when the first of the expeditions aimed at expansion of the defensive perimeter — the occupation of Port Moresby — was set in train, only two of the fast fleet carriers, *Zuikaku*, flagship of Rear-Admiral Hara, and *Shokaku*, could be spared to form a covering force.

Nevertheless to the Japanese, their judgment warped by their underestimation of American capabilities, this seemed sufficient, particularly as they believed that only one American aircraft carrier was in the South Pacific. In fact the Americans, able to decipher many of the Japanese operational signals, had been forewarned as early as 16 April of an impending operation to begin on 3 May and the Commander-in-Chief Pacific, Admiral Chester Nimitz, had at once despatched the *Lexington* group (Task Force 11 under Rear-Admiral Aubrey Fitch) from Pearl Harbour to join the *Yorktown* group (Task Force 17 under Rear-Admiral Frank Fletcher) in the south. Orders followed for the two forces to rendezvous on 1 May in the Coral Sea approaches to the westward of the New Hebrides. In addition, a force composed of the Australian cruisers *Australia* and *Hobart*, the U.S. cruiser *Chicago* and two U.S. destroyers, under the command of Rear-Admiral J. C.

Crace, R.N., was to join Admiral Fletcher's flag in the Coral Sea by the 4th.

The Japanese operational plan was an elaborate one calling for the co-ordinated movement of a number of separate groups, the whole operation being commanded by the Commander-in-Chief Fourth Fleet, Vice-Admiral Shigeyoshi Inouye from his light cruiser flagship *Kashiwa* at Rabaul. From that base, two occupation forces were to set out, the first a small group with a single transport which would carry troops to seize the anchorage at Tulagi on Florida Island on 3 May and set up a seaplane base. Then the main occupation force with five transports for Port Moresby would leave, routed via the Jomard Pass through the Louisiades. Both of these groups would be shepherded by a Covering Group, under Rear-Admiral Goto, coming from Truk in the Carolines and composed of four heavy cruisers and the light aircraft carrier *Shoho*, with 12 Zero fighters and nine torpedo-planes embarked. Yet another group of two light cruisers and a seaplane carrier, under Rear-Admiral Marushige, also from Truk, was to operate in support and establish a seaplane base in the Louisiades. Finally, to take care of the American carrier group when it arrived to intervene, Vice-Admiral Takagi's Striking Force of two heavy cruisers and Rear-Admiral Hara's carrier squadron were to come south from the Carolines, circle the Solomon Islands and enter the Coral Sea from the east, catching the Americans between the hammer of Hara's air squadrons and the anvil of Goto's force.

This plan, with its elaborate organisation of numerous groups, setting off from widely separated starting points and working to a pre-arranged time-table to trap the enemy into an unequal battle, was a favourite one with the Japanese and would be repeated in the time to come. Such a division of force is strategically dangerous and in this case only justifiable on the assumption that surprise could be achieved, and that the Americans would have only the one carrier group available, which they would obligingly send to slaughter in the Solomon Sea. Initially, however, the Japanese plan proceeded according to schedule. While the American carrier task force, which, unknown to the Japanese, had duly made rendezvous to the northward of New Caledonia on 1 May, was engaged in refuelling at sea (a process which would take three days to complete), the small expedition for Tulagi sailed from Rabaul. From Truk arrived Goto's Covering Force and Marushige's Support Force to hover protectively to the southward of New Georgia.

Aircraft of General MacArthur's South-West Pacific Command on reconnaissance over the Solomon Sea sighted some of these units during the 2nd. Their reports reached Admiral Fletcher in the *Yorktown* in the evening of that day but were insufficiently detailed to make the situation clear; nor did they seem to refer to the expedition expected to be directed towards Port Moresby. As senior officer of the combined Task Force he therefore gave Fitch a rendezvous for dawn on the 4th, and set off with his own group north-westward to bring the area within the reach of his own reconnaissance planes. No further news came in during the 3rd until, at 1900, the quite unexpected report by one of MacArthur's planes that transports were disembarking troops at Tulagi. Fletcher at once headed north at full speed to catch the Japanese ships with a dawn air-strike from the *Yorktown*. For the first time in the war American naval aviators were to have a chance to repay some of Nagumo's blows in kind. During 4 May on three separate occasions the *Yorktown*'s torpedo-planes and dive-bombers, nearly 40 in all, swooped on the ships in Tulagi harbour. Pilots

68

returned with glowing tales of the damage they had wrought. Well satisfied, Fletcher gathered in his planes, of which only three had been lost, and headed south at high speed to rejoin the *Lexington* group. In fact, however, his flyers, lacking the experience of Nagumo's veterans, had achieved very little. One destroyer, three small minesweepers and five seaplanes were their total score.

By the morning of the 5th, the Allied force had regrouped and, while waiting for further news of enemy forces, it refuelled from the tanker *Neosho*. Reconnaissance planes provided a confusing picture of the situation, reporting ships of every sort, including three aircraft carriers, south of the Solomon Islands. The only certainty was that a force making for Port Moresby must have been amongst those sighted, and during the night Fletcher made ground to the north-west towards its expected route. He had no knowledge as yet of Takagi's Striking Force which that evening rounded San Cristobal and turned north-westerly into the Coral Sea. Nor, as yet, had the Japanese any information about the size or position of the Allied fleet.

During the 6th Fletcher resumed fuelling on a south-easterly course, while waiting for further enlightenment. Takagi's carrier force had turned southwards at 0930, a collision course with Fletcher had it been persisted in; but that evening, when only 70 miles separated the two forces, Takagi turned to refuel his ships on a northerly course. For some reason no air search had been sent out from the Japanese force. One of Admiral Inouye's scouting planes from Rabaul did locate and report the Allied force, but the message did not reach Takagi until the next day. Fletcher remained similarly ignorant of his principal enemy's position. Searches were flown from his carriers but during the forenoon they turned back just short of Takagi's force; later in the day the Japanese were shrouded by the belt of low cloud of a cold front stretching east and west across the Coral Sea.

It was shore-based aircraft that brought Fletcher his first concrete news of other enemy groups, reporting both Goto's Covering Group, which was ineffectively bombed by U.S. Flying Fortresses, and the Port Moresby Invasion Group. By the evening Fletcher could be confident that the latter would be threading the Jomard Pass the next morning. Sending the *Neosho* and her escorting destroyer *Sims* away with orders to make for their next fuelling rendezvous, he turned north-west again for a position from which the enemy would be in range for a dawn air-strike.

A feeling of great events pending gripped the men of Fletcher's force when dawn arrived on 7 May. A decision, one way or the other, was likely to be reached before the day was over, for Japanese reconnaissance planes were soon in touch and reporting the position of the American carriers. To make doubly sure that the Port Moresby expedition was headed off from its objective, Fletcher now detached Rear-Admiral Crace with the *Australia, Hobart, Chicago* and three destroyers to intercept them should they get through the Jomard Pass. The carrier groups turned north and launched ten scout-bombers to search over a wide arc. Once again the planes which might have contacted Takagi's force were turned back by the bad weather in which it was shrouded. At 0815, however, came an electrifying signal from another scout from the *Yorktown*, which reported two carriers and four heavy cruisers 225 miles distant, to the northward of Misima Island in the Louisiades. The elusive Japanese fleet carriers had been located at last — or so it seemed. From the deck of the *Lexington* 28 dive-bombers and 12 torpedo-planes with an escort of ten fighters were soon streaming off, forming up and steering away to the attack. Half-an-hour later 25 dive-bombers, ten torpedo-planes and eight fighters from the *Yorktown* followed them.

But now the scouting planes began returning. As each landed on, the pilots reported for de-briefing. There was dismay when it was discovered that the report of 'two carriers and four heavy cruisers' had been intended to read 'two heavy cruisers and two destroyers'. A coding error had been made. Almost the whole air-striking force had been launched against a minor target and had taken with them a large proportion of the defensive fighters. Until they returned, Fletcher's carriers would be very vulnerable to any massive air attack mounted against them, whether by shore-based bombers or Hara's carrier planes — and such an attack was more than likely. Nevertheless, encouraged by a further report from one of MacArthur's Australia-based reconnaissance planes that a force comprising one carrier, 16 other warships and ten transports had been sighted not far from the target position given to his attack planes, Fletcher decided to let them continue on their mission. Though this reported armada was in fact the Port Moresby invasion group and Goto's covering group, his calculated risk was to be justified.

Admiral Takagi's Striking Force which, all unaware of the American carriers only 70 miles distant, had turned away on a northerly course at dusk the previous evening, reversed course again at 0200 on 7 May. At dawn, when some 200 miles to the east of Fletcher, an air search southward had been launched. At 0736 one of Hara's planes reported a carrier and a cruiser about 200 miles south-south-west. Never doubting that this was the enemy for whom he had been looking, the Japanese admiral immediately ordered a full-scale air-strike to be despatched. Half-an-hour later 36 'Val' dive-bombers and 24

'Kates' armed with bombs, with a fighter escort of 18 Zeros, were on their way, led by Kakuichi Takahashi, leader of the dive-bombers at Pearl Harbour and veteran of all Nagumo's subsequent strikes. Like Fletcher, Hara was now to find himself similarly bereft of many of his aircraft for the sake of a target of minor importance. For, when Takahashi reached the area of the reported contact, he found only the tanker *Neosho* and her escorting destroyer *Sims* which had been mistaken for a carrier and a cruiser by the reconnaissance pilot. When no other target could be discovered, Takahashi gave the order to attack and the two ships were quickly overwhelmed and sunk. And meanwhile Fletcher's real position had at last reached Admiral Hara from a reconnaissance plane flown from one of Goto's cruisers. Nothing could be done about it, however, until the strike aircraft returned.

Fletcher's attack planes had, in the meantime, been having better luck. Led by Commander William B. Ault, the *Lexington*'s air group commander, they had taken off in dirty, gusty weather between rain squalls, but had broken out into a cloudless blue with visibility clear to a sharp horizon. By 1100 they were at 15,000 feet and were flying up the island chain of the Louisiades when far away on the starboard horizon ships were sighted. Behind Ault and his two supporting wing men, the air group swung round in their direction. As they approached, the flat, flush-deck shape of an aircraft carrier could be distinguished from amongst the medley of cruisers and destroyers. It was the little *Shoho* and she was at once selected as the target. In such clear weather no surprise attack was possible. The *Shoho*'s fighters were already in the air and the ship manoeuvred violently to evade the bombs aimed by the dive-bombers, plummeting down from 18,000 feet to release at 2,500 feet, and the torpedoes launched by the low-flying torpedo-planes. But escape was impossible. The Japanese fighters proved strangely ineffective on this occasion, shooting down only one American bomber during the attacks and damaging another so that it was forced to land on Rossel Island in the Louisiades, while eight of their own number were shot down by the Wildcats. As the *Lexington*'s bombers pulled away, the *Yorktown*'s roared in, concentrating on the carrier already crippled by bombs and torpedoes. Thirteen bomb hits and seven torpedoes sent her to the bottom within three minutes of the last attack. Over the air was heard the excited voice of Lieutenant-Commander Dixon, commanding one of the *Lexington*'s squadrons: 'Scratch one flat-top. Dixon to Carrier. Scratch one flat-top.'

So far so good. By 1338 Fletcher's aircraft, less three lost, had landed on their carriers again. Already Admiral Inouye, appraised of Fletcher's position and strength and of Crace's squadron waiting south of the Jomard Pass, had ordered the Port Moresby Invasion Group to turn back until the way through had been made safe. Goto followed suit with the remainder of his covering force. But meanwhile an effort to eliminate Crace was under way. From Japanese shore bases squadrons of aircraft had been despatched. From 1400 onwards the Allied squadron was repeatedly attacked by high bombers, low bombers and torpedo-planes. Bomb-bursts straddled them and torpedo tracks sped close by. The Japanese aviators believed they had sunk a battleship and a cruiser and torpedoed a second battleship. But by skilful manoeuvring Crace's ships emerged unscathed from their attacks — and from another by three over-enthusiastic U.S. Army planes from an Australian base.

The two main opposing units — the carrier squadrons — shrouded in the driving drizzle of the cold front stretched east and west across the Coral Sea, had still no contact with one another, though each knew the other was within range of an air strike. By the time the American carrier aircraft had been refuelled and re-armed after their attack on the *Shoho*, it was too late in the day for Admiral Fletcher to contemplate launching a second strike even if Takagi's force were located. At that time American carriers were not yet capable of air operations by night. Trusting to the searches being carried out by MacArthur's shore-based aircraft to locate his enemy for him, Fletcher decided to wait for the morrow.

Not so the Japanese admirals. The unbroken run of spectacular success of the past five months, and the quality of their highly-trained and experienced flyers, inspired them with confidence. Takahashi was ordered out again, leading 12 dive-bombers and 15 torpedo-planes, to locate the enemy and attack at dusk. The Zero fighter escorts, untrained for night operations, had to be dispensed with. The remainder took off at 1630. Steering westward under the low overcast and through intermittent squalls of rain, they sighted nothing. With the approach of dusk they jettisoned their bombs and torpedoes and turned for home. They could not know that their return track was to take them directly over their long-sought target. Suddenly, amongst their somewhat scattered formation, Wildcat fighters were whirling, their guns blazing. The 'Val' dive-bombers, highly manoeuvrable, turning to mix it with their attackers escaped lightly, only one of them being shot down. But the staid 'Kate' torpedo-bombers made easy victims; one after the other, eight of them plunged flaming into the sea. Wildcats from the *Lexington* had been patrolling over the American task force when radar detected the Japanese formation. They had at once been directed out to intercept while more Wildcats were launched from the *Yorktown*. In the brief, fierce fight that ensued, two of them were shot down.

It was now almost dark. The American fighters were recalled and began landing on. Some were still circling, waiting their turn, when three strange aircraft joined the circuit, switching on their lights and signalling to the carriers. Japanese bombers had mistaken the *Yorktown* for one of their own and were shaping to alight on her! Awakening came simultaneously to both sides. The Japanese sheered hastily away and vanished into the gloom pursued by a burst of gunfire. Twenty minutes later three more made the same mistake and were driven off. As the author of *Zero!* records

> Our air-crews were disgusted. They had flown for gruelling hours over the sea, bucked thunder squalls and, finally, had lost all trace of their positions relative to their own carriers. When finally they did sight the coveted American warships, cruising unsuspecting beneath them, they were without bombs or torpedoes — having previously jettisoned them into the sea.

Admiral Hara was now regretting the easy confidence with which he had sent his airmen out into the dirty weather. Lacking radar or radio homing beacons, he switched on his searchlights to guide the pilots home. Only seven straggled back including the group leader, Takahashi, and were gathered in with petrol almost exhausted; the remaining 11 failed to make it and splashed into the sea as their engines spluttered and died. It had been a shaming day for the vaunted Japanese naval air service. They had lost their first carrier, though only an auxiliary. Their proud veterans of a dozen successful battles had failed ignominiously under the eyes of an amused enemy. 'Face' had been lost. Takagi contemplated seeking a night action with his cruisers, in which the disgrace might be wiped out; but a plaintive request from Rear-Admiral Abe, commanding the Port Moresby transport convoy, for air cover since the *Shoho* was no longer there to provide it, reminded him of his primary duty under the operation orders. To close the Port Moresby force he steamed away to the north.

Nevertheless it was still dark the next morning, when aircraft took off from Hara's carriers and fanned out on a search between southeast and south-west to a distance of 200 miles. At about the same time, on the deck of the *Lexington*, some 180 miles to the southward, 18 Dauntless scout-bombers were warming up before taking off on a similar mission in search of the Japanese carriers. Confident that his search would soon reveal the position of the enemy carrier force, Hara ordered a striking force of 33 dive-bombers and 18 torpedo-planes with an escort of 18 fighters to be ranged up and, as daylight spread across the dappled sea, over which swept a succession of rain squalls, they roared off the decks of the *Zuikaku* and *Shokaku* and headed south. Hardly had they gone out of sight when the expected sighting report from one of the scouting planes reached Hara and was relayed to Takahashi, once again leading the strike formation.

Almost simultaneously, Lieutenant J. G. Smith, pilot of one of the *Lexington*'s scouts, on his way back after completion of an apparently fruitless search, caught sight of Hara's carriers through a curtain of rain and passed the great news for which Fletcher had been so anxiously waiting. By 0915 24 Dauntless dive-bombers, nine Devastator torpedo-planes and six Wildcats from the *Yorktown* were on their way, followed ten minutes later by 22 dive-bombers, 12 torpedo-planes and nine fighters from the *Lexington*.

Though launched nearly an hour later than the Japanese striking force, the Americans were to be the first to locate their target. The *Yorktown*'s dive-bombers, circling at 17,000 feet and making use of cloud cover, waited for the slower torpedo-planes to arrive. While they waited, the *Zuikaku* disappeared into a large rain squall, but the *Shokaku* remained in the clear, launching Zero fighters to bring the defensive patrol already in the air up to 18. It was just 1057 when Torpedo Squadron 5, led by Lieutenant-Commander Joe Taylor, started down the long slope to the torpedo-launching position, while the dive-bombers peeled off in succession into their plummeting seaward plunge. Six Zeros racing in to pick off the lumbering Devastators were met and repulsed by four escorting Wildcats. The torpedo-plane pilots were left unmolested. But even so they suffered under the crippling handicap of slow and unreliable torpedoes, which had to be dropped at a low speed from only a few feet above the surface of the sea. Experiencing for the first time the daunting sight of tracer shells converging from the scores of guns aimed at them from the carrier and her screen of cruisers and destroyers, and the barrage of high-explosive bursts between them and the target, it is not surprising that they launched at too great a range to ensure success; furthermore many of the torpedoes ran wild. The *Shokaku* had no trouble avoiding them. The dive-bombers, pulling out of their vertical dives at 2,500 feet to send their 500-lb. bombs whistling down, did better. Though they, too, discovered a flaw in their equipment when their bomb sights and windscreens fogged up with the sudden change of temperature in the dive, two of them scored hits on the *Shokaku*, damaging the flightdeck and starting a blaze forward as petrol caught fire.

Meanwhile the air group of the *Lexington*, ten minutes behind the *Yorktown*'s, had lost cohesion in the rolling rain clouds. Many failed to locate the enemy and turned back after a fruitless search. Only the four dive-bombers of the section led by the air group commander, Commander Ault, 11 of the torpedo-planes and six Wildcats arrived over the target and attacked through a hole in the overcast. The Wildcats, drawing off the more numerous Zeros, lost three of their number. Five of the torpedo-planes, no more successful than the *Yorktown*'s, were shot down. Once again the Dauntless dive-bombers scored the only hit at the cost of two shot down and three more that ran out of fuel and failed to get back to the carrier. The *Shokaku* had suffered more than 100 men killed and was put out of action. The fires which raged for a time were brought under control, however, and she limped away, riding low in the water, for Japan, which she reached after a perilous journey.

While the flyers of the United States Navy were thus discovering that they had much leeway to make up in both material and skill, 180 miles to the south the American carriers were experiencing their first attack by pilots who had behind them long experience and had seen the *Cornwall, Dorsetshire* and *Hermes* go down under their bombs. The pilot who had located Fletcher's Task Force, Warrant Officer Kenzo Kanno, remained to shadow and report its movements until, with fuel running low, he set course to return to his carrier. On his way he sighted Takahashi's formation. Accepting the suicidal certainty of his actions, Kanno ranged himself alongside the leader's plane to guide him through the barrier of bad visibility to where the target was to be found in the clear, blue weather beyond, only breaking away when it came in sight. On a sparkling blue sea, white-flecked by the fresh trade wind, the

American Task Force could be seen in circular formation, an inner ring of the five cruisers at one-and-a-half miles from the carriers, the seven destroyers making an outer ring half-a-mile beyond.

The signal to attack was given. The 'Kate' torpedo-aircraft broke into small formations and, as they planed down, fanned out in oft-practised fashion to approach from various points of the compass. The 'Val' dive-bombers, high above them at 17,000 feet, flew on till they were over the target before banking steeply over to begin their vertical dive one after the other. Both groups found themselves strangely undisturbed by any fighter opposition. In spite of the advantage of possessing radar which had given 20 minutes' warning of the impending attack, the Americans had been caught off balance. Eight Wildcats had been airborne at the moment of alarm but they were low in fuel. Nine more had been hastily launched but were either drawn into dogfights by Zeros or were still clawing their way upwards when the 'Vals' began their dives. Thus the Japanese aircraft had only the efforts of the inexperienced and unpractised anti-aircraft gunners to face as they swooped. The *Lexington* found herself amongst a pattern of criss-crossing torpedo wakes. Captain Sherman swung the unwieldy great ship as best he could to 'comb' the tracks of as many as possible; but others could not be avoided. Two slammed into her port side at the very moment that bombs from the diving 'Vals' began exploding all round her, two hits and a number of near misses rending and shaking her. The *Yorktown*, a handier ship than the 'Lady Lex', having a smaller turning circle, fared better. The eight torpedoes aimed at her all came from her port side. Streaking through the water at 30 knots she avoided them all. The dive-bombers which selected her for target scored only a solitary hit. The 800-lb. bomb, penetrating to the fourth deck before exploding, inflicted heavy casualties; but the flight deck remained serviceable for flying operations.

The Japanese airmen pressed home their attacks with their usual valour. At the very end a solitary torpedo-plane, coming late to the battle, flew unswervingly up the starboard side of the *Yorktown*, fired at by every five-inch gun and machine gun, until the launching position on the carrier's bow was reached, when it turned, dropped its torpedo and swung away, apparently unscathed. The defences had proved ineffectual even to hamper the assault seriously; but as the attackers turned away, their mission accomplished, the Wildcat fighters and the Dauntless scout-bombers forced them to pay heavily for such success as they had achieved. The latter could hardly be considered fighter aircraft and though they boldly challenged any 'Kates' they could find, shooting down four of them, they, too, lost four of their number. The majority of the 26 other aircraft that the Japanese lost that day in combat went down before the guns of the Wildcats. They included the air group commander Kakuichi Takahashi. Twelve more Japanese aircraft, besides that of Warrant Officer Kanno, failed to return to their carrier. On the American side, 33 aircraft in all were lost during 8 May.

The aerial battle was over before noon. Both sides could take stock. The Japanese had lost the *Shoho* and, as mentioned above, had been forced to send the *Shokaku* to seek shelter and major repairs. She was to be out of action for two months. The *Zuikaku* was undamaged; but she had lost so many aircraft with their experienced crews that she, too, would be non-operational for more than a month. Thus neither of Japan's two most up-to-date fleet carriers would be available for the next operation planned. On the fateful 4 June off Midway, their absence was to have decisive consequences. Meanwhile the Japanese triumphant progress had received its first check at the Battle of the Coral Sea. Admiral Inouye now postponed the Port Moresby operation, a postponement that was eventually to become a cancellation.

In Admiral Fletcher's Task Force, as the gunfire and the crump of bombs died away, the situation appeared reasonably satisfactory. The *Yorktown's* damage was not enough to affect her ability to operate her aircraft and by 1300 she had gathered them all in. The *Lexington*, to be sure, was on fire in four places and listing seven degrees to port, but the fires were being contained and the list corrected by transferring oil. Her lifts were jammed in the 'up' position but she was able to land her returning aircraft and park them on deck. Commander R. H. Healy, her damage control officer, felt confident enough to suggest light-heartedly to Captain Sherman that, though the situation was well in hand, he would be well advised to take any further torpedo hits on the starboard side. Even discounting the oversanguine reports of some of the returning American bomber pilots, that they had left one of the Japanese carriers 'on fire and settling fast', it seemed that the balance of success lay clearly with Task Force 17.

Then at 1247 came a sudden, unexpected shock as the *Lexington* staggered under a violent internal explosion. The supreme peril to which a carrier in action was subject, the spread of petrol fumes between decks as a result of torpedo or bomb damage, had been insidiously growing. Now it reached the motor generator room. A sparking commutator set off the explosion. Even now the situation did not seem catastrophic and landing operations were still taking place as late as 1400. But, as further explosions took place, fires blazed up, communications failed, electric power and steering control were successively lost, and fire main pressure fell away, the flames could no longer be fought. At any moment the great ship might blow up. By 1630 the engine and boiler rooms had to be evacuated. At 1707 the order to abandon ship was given. The wounded had already been transferred to boats alongside. The remainder of the crew now went over the side and were picked up by destroyers without loss. Captain Sherman and his Executive Officer, Commander Seligman were still on board 45 minutes later when a heavy explosion hurled aircraft on deck high into the air. It was time to make an end. As soon as they had left her, the *Lexington* was given the *coup de grâce* with five torpedoes from the destroyer *Phelps* and at 1853 she plunged to the bottom. Of her crew, 216 had been killed by the Japanese bombs and torpedoes, and 35 of her aircraft were still on board when she went down.

Petrol fires had proved to be the Achilles Heel of the aircraft carrier, turning otherwise repairable damage into a mortal wound. Japanese carriers were soon to suffer the same fearful fate. The loss of the 'Lady Lex' robbed the Americans of any claim to a victory in the Battle of the Coral Sea. If ships lost were the only criterion, indeed, it would be rated as defeat. But other factors must be taken into account — the halting of Japanese conquest in the South Pacific, the temporary elimination at a crucial moment of both *Shokaku* and *Zuikaku* and, above all, the heavy losses amongst Japan's irreplaceable, highly-skilled veteran carrier airmen. On the morrow of the battle, both sides withdrew their naval forces from the Coral Sea, to lick their wounds. For the time being, at any rate, Japanese ambition in that area had been contained. The Americans, informed through cryptography of Japanese plans, were able to concentrate their available forces in Hawaiian waters. It was not yet the turn of the tide in the Pacific War, but at the Battle of the Coral Sea Japanese victory was seen to have reached high water. A limit had been set to expansion southwards. In the following month, at Midway, the eastward lunge was to be bloodily repulsed.

5. MIDWAY — GUADALCANAL: SAVO ISLAND

Hindsight shows the Battle of the Coral Sea to have been a strategic victory for the Allies, though tactically a drawn battle at best. Japanese southward expansion was halted and the threat to the Antipodes removed; but the cost in ships was greater to the U.S. Fleet both actually and proportionately. Not only had the Americans lost a fleet carrier as against a Japanese auxiliary carrier, but, with the *Yorktown* out of action and the *Saratoga* not yet operational after repairs and modernisation, they were left with only the *Hornet* and *Enterprise* in the whole Pacific to oppose the four fast carriers of Nagumo's squadron, *Akagi*, *Kaga*, *Hiryu* and *Soryu*, fresh from their period of rest and re-equipment after their return from the Indian Ocean. As for battleships, an American squadron had been assembled on the U.S. west coast, but they were too slow to operate with the carriers and they were left out of the Commander-in-Chief's consideration. The initiative still lay with the Japanese. How should Admiral Nimitz deploy his exiguous force to parry the next blow? The alternatives were 3,000 miles apart.

The problem would have been insoluble but for the important advantage held by the Allies — the ability (unknown to the Japanese) to decipher many of the Japanese operational signals. By 10 May the Commander-in-Chief Pacific Fleet, Admiral Nimitz, knew that an expedition to capture Midway Island would be getting under way about the 24th, and he made preparations to meet it. The whole of his force, other than the battleship squadron, was concentrated at Pearl Harbour where dockyard engineers were working at breakneck

84

pace round the clock to make the *Yorktown* battleworthy again. Besides knowing the main objective for the next Japanese thrust, Nimitz was also in possession of the principal details of Admiral Yamamoto's plan. As this depended for its success firstly upon surprise and then on deception to lure the American Fleet into decisive action against a superior concentration of force, this advantage was crucial. The ingenious and elaborate Japanese plan, with its division of the fleet into a number of independent task forces, could only justify its disregard of the principle of concentration of force if secrecy were preserved and surprise achieved.

The Japanese Fleet was divided into no less than eight such task forces for the Midway operation. Two of these were small expeditions to occupy Attu and Kiska at the western end of the Aleutian island chain. A third, centred round the light carriers *Ryujo* and *Junyo*, was to deliver a paralysing air bombardment on Dutch Harbour at the other end of the chain. Though the occupation of Attu and Kiska was part of the strategic plan to expand the perimeter defences, these northern expeditions were also expected to bring American forces hurrying to the rescue. A fourth force of four battleships, the Aleutian Support Force, was therefore to be stationed to intercept them halfway between the Hawaiian islands and the Aleutians. Meanwhile, from the Marianas, would sail a transport group carrying occupation troops to Midway with a close support group of cruisers and destroyers; from Japan a covering group of two battleships, four cruisers and a destroyer screen. These three groups comprised the Occupation Force, commanded by Vice-Admiral Nobutake Kondo.

The territorial objectives were those of the victory-drunk Japanese High Command. The more clear-sighted naval Commander-in-Chief, Yamamoto, realised that the outcome of the war depended rather upon bringing to action and decisively defeating the United States Fleet before the massive reinforcements of modern battleships and aircraft carriers under construction reached it. Admiral Nagumo's force of four large carriers, therefore, having delivered its customary whirlwind air-strike on Midway to soften it up for the amphibious assault, would then be free to join Yamamoto's Main Body centred round the three splendid battleships *Yamato* (biggest in the world, mounting nine 18-inch guns), *Mutsu* and *Nagato* and to engage the fleet which Nimitz must inevitably send to the support of Midway.

Had Nimitz not possessed knowledge of the plan in considerable detail, it could well have been successful. Between 26 and 29 May the eight Japanese task forces got under way from their scattered points of departure. A spirit of boastful confidence permeated the whole fleet, engendered by memories of past easy victories. Commander Fuchida, hero of the Pearl Harbour exploit, and still Nagumo's air group leader, was to record that 'We were so sure of our own strength that we thought we could smash the enemy fleet single-handed, even if the battleship groups did nothing to support us.' In Yamamoto's flagship, according to one of his office staff captured later, all hands 'were singing war songs at the top of their lungs'. Only the Admiral himself 'seemed in unusually low spirits'. On board the *Akagi*, where his trusted operations officer, Minoru Genda, lay sick of a fever, the ever-cautious Nagumo was doubtful of the quality of the unfledged aviators who had come to fill the vacancies left by earlier casualties.

The Japanese Admiral's gloom was more justified than they knew. Fully apprised of their intentions, the American Task Force 16 — the carriers *Enterprise* and *Hornet* commanded by Rear-Admiral Raymond Spruance — had cleared Pearl

Harbour, to be followed on 30 May by Rear-Admiral Fletcher's Task Force 17 centred on the *Yorktown*, now fully battleworthy after a tremendous feat of rapid repair by dockyard technicians. On 2 June the two forces made rendezvous 325 miles north-east of Midway and prepared to counter the blow they knew to be scheduled for the 4th.

The Battle of Midway which followed, a decisive victory for the Americans and the great turning-point of the Pacific War, has been too often recounted from Japanese as well as American viewpoints to require repetition in detail in the restricted space of this volume. A summary must suffice. Never dreaming that an American carrier task force would be poised waiting for him in the Midway area, and badly served by the scouting seaplanes sent out from his attendant cruisers, Nagumo was caught off balance: his planes were still being refuelled and re-armed after attacking Midway when the massed airstrike from the American carriers swooped on him. Though the American torpedo-planes failed to achieve any hits and their crews suffered cruel casualties attacking with the same ineffective torpedoes as at the Coral Sea and in the same low-performance Devastators, they drew off the Japanese defences to allow the Dauntless dive-bombers to deliver mortal blows to all four of Nagumo's carriers. The same fatal sequence occurred in each as petrol fires spread uncontrollably, forcing the crew on deck or trapping them below. Finally, when the Emperor's portrait had been reverently wrapped and transferred to safety, the order to abandon ship was given and the carrier's end hastened by torpedoes from an attendant destroyer.

From one carrier only, the *Hiryu*, put out of action later than the others, was it possible to launch counter-attacks. The first, of 18 dive-bombers with an escort of six Zeros, though intercepted by Wildcat fighters and losing 13 'Vals' and three Zeros, succeeded in getting two bomb hits on the *Yorktown*, These inflicted no fatal damage and within two hours the carrier was able to steam at 19 knots and operate aircraft. A second strike, however, comprising ten torpedo-planes and six fighters, scored two torpedo hits on the *Yorktown*, bringing her to a halt with all power gone. As the ship heeled far over to port and seemed about to capsize, the order to abandon her was given. She remained afloat, nevertheless, and on the following day was taken in tow, only to be torpedoed and sunk during the afternoon of the 6th by the Japanese submarine *I-168*.

Appreciation of the disastrous outcome of the carrier battle did not come to Admiral Yamamoto for some time after Nagumo had transferred his flag from the doomed *Akagi* to the cruiser *Nagara*. On the other hand, from distorted accounts reaching the Commander-in-Chief he believed that the Americans had lost the only one of their carriers present. The time had come to bring his overwhelming force of battleships and cruisers into action. Orders went out for the heavy ships to concentrate with the Main Body and join in pursuit of the defeated enemy. But during the evening of the 4th, details of his own losses and of the enemy's carrier strength reached Yamamoto from Nagumo and in the early hours of the 5th he accepted defeat. The Midway operation was abandoned and a general retirement ordered. Rear-Admiral Spruance's Task Force 16 had prudently withdrawn eastwards at dusk to avoid any night encounter with the greatly superior Japanese surface forces. Returning to renew action on the morning of the 5th, planes from his two carriers found only two Japanese heavy cruisers, *Mogami* and *Mikuma*, to receive their attentions. These two ships had been part of the Close Support Group of four cruisers, whose part in the Midway operation was to have been a bombardment of the island installations prior to the landing operation. Recalled by the Commander-in-Chief, they had been steering to rejoin the Main Body when an American submarine had been sighted in the moonlight. Swerving hastily away in an emergency turn, the *Mogami* and *Mikuma* had collided. Left by the remainder of their squadron to limp home as best they could, they were discovered early on the 5th by a scouting plane and were then set upon by no less than 81 dive-bombers from the *Hornet* and *Enterprise* attacking in three waves. The *Mikuma* was battered to a wreck and sunk, but the *Mogami* amazingly survived to reach Truk.

This brought the Battle of Midway to an end. Overnight, the Japanese Navy's daunting carrier superiority had been wiped out. With Nagumo's ships had gone some 250 aircraft and several hundred crack air-crew, irreplaceable under war-time conditions and the unceasing press of operations. Only in the rolling mists of the Aleutians did the Japanese plan go, for what it was worth, according to schedule. The light carriers *Junyo* and *Ryujo* evaded the sea and air reconnaissance searching for them and launched two sharp raids on Dutch Harbour. Japanese troops occupied the undefended islands of Attu and Kiska. But Admiral Nimitz did not rise to the bait offered by sending reinforcements into the waiting arms of the battleships of the Aleutian Support Force. It was with only a hollow victory in the north to their credit that the Japanese naval forces left in the middle of June.

The Japanese oversanguine ambitions to extend their conquests had been halted at both ends of the huge perimeter. In the south, though a fresh attempt to capture Port Moresby, by means of a land operation across the Owen Stanley mountains, was soon to be initiated by landings near Buna on the northern shore of Papua, and was to come near to success before being finally thrown back by Australian troops, other far-seeking plans to occupy New Caledonia, Fiji and Samoa were now abandoned. The Japanese reverted to their original plan to halt and consolidate at this stage. For this purpose Rabaul was to be built up as the main naval and air base. Command of the area and of the naval forces based on Rabaul was assigned to Vice-Admiral Gunichi Mikawa. He had at his disposal the four heavy cruisers of the 6th Cruiser Squadron, *Aoba* (flagship) *Kako*, *Kinugasa* and *Furutaka*, each mounting six eight-inch guns, commanded by Rear-Admiral Aritomo Goto who fought at the Battle of the Coral Sea, the light cruisers *Tenryu* and *Yubari* and a few destroyers, while the heavy cruiser *Chokai* mounting ten eight-inch guns was available as fleet flagship when required. Rear-Admiral Yamada's 25th Naval Air Flotilla — 24 twin-engined bombers and 30 Zero fighters — provided the air component of the fleet. Mikawa had previously commanded the force of fast battleships and cruisers supporting Nagumo's carriers in their meteoric course from Pearl Harbour to Ceylon. During the Midway operations he had commanded the battleships of the Covering Group.

The American Joint Chiefs of Staff, though bound by inter-Allied agreement to give preference to the war in Europe and therefore confined by their limited naval and military strength in the Pacific to a strategic defensive, had no intention of leaving the Japanese free to consolidate unhindered. Plans had been for some time under consideration for an advance through the Solomon Islands chain, starting with an occupation of the Santa Cruz Islands, to be followed by the recapture of Tulagi and the area adjacent to it. Preparations had included the setting up of a naval and air base on the island of Efate and a seaplane base, to which an airstrip was being added, on Espiritu Santo, and the despatch of two regiments of the 1st Marine Division to New Zealand. Its third regiment had been sent to Samoa in March 1942. In command of the operational area (South Pacific) and of whatever Allied forces were assembled there (South Pacific Force), Vice-Admiral R. L. Ghormley was appointed. From his adjoining South-West Pacific Area, General MacArthur would provide reconnaissance by his air forces based in Queensland and at Port Moresby. Under Rear-Admiral John McCain, a land-based air component of the South Pacific Force, composed of U.S. Navy and Marine seaplanes and fighters, U.S. Army bombers and fighters and some Royal New Zealand Air Force bombers, was deployed on bases at Espiritu Santo, Efate, New Caledonia, Fiji, Tongatabu and Samoa. Tulagi, however, was 560 nautical miles from the nearest of these bases, Espiritu Santo, and therefore beyond the range of McCain's fighters. Thus the essential close air support during the landings could only be supplied from carriers. The triumphant outcome of the Battle of Midway fortunately enabled the Commander-in-Chief Pacific to deploy three of these ships, *Saratoga*, *Enterprise* and *Wasp* (recently joined from the Atlantic), in the South Pacific with their cruiser and destroyer screens.

The spearhead of the whole great enterprise would be the South Pacific Amphibious Force comprising 19,000 officers and men of the U.S. Marines, commanded by Major-General Alexander Vandegrift. These would be carried in 23 transports, with five American and three Australian cruisers, with 15 American destroyers providing escort and fire support, under the command of Rear-Admiral V. A. C. Crutchley, R.N., flying his flag in the cruiser *Australia*.

With these various resources earmarked, Admiral Ghormley received his directive on 2 July 1942, which laid down as his first task, with target date 1 August, the occupation of the Santa Cruz Islands[7], Tulagi and adjacent positions. Two days later came startling news. Air reconnaissance had revealed a Japanese airstrip under construction on the grassy plain eastward of Lunga Point on the north coast of the island of Guadalcanal, opposite Tulagi, virtually the only piece of terrain suitable for an air base in the whole of the mountainous, jungle-clad Solomon Islands group. It was at once appreciated that Guadalcanal was the key to the whole area. Everything must be subordinated to its speedy capture. And, indeed, for the next six months the whole Pacific War was to be distilled into a bloody struggle for possession of this one almost uninhabitable island of mountain, jungle and swamp. The outcome would depend upon which side could establish control of the adjacent seas to supply and reinforce the land forces contending ashore for mastery.

While Ghormley and his staff planned and organised at a furious pace (and even so found it necessary to postpone D-day to 7 August), and while the bulldozers and mechanical diggers of construction battalions tore down the jungle and prepared the new island airfields, the Marines of the expeditionary force were being concentrated, some coming from New Zealand, others directly from the United States, in their combat-loaded transports. On 26 July the whole huge armada — the Amphibious Force with its cruisers and destroyers and Rear-Admiral Leigh Noyes' Air Support Force (*Saratoga*, *Enterprise* and *Wasp*) with its attendant fast battleship, *North Carolina*, six cruisers and 16 destroyers — gathered at an ocean rendezvous south of Fiji. The several flag officers met in conference on board the *Saratoga*, flagship of the Task Force

---

[7] The Santa Cruz Islands were to prove unsuitable as a base, and were in fact never effectively occupied.

Commander, Vice-Admiral Frank Fletcher. The 48 hours allowed for ironing out details of the coming operation was little enough time to ensure smooth co-operation. In particular the mixed force of American and Australian cruisers, concentrated under the command of Rear-Admiral Crutchley, had little opportunity to exchange ideas or standardise methods. Indeed some of the American cruiser captains were soon to be in action commanded by a foreign admiral they had never met. Similarly the impromptu landing rehearsals carried out by the Marines in the Fijis between 28-31 July were far less than adequate. But there was no time for more. The airstrip on Guadalcanal was growing apace. It must be in American hands before Japanese aircraft arrived to occupy it.

Speed and surprise were the two essentials. The former was achieved, though at the expense of thorough preparation, and at sundown on *6* August the Amphibious Force was approaching the eastern entrance to Indispensable Strait between Guadalcanal and Malaita. That ultimate arbiter of many naval operations, the weather, ensured surprise, shrouding the expedition in rain and low cloud and hiding it from Japanese air reconnaissance. The first warning of the approach — indeed of the existence — of the invasion force came to Admiral Mikawa in a wireless message from Tulagi at 0725 on the morning of the 7th, at which time U.S. Marines were already landing on Guadalcanal. Speed and surprise had brought rich dividends. Though the airfield which quickly fell into American hands was almost ready to accept planes, no Japanese aircraft had yet arrived; nor had occupation troops, so that almost negligible opposition from the Japanese labour battalion was encountered. At Tulagi, the 6,000 Marines employed suffered more than 300 casualties before the base was in their possession but this was owing to the fanatical resolve of the 750-strong garrison to die rather than surrender.

Caught by surprise as they were, the Japanese were not slow to react. Within two hours of Mikawa's receipt of the message from Tulagi, 27 twin-engined bombers escorted by 18 Zeros were roaring off the Rabaul runways for the 560-nautical-mile flight to Guadalcanal. They were followed by 16 single-engined dive-bombers which were to be staged through the refuelling airstrip on Buka island. At 1045 on Bougainville Island, two young Australian naval officers, Lieutenants P. E. Mason and W. J. Read, in their jungle hide-outs in the lonely, dangerous role of 'coast-watchers', as such devoted spies were un-romantically called, saw the bombers passing overhead. On their portable wireless sets they tapped a warning, the first of the innumerable invaluable messages by which the various coast-watchers would keep the Allies alerted to every Japanese move in the campaign ahead. From Admiral Noyes' carriers operating to the south of Guadalcanal, 60 Wildcats in groups of six or eight were flown off. Over the anchored transports a furious air battle developed, in which 11 American fighters were lost against 14 Japanese bombers and two Zeros. The transports emerged unscathed. On the following day Yamada's bombers were armed with torpedoes. Admiral Turner, warned again by the coast-watchers, had his ships under way to meet the attack. Of the 26 attackers, four were shot down by fighters from the *Enterprise*, 13 more fell to the storm of gunfire from the ships. The only torpedo to strike home hit, but did not sink, the U.S. destroyer *Jarvis*. One burning 'Betty' however was crashed into the transport *George F. Elliott*, which was set ablaze and eventually became a total loss.

So far the operation, the first of the many American amphibious assaults that were to play so large a part in the

Pacific War, had proceeded with a smoothness beyond expectation by a force the majority of which had previously seen no action of any sort. Admiral Turner, who was to go on to become the most successful amphibious commander of the war, could already congratulate himself. By the afternoon of 8 August the last resistance at Tulagi was flickering out, while on Guadalcanal 11,000 U.S. Marines had been landed and had advanced inland, capturing the airfield. One more day and the unloading of the transports would be complete; meanwhile, as a hot, steamy darkness fell, the cruisers and destroyers of Admiral Crutchley's force took up their defensive patrol positions. Dividing the westward entrance to the strait between Guadalcanal and Florida Island, lay Savo, a steep, jungle-clad little island. An enemy force coming from the west to attack the transports at their anchorage would have to pass north or south of Savo. A third possible route was from the east through the Lengo and Sealark Channels between Florida Island and Guadalcanal. To block each of these Crutchley divided his force. A Southern Group, composed of H.M.A.S. *Australia* and *Canberra* (eight eight-inch guns), the U.S.S. *Chicago* (nine eight-inch guns) and the destroyers *Patterson* and *Bagley*, was allocated the area between Guadalcanal and Savo. The American cruisers *Vincennes*, *Quincy* and *Astoria* (each mounting nine eight-inch guns), with the destroyers *Helm* and *Wilson*, formed a Northern Group to the east and north of Savo, while farther away to the eastward patrolled the light cruisers U.S.S. *San Juan*, flagship of Rear-Admiral Scott, and H.M.A.S. *Hobart* with the destroyers *Monssen* and *Buchanan*. Two destroyers equipped with radar, though of a type designed primarily to detect aircraft, were directed to patrol beyond Savo Island across the western approach routes, the *Blue* to the south and the *Ralph Talbot* to the north.

There seemed little reason to expect that this force would be called upon to repulse any night attack on the Amphibious Force by surface ships. All approach routes were believed to be under aerial observation by aircraft of MacArthur's or McCain's command. U.S. submarines were on patrol in the vicinity of Rabaul. There would surely be timely warning. And, indeed, several messages had been received by Admirals Turner and Crutchley. Shortly before midnight the previous day, they had learnt that one of MacArthur's Fortresses had sighted 'six unidentified ships' steering south-east in the St George's Channel between New Britain and New Ireland. Early on the 8th a report from the submarine *S-38* had come in. She had sighted at 2000 on the 7th 'two destroyers and three larger ships of unknown type' emerging from the St George's Channel at high speed. Nothing more had been heard during the day. A few naval units at sea near the Japanese main base at Rabaul, some 550 miles away, hardly seemed an immediate threat. If they were heading for Guadalcanal they could not fail to be sighted by the reconnaissance aircraft covering the area; and so, indeed, they were — on two occasions during the forenoon of the 8th by two Australian Hudson aircraft, which shadowed them as they steamed south-easterly to the north of Bougainville. But unfortunately the pilots considered the sighting insufficiently important to break radio silence to report it or even to return at once to their base to do so verbally. It was not until 1845 on the 8th that Turner knew that they had sighted 'Three cruisers, three destroyers and two seaplane tenders', and even this hardly painted a picture of a striking force heading to deliver a night attack. Seaplane tenders were most likely to be moving to set up a new seaplane base. Besides, Turner had earlier requested McCain to augment his planned air-search programme by sending a flying boat up the 'Slot' — the name given by the Americans to the long sea channel running between the two island chains comprising the Solomons — down which any force from Rabaul would come. He did not know that this had been only partially fulfilled. Thus there was no sense of alarm in the Allied command when, at 2032, Turner urgently summoned Crutchley and General Vandegrift to meet him aboard his flagship *McCawley* for a conference on another matter — the professed intention of Vice-Admiral Fletcher to withdraw his carrier force immediately, leaving the Amphibious Force unprotected against air attack on the following morning. Crutchley at once gave orders for his flagship to be taken to the Lunga Roads, where the *McCawley* lay amongst the transport fleet. Captain Bode of the U.S.S. *Chicago* assumed tactical command of the Southern Group.

Crutchley would no doubt have acted differently if he had had any suspicion of what was in store. Since early afternoon Mikawa's force of five heavy, two light cruisers and one destroyer had been racing down the Slot, intending to burst upon the unsuspecting Amphibious Force during the black early hours of the 9th. When Vice-Admiral Mikawa had heard the first startling news early on the 7th of an Allied expeditionary force thronging the waters between Guadalcanal and Florida and Marines pouring ashore at Tulagi, he had been at his headquarters at Rabaul. The five heavy cruisers of his command had been absent at Kavieng at the northern end of New Ireland. He had hastily recalled them and it was they that the Flying Fortress had sighted and reported. The *Chokai* was brought into Rabaul harbour, where Mikawa embarked and broke out his flag. With the light cruisers *Tenryu* and *Yubari* and the destroyer *Yunagi*, the *Chokai* hurried to sea and joined the *Aoba, Kako, Kinugasa* and *Furutaka* in the St George's Channel.

As they debouched from it they swept so closely past the submarine *S-38* that her captain, Lieutenant-Commander Munson, found himself unable to fire torpedoes. In the darkness, too, he underestimated the strength of the force and made the misleading report quoted above.

Through the night Mikawa led his force on an easterly course, passing to the north of Buka and turning again south-easterly at 0200 on the 8th, so as to spend the forenoon on the northern side of Bougainville. There he loitered while scout seaplanes, catapulted off from the cruisers at dawn, searched ahead. By noon he had the information he wanted. Fifteen transports were reported off Guadalcanal, another three off Tulagi. But supporting them, besides six cruisers and a large number of destroyers, his pilot reported a battleship. This gave Mikawa food for thought, especially as during the forenoon his force had been twice 'snooped' by enemy reconnaissance planes and hope of surprising the enemy seemed to have been dashed. He weighed the possibilities. He could have supreme confidence in the Japanese Navy's skill and equipment for night fighting. Training for it had been pressed ahead in peace-time with an intensity and disregard for risk far beyond anything known to other navies. Their ships had no radar, but look-outs specially selected for extraordinary night vision were provided with powerful night binoculars. The huge size of these instruments had on occasion made them objects of derision to foreigners who saw them and dismissed them as further evidence of the chronic myopia of the Japanese. The advantage they gave to the Japanese was very real, however. It was supported by the weapon best suited to night action which had already proved itself in the Battle of the Java Sea, the deadly, 'Long-Lance', oxygen-propelled 24-inch torpedo with which every cruiser and destroyer was lavishly equipped. For closer range work powerful searchlights were fitted, their control linked to that of the eight-inch guns of the heavy cruisers and the 5.5-inch guns of the light cruisers. Crews well practised in night fighting served them.

Mikawa thus had no fears as to the outcome of a night battle with Allied warships, even if he found himself unable to slip by them to get at his hoped-for target, the transports off Guadalcanal. His withdrawal in daylight was another matter. The American carrier force had not been located but carrier aircraft had been in action over the beaches. Mikawa had been at Midway. He had a healthy respect for American naval dive-bombers. He could not know that Admiral Fletcher had made the much criticised decision to withdraw his carriers on the evening of the 8th. Nevertheless he did not hesitate for long. He would attack that night and destroy the invasion force before it was strongly established ashore. At 1300 signal flags sped to the *Chokai*'s masthead. At 24 knots she led the way southward through the Bougainville Strait into the Slot. Before sunset Mikawa's intentions had been signalled down the line of ships. In single line ahead, with the *Chokai* leading the heavy cruisers and the light cruisers and solitary destroyer bringing up the rear, the Japanese force was to race at 24 knots between Savo Island and Guadalcanal, brush aside any opposition and fall upon the enemy transports in the anchorage. Then, turning north-west it would repeat the process off Tulagi before returning north of Savo. Lest any confusion should occur in the darkness long white pendants were to be streamed from ships' bridges as means of mutual recognition.

When the swift tropical darkness fell, no enemy reconnaissance plane had sighted the squadron. Mikawa signalled his men: 'Let us attack with certain victory in the traditional night attack of the Imperial Japanese Navy. May each one calmly do his utmost.' On into the dark, oppressive tropical night sped the eight ships. At 2313, with 90 miles to go, the seaplanes from the *Chokai*, *Aoba* and *Kako* were launched. Their task was to report the positions of enemy ships and at the crucial moment to illuminate them with flares.

In the Allied fleet the middle watch was dragging on uneventfully towards its end, longed-for by watch-keepers deadly tired after the long, hot, steamy day at action stations. The night was clear except to the westward where tropical rainstorms drifted across Savo Island, but heavy clouds overhead made it very dark. Beyond Savo the *Blue* and the *Ralph Talbot* steamed back and forth on guard. Look-outs stared into the darkness, but, falsely reassured by the knowledge that overhead the radar aerials were sending out their probing beams, their gaze was less than keen. The Southern Group, *Canberra* and *Chicago* in line ahead with the *Patterson* and *Bagley* screening on either bow, patrolled on a NW-SE line to seaward of the anchored transports at 12 knots. The cruiser captains had turned in, as had half the ships' companies. The Northern Group, *Vincennes*, *Quincy* and *Astoria*, also in line ahead, and the destroyers *Helm* and *Wilson*, jogged along at ten knots on a square patrol east of Savo Island, some ten miles from the Southern Group. The senior officer, Captain Riefkohl of the *Vincennes* knew nothing of Admiral Crutchley's departure. All was quiet and he, too, yearned for his bunk for some badly needed rest. He was about to leave the bridge when, through the crackle of static on the radio telephone (T.B.S. — 'Talk Between Ships') came the words 'Warning. Warning. Plane over Savo headed east' from the destroyer *Ralph Talbot* on picket duty north of Savo. A little later the plane was sighted by several ships, flying serenely overhead, with navigation lights burning, followed shortly by another. It could only be a 'friendly', it seemed. Riefkohl, reassured, turned in as his fellow cruiser captains had already done.

For the next two hours these planes droned overhead. The brief alarm died away. Around midnight, the conference concluded, Admiral Crutchley left the *McCawley* in his barge taking General Vandegrift to deliver him to the minesweeper waiting to transport him to Tulagi. Crutchley regained his flagship soon after 0100; but rather than search for his force in the black night he decided to keep the *Australia* patrolling off the anchorage until daylight. Nowhere in the Allied force was there any anxiety about what the night might bring forth. Admiral Turner's thoughts were on the morrow, when his Amphibious Force would be bereft of fighter cover, owing to the Task Force Commander's decision to withdraw his carriers. Neither he nor Crutchley had received the *Ralph Talbot*'s report of aircraft overhead. Crutchley had discussed with Turner the belatedly received reports of an enemy squadron off Bougainville that morning. He was reassured by Turner's assessment of it as merely an expedition to set up a seaplane base. The possibility of a surface raid was not entirely dismissed, but both admirals felt confident that their available force was adequate to meet it and sensibly deployed. In the busy weeks since the conception of the operations, filled with planning and organisational activities, there had been no opportunity to perfect co-operation amongst the warships of Crutchley's command — another good reason for dividing them into semi-independent units of ships familiar with each other, the Southern Group having operated together for some months under Crutchley's predecessor, Rear-Admiral Crace. Nor had the state of training for night action of the hastily gathered force been given much consideration. In fact none of the cruisers had fired their guns at a target by night in the last eight months or had had recent practice in night-encounter procedure. But this seemed of no great account when the enemy were the myopic Japanese, who, peering owlishly through thick-lensed spectacles, were officially judged to be indifferent night fighters.

Even as Crutchley was re-embarking in the *Australia* the first contact between the opposing forces was taking place. At 0054, on the bridge of the *Chokai*, racing forward at 26 knots at the head of Mikawa's line of ships, a look-out staring through his huge binoculars reported a ship in sight fine on the starboard bow. A brief scrutiny and it was identified as an enemy destroyer steering away south-westerly, having crossed ahead. Incredibly, she had apparently not sighted the bulky cruiser with its massive hop-hamper and white curling bow wave charging towards her. Reducing speed to 22 knots, however, to cut down his conspicuous bow wave, Mikawa led away to port, deciding to pass to the north of Savo. But once again a look-out warned — another destroyer on the port bow. As there was still no challenge from the *Blue* — for such was the first sighting — Mikawa reverted to his original intention of passing south of Savo and altered course once again to starboard. Hardly daring to imagine that they could pass unobserved, the Japanese cruisers filed across the *Blue*'s wake at a distance of five miles. No challenge, no searchlight; in the American destroyers the radar screens remained blank; inexperienced, tired look-outs could distinguish nothing against the black curtain of the night; and now Mikawa increased speed again to 26 knots. By 0130 the *Chokai* was leading through the channel between Savo and Guadalcanal. Four minutes later the port look-outs reported another destroyer to the northward steering slowly westward. Once again the

Japanese held their fire and passed undetected by the *Jarvis*, damaged in the previous day's air attacks and now departing for Sydney for repairs. Mikawa's lone destroyer, *Yunagi*, was ordered away to see she did not interfere and to act as picket beyond Savo. Bigger game was in sight for the remainder — silhouetted against the clear horizon ahead, the cruisers *Canberra* and *Chicago*, closing fast on an opposite course. Mikawa gave the order to attack, ships firing independently. At 0138 the first of a stream of torpedoes sped away towards their unsuspecting victims. For another five minutes no inkling of impending action reached the four ships of Crutchley's Southern Group slipping through the calm water at their stately 12 knots. Then events piled thickly on one another. At about 0143, on the bridges of the *Patterson*, *Bagley* and *Canberra*, almost simultaneously look-outs reported ships right ahead. Over the *Patterson*'s voice radio a warning went out 'Strange ships entering harbour', but it was not received in any Allied ship. All night, atmospheric conditions combined with disorganised chatter on the T.B.S. circuit had been making communications a bedlam. Both destroyers turned at once to port to bring their starboard torpedo tubes to bear; but in the surprise and confusion neither launched torpedoes as they swung past the firing course, though the *Bagley* was able to do so a few minutes later at a dimly seen, disappearing enemy. At the same moment, over the anchorage astern, bright flares suddenly blossomed in the sky, dropped by Mikawa's aircraft illuminating the huddled transports, but, more significantly, silhouetting the Allied cruisers for the Japanese, themselves almost invisible against the loom of Savo Island with its cloak of rain cloud.

On the *Canberra*'s bridge the officer of the watch was still trying to identify the object reported by his look-out. The startled watch below was stumbling, sleep-sodden, to their action stations in response to the urgent clanging of the alarm bell when torpedo tracks were sighted passing down either side. To bring her full gun armament to bear, the cruiser began to turn to starboard, but her turrets were still trained fore and aft when a storm of shells, eight-inch and smaller, smothered her upper works and tore open her high, unarmoured hull. Captain Getting fell mortally wounded amongst a shambles of dead and wounded on the bridge. Down below, steam-power was lost and the ship came to a stop, a blazing wreck.

Astern of the *Canberra*, equally dazed incomprehension governed actions on the *Chicago*'s bridge where Captain Bode had been summoned when the aircraft flare blazed out and the *Canberra* was seen to swerve to starboard. Torpedo tracks were seen coming from the starboard bow and the wheel put over to comb them; but the ship had barely begun to swing when others were seen to port and the wheel was reversed. It was to no avail and at 0147 a torpedo exploded on the cruiser's port bow. It tore a large hole for some 16 feet abaft the stem, blowing out the bottom of the chain locker leaving the anchor cable hanging down. At the same moment a shell hit high up on the foremast. A storm of splinters sprayed the deck causing a number of casualties. The structural damage was not crippling, however, nor was the cruiser's armament affected. But no enemy could be seen to shoot at. Bode ordered starshell to search ahead. Four salvoes were fired — 16 shells in all — but not one ignited. Unseen from the American cruiser, Mikawa's force had crossed ahead and was now moving away northeast. But at this moment, to the westward, ahead of the *Chicago* a searchlight beam stabbed out momentarily — it was presumably the *Yunagi*. Stepping up his speed to 26 knots Bode chased blindly westwards, and finding nothing, the *Chicago* passed out of the action; on returning to the battle area three hours later there was a brief and fortunately inaccurate exchange of fire with the *Patterson*, which was standing by the shattered *Canberra*.

Meanwhile Mikawa's force had run foul of the Northern Group. On turning north-east to engage the Southern Group, the Japanese force had divided into two sections with the two light cruisers and the *Furutaka* following a route closer to Savo Island than the remainder. And now crossing some four-and-a-half miles ahead of them, could be seen the *Vincennes* leading the *Quincy* and *Astoria*, with the *Helm* and *Wilson* on the port and starboard bow respectively. The two Japanese sections steered to engage them from either quarter, *Chokai* to starboard, *Furutaka* to port.

No word of warning had reached Captain Riefkohl. Admiral Crutch-ley had not told him of his absence. Captain Bode had been too stupefied by the calamitous turn of events to pass the alarm. Nevertheless the aircraft flares at 0143, followed by gunfire to the south-west, had alerted the Northern Group and speed had been increased to 15 knots. In each of the cruisers, the captain was shaking off the stupor of deep sleep and stumbling to the bridge from his sea cabin. Before they reached it, however, the blinding bedlam of night action had broken out.

The *Astoria*, at the rear of the line, was the first to receive the attention of the enemy as at 0150 the *Chokai*'s searchlight beam stabbed out, bathing her in its harsh white light, and the tall columns of shell splashes rose out of the sea close alongside. At the same moment the *Vincennes* and *Quincy* ahead of her were similarly illuminated. Though only now was the general alarm sounded, the Gunnery Officer of the *Astoria*, Lieutenant-Commander Truesdell, had ordered General Quarters some minutes earlier. Within two-and-a-half minutes his guns replied with a salvo of six eight-inch shells. At this moment the bemused Captain Greenman reached the bridge. Convinced that a fearful mistake was being made and that his guns were firing on the Southern Group, he gave the order to cease fire. While the appalled Gunnery Officer pleaded with him to reverse this order, three more salvoes from the *Chokai* fell, each one closer than the last. Remarking that 'Whether our ships or not, we will have to stop them', Greenman finally gave way. But it was too late to save the situation. The next Japanese salvo plunged squarely into the *Astoria*'s superstructure, setting her ablaze, the flames fed by petrol from her scout plane amidships on its catapult. Under the hail of shells from the *Chokai* on her starboard quarter and from the *Furutaka*, *Yubari* and *Tenryu* to port, the American cruiser could reply but feebly, though before her guns fell silent one eight-inch shell hit the Japanese flagship near the bridge killing 30 men. Pounded to a wreck, suffering fearful casualties, the *Astoria* followed the ships ahead as best she could until she finally came to a stop, blazing from bow to stern, just as the enemy ships vanished into the night.

Ahead of the *Astoria*, the other two cruisers had suffered the same searing agony. The *Quincy* was caught with her turrets still trained fore-and-aft as the searchlight of the *Aoba* flashed on to her and shells began to fall alongside. Gun control teams were still stumbling to their stations and Captain Moore could only order the turret crews to 'Fire at the ships with searchlights on'. With these vague instructions two salvoes were fired hopefully but ineffectively, before shells from the *Aoba* and the *Furutaka*'s section smothered the luckless *Quincy*, blowing up one of her turrets, making a shambles of her bridge and secondary batteries. To complete her destruction a torpedo exploded against her port side abreast a boiler-room. At 0235 she capsized to port and sank bows first. Some 370 of her crew, including Captain Moore, were killed or died of wounds; another 167 were wounded.

Aboard the leading ship *Vincennes*, Captain Riefkohl, senior officer of the Northern Group, had been called to the bridge by his executive officer, Commander Mullan, to see the aircraft flares hanging in the sky. When to the southward flashes were seen, followed by the thud of guns, and through the hull under his feet were felt the shock of distant underwater explosions, it still did not enter his mind that a surface action was in progress. No doubt the Southern Group was firing at aircraft. Ordering an increase of speed to 15 knots he awaited developments.

They came with the sudden dazzling light of searchlights glaring into his eyes. Never doubting that they must be from the Southern Group, Riefkohl over the voice radio demanded they be shut off.

Lieutenant-Commander Adams, the *Vincennes'* Gunnery Officer, was less certain and ordered the turrets on to the bearing. In reply came a salvo from the *Kako* plunging into the sea 500 yards to starboard. The *Vincennes'* five-inch battery fired a salvo of star shells and then the eight-inch battery thundered out twice. It may have been one of these latter that hit and damaged the *Kinugasa*. If so, it was the last effective blow struck by the American cruiser; for simultaneously with the second salvo she staggered under the shock of shells hitting amidships. Her aircraft blazed up offering a perfect aiming mark. The Japanese searchlights, no longer necessary, were shut off. Shell after shell crashed home as the ship swerved this way and that, trying to escape the destructive hammer blows. Then torpedoes exploded against her port side, to complete the devastation. Steam pressure dropped and her speed fell away till, burning fiercely, she finally stopped. Even now, when two fresh searchlights opened up, it was thought they must be from 'friendly' ships and Captain Riefkohl ordered a large battle ensign hoisted at the foremast. It brought only a renewed hail of shells. Then at 0215 the searchlights were suddenly dowsed, the shattering shellfire ceased. For the next 45 minutes the crew of the *Vincennes* fought the fires engulfing their steeply listing ship, lowered the wounded into life-rafts and at last abandoned ship as she rolled over on her beam ends before sinking. Her casualties totalled 332 killed, with a further 258 wounded.

The cruisers of the Northern Group had been wiped out, though the *Astoria* was to survive, a shattered wreck for some hours. Mikawa could feel well satisfied as his force hurried off, circling Savo Island, though his original intention of attacking the transport fleet remained unfulfilled. It seems that he did try to lead his cruisers towards the anchorage at 0200, but in the turmoil and confusion of the gun action at that time in full swing they failed to follow him. Once action had been joined, indeed, with the glare of searchlights and the flash of gunfire dazzling all eyes, the concussion of eight-inch gun salvoes drowning spoken orders and all the while his ships racing through the night at 26 knots, little detailed control was possible. He therefore turned the *Chokai* back to follow the remainder northwards and at 0220 signalled for all ships to withdraw. The battle flared up again for a while when the *Furutaka*'s section ran across the *Ralph Talbot*. Naked under the glare of searchlights the destroyer was savagely hammered before escaping into a rain squall, listing steeply and on fire. She survived, heavily damaged and with 22 casualties, to limp into Tulagi the following morning. Just 50 minutes after the action had opened with torpedoes fired at the Southern Group, the Japanese squadron vanished, leaving the darkness lit by the flickering flames of burning ships. Only the *Chokai*, hit four times and the *Kinugasa* and *Aoba* once each, had suffered any damage. Japanese casualties totalled in killed and wounded. In reply, they had virtually annihilated an enemy force of approximately equal strength — at 0800 the *Canberra* was to join the three American cruisers on the floor of what was soon to be ironically dubbed 'Ironbottom Sound'. Mikawa was nevertheless to be criticised in time to come by Admiral Yamamoto for not staying to attack the transports. The criticism is hardly fair. Reforming his divided force in the black, overcast night would have been a lengthy process not unaccompanied by risk of mistaken identity and surprise encounter with other Allied ships known to be in the vicinity. Dawn would have found him still within easy range of strike aircraft from the American carriers which he believed to be nearby. Though hindsight reveals the peerless opportunity for a clean sweep missed by Mikawa, his prudence is justified taking into account the situation as he saw it. At 30 knots his force sped away up the Slot.

Behind him, Admirals Turner and Crutchley had been seeking the meaning of the flurry of gun flashes dimly seen through rain squalls in the direction of Savo Island and of the garbled messages cluttering the ether. Crutchley, in complete ignorance of the number or the nature of the enemy force and the progress of the action being fought, radioed the senior officers of his three groups, 'Are you in action?'. No reply could come from the shattered ships of the Northern Group. Rear-Admiral Scott in the *San Juan*, still guarding the eastern approaches, could only report that there 'appears to be surface force between Florida Island and Savo'. The luckless Captain

Bode of the *Chicago* who had followed some unexplained wild-goose chase to the westward, at first replied, pithily but hardly informatively 'Were but not now'. It was not until 0250, by which time Bode had brought the *Chicago* back south of Savo, that Crutchley learnt from him that his ship had been damaged by a torpedo and that the *Canberra* was crippled and burning. Hoping to gather together the seven destroyers he had previously instructed to act as a striking force when ordered, he had signalled them to concentrate on his flagship to seaward of the anchorage. In the general signal confusion this was misinterpreted as an order to proceed to a previously arranged rendezvous five miles to the north-west of Savo Island, and a number of the destroyers had thus sped away off the scene of action.

Daylight brought full realisation of the catastrophe. *Vincennes* and *Quincy* had gone; *Astoria* and *Canberra* were immobilised, burning and doomed. Renewed heavy air attacks were to be expected and there would be no fighter defence coming from Fletcher's carriers — by this time far away to the south of San Cristobal. The prospect facing Admiral Turner was a daunting one and he could hardly have been blamed if he had decided to withdraw at once. Courageously he decided to continue unloading supplies until 1600. Fortune favoured the bold decision. The 16 torpedo-planes and 15 fighters despatched by the 25th Air Flotilla ignored the Amphibious Force. Instead they sought in vain for the American carrier force, finally expending their concentrated fury on the crippled destroyer *Jarvis*, limping southward, bound for Sydney and mistaken for a cruiser. The *Jarvis* was sunk with all hands; but far greater Allied losses might have been suffered had the torpedo-planes swooped on Turner's weakened force off the beachheads.

The *Canberra* received her quietus from an American torpedo at 0800. On board the *Astoria* heroic efforts to save her continued until noon, but by then, following a magazine explosion, it was clear she was doomed. Fifteen minutes after Captain Greenman followed the survivors of his crew over the side, she heeled over and sank; 216 officers and men had died and 186 were wounded. At sunset the Amphibious Force weighed anchor and set course for the New Caledonia base, leaving the Marines to hold on as best they could until, with a renewal of confidence after the nerve-shattering lessons of Savo Island had been absorbed, supplies and reinforcements would begin to flow again.

A tail-piece to the battle remains to be told. By the afternoon of the 9th, the victor was through the Bougainville Strait and felt secure from any serious air attack. Detaching Goto with his four heavy cruisers to make for Kavieng, he headed with the remainder for Rabaul. Before they reached harbour, Mikawa's satisfaction was to some degree to be marred.

On patrol to the eastward of Kavieng in the old submarine *S-44* Lieutenant-Commander John R. Moore sighted, early on 10 August, the sort of target that comes once in a lifetime to a submariner — four large cruisers formed in a rectangle steaming towards him at 16 knots with a solitary aircraft aloft and no anti-submarine screen. Moving in to the attack, Moore closed to within 700 yards of the *Kako* undetected. Only when the white tracks of four torpedoes were sighted was the alarm raised in the Japanese ships. It was too late. The *Kako* leapt in violent eruption, broke in half and within five minutes had sunk.

6. GUADALCANAL: THE EASTERN SOLOMONS — CAPE ESPERANCE

The Battle of Savo Island had been a rude shock to Allied confidence and self-esteem. On top of the revelation of inferior American naval aircraft and ineffective aerial torpedoes which had emerged from the Coral Sea and Midway battles, the Japanese had now shown themselves to be the Allies' masters in the form of sea warfare in which they had been considered weakest. Without benefit of radar with which some American ships were by this time fitted, they had achieved complete surprise in a night encounter. The Allied forces concerned being, for the most part, American, there was much earnest soul-searching in the U.S. Navy.

Inevitably, mutterings were heard in some quarters that the disaster was the result of placing American ships under foreign command and that Crutchley's failure to delegate command when he left the scene to confer with Admiral Turner was a blameworthy contributory cause. That a mixed force, subject to differing doctrines and methods and employing different communication systems, suffers from inherent weaknesses is true enough. But the defeat off Savo Island was the result primarily of inefficiency in night fighting by the individual ships concerned and of signal confusion amongst the American ships, neither of which could have been rectified by a flag officer so recently placed in command as Crutchley. So far as fighting efficiency was concerned, in the press of events since the outbreak of war, there had been no opportunities for training. The communications muddle was another matter. The U.S. Navy relied to a very great extent for intercommunication upon the excellent voice radio equipment — T.B.S. (Talk Between Ships) — fitted in every ship. British Commonwealth ships did not at this time have such a radio telephone system and though they were deeply envious of their American comrades, it is true to say that they kept up a higher standard of operating efficiency with the alternative systems — morse-code radio and visual light signalling — and that discipline in the use of these systems was more easily imposed than with voice radio. In American ships where an operator could come on the air by the simple process of uncradling a telephone and speaking into the mouthpiece, even the strictest control from the senior officer's ship could not always prevent a bedlam of cross-talk, misunderstandings and missed messages occurring. Such was the situation for much of the time on the night of Savo Island when a number of separate units were operating at nearly the extreme T.B.S. range from each other.

In December 1942 an enquiry into the causes of the Savo Island debacle was set on foot. From it emerged criticisms of a general lack of alertness and night-fighting efficiency as well as signal shortcomings. Nevertheless fighting efficiency at sea, particularly night-fighting, depends more than anything on clear, reliable, unambiguous signals. Before the findings of the enquiry were promulgated, further night actions were to take place in the waters off Guadalcanal in which this was to be demonstrated.

When Admiral Turner's Amphibious Force, bereft of air cover by day owing to Admiral Fletcher's much criticised decision to withdraw his carriers, and inadequately defended against night surface attack since the losses of the previous night, steamed away from Guadalcanal on the evening of 9 August 1942, the 17,000 Marines on Guadalcanal were left short of ammunition, barbed wire, entrenching tools and sandbags. Heavy equipment such as bulldozers, mechanical diggers for construction of their base and coast defence guns were still in the holds of the departing transports. Food was only sufficient for 30 days. No aircraft could yet use the airfield. Only small quantities of petrol, ammunition and rations could be run in aboard a few old destroyers converted to the transport role. For the time being the troops were a beleaguered garrison exposed to unopposed air attack and naval bombardment.

Using hand tools and some antiquated equipment captured from the Japanese the Marines worked feverishly to lengthen the airstrip. By 20 August it was done and 19 Marine Wildcat fighters and 12 dive-bombers were flown in from the escort carrier *Long Island* to inaugurate the airfield, now named Henderson Field after a Marine hero of Midway. With this cover the Navy was able to reopen a sea supply route, two transports arriving under escort of the destroyers *Blue*, *Henley* and *Helm*.

On the Japanese side, efforts to throw reinforcements into Guadalcanal had begun as soon as news of the American landings reached Rabaul. Admiral Mikawa had at once sailed 500 Marines in transports; but when the largest of them was torpedoed and sunk by the U.S. submarine *S-38* before it had got very far, he had recalled the remainder. The task of recapture of Guadalcanal was now taken over by Lieutenant-General Hyakutake commanding the 17th Army from headquarters at Rabaul. The majority of his troops were committed to the operation to capture Port Moresby across the Owen Stanley Mountains. He thus had less than 2,000 available for Guadalcanal besides a further 1,000 Marines of the 5th Special Naval Landing Force. He was by no means dismayed, believing that the Americans had only about 2,000 men ashore on Guadalcanal.

On 17 August, elements of the Naval Landing Force were put ashore at Tassafaronga to the west of Henderson Field. The following night six destroyers bringing 1,000 troops from Truk made a fast run down the Slot to land them to the eastward, inaugurating the almost nightly schedule of what was to be called by the exasperated U.S. Marines the 'Tokyo Express'. Under the indomitable leadership of Rear-Admiral Tanaka, who took his destroyers with such dash into action in the Java Sea, this flotilla was to persist with great gallantry, in the face of inevitable ultimate annihilation, throughout the Guadalcanal campaign, immune by night, but harried by air attack when dawn found them retiring up the Slot. The U.S. Marines were quickly aware of the newly arrived enemy troops, and moving out to the attack were able on this occasion to wipe them out. With this began the grim, bloody campaign amongst the jungle and swamps of Guadalcanal that was to continue for six months as each side strove for possession of an island they loathed, but on which the outcome of the war in the South-West Pacific depended. And while the soldiers fought savagely ashore, an equally desperate, long-drawn struggle was to take place at sea to control the sea approaches and deliver supplies and reinforcements.

The Japanese destroyer *Kawakaze* had just completed her task as the 'Tokyo Express' on the night of the 20-21 August and was slipping secretly away again when, shortly before dawn, she encountered the *Blue*, one of the destroyers bringing in the two American transports. The *Blue*, though warned by her radar, was no more discerning than she had been at Savo Island. A torpedo from the invisible enemy blew off her stern, leaving her immobilised, eventually to be scuttled.

Hasty, clandestine deliveries by the Japanese of men and material, were not enough by themselves to affect the situation. The Japanese Commander-in-Chief, Yamamoto, had brought the Combined Fleet south to Truk and he now decided to use the whole of it to cover the landing of the available troops, even though these were a mere 1,500 men. Transported in four old destroyers and a converted light cruiser, *Kinryu Maru*, they would be escorted by Rear-Admiral Tanaka's flagship *Jintsu* and the destroyers of his 'Tokyo Express'. In support, Admiral Mikawa would bring the four surviving cruisers of the Savo Island battle. Covering the operation against interference by the American carrier fleet would be the *Zuikaku* and *Shokaku*, the latter flying the flag pf Admiral Nagumo, athirst to avenge Midway and recover lost 'face'. Still hoping that the Americans might allow themselves to be drawn into close action, Yamamoto added a Vanguard Group of two battleships and three heavy cruisers under Rear-Admiral Abe to steam close ahead of the carriers, while an Advance Force of six cruisers with the overall tactical commander, Vice-Admiral Kondo, flying his flag in the *Atago*, and the seaplane carrier *Chitose*, would scout far in advance. Finally the concept of a sacrificial decoy, which was so regular a feature of Japanese plans, was to be provided for by a Diversionary Group under Rear-Admiral Hara comprising the small carrier *Ryujo*, a cruiser and two destroyers. Six submarines would form a broad scouting line far ahead of the fleet. Others were given patrol stations to cover the area in the Coral Sea in which the American carriers were expected to operate and which was soon to gain an unsavoury reputation as 'Torpedo Junction'.

Such a concentration of force could not escape the notice of American long-range air reconnaissance. Some major operation was obviously in preparation. Admiral Fletcher's Task Force

61, the carriers *Saratoga*, *Enterprise* and *Wasp*, with their attendant battleship, *North Carolina*, nine cruisers and 17 destroyers moved up into the eastern approaches to the Coral Sea. By 21 August they were in position, with their planes fanning out on searches to the northward of the Solomon Islands, augmenting the regular coverage provided by Admiral McCain's island-based aircraft. For two days all reports were negative. Then early on the 23rd, by which time Task Force 61 had advanced expectantly beyond the Solomons island chain, came the first contact. *Enterprise* planes sighted and attacked two of the Japanese submarines which, heading southwards at high speed on the surface, were correctly assessed as outriders of the main fleet. A few hours later one of McCain's seaplanes reported Tanaka's troop convoy some 300 miles north of Task Force 61, heading south.

Fletcher did not wait for bigger game to be detected. The *Saratoga* was ordered to launch a striking force and at 1445 31 dive-bombers and six torpedo-planes thundered off her deck, formed up and set off to intercept. However, the lessons of the Coral Sea battle had not been forgotten. The carrier's fighters were held back against the possibility of an enemy attack developing while the striking force was absent. From Henderson Field further Marine dive-bombers also set out. But Tanaka had only waited for the enemy reconnaissance plane to leave before reversing course, as did the main body of the fleet. In driving rain and low cloud the American airmen sought in vain for their prey and at dusk the carrier planes followed the Marines back to land at Henderson Field for the night, rejoining the *Saratoga* the next morning. Suspecting a mare's nest, Fletcher had decided the previous evening that it was a suitable moment to detach the *Wasp*'s group to top up with fuel at a tanker rendezvous 240 miles to the south, unaware that during the night the whole Japanese Fleet, which had once again reversed course, was heading directly for him and that a day of fierce air battle impended. Shortly after 1000 on 24 August a report from a shore-based aircraft reached Fletcher that a carrier group had been sighted some 300 miles north of him and steering south. This was the *Ryujo* and her escort which had been detached from the Japanese main body during the night to create the diversion called for by Yamamoto's plan. Fletcher manoeuvred his force to close the enemy as much as possible, but with the wind blowing from the south-east, into which his carriers had repeatedly to turn to operate aircraft, he made only slow progress northwards. During the forenoon, radar detected Japanese reconnaissance planes on three occasions: each time Wildcats on patrol were directed out and shot down the snoopers before they had been able to get a report away, though this was not realised at the time and Fletcher had to assume his position was now known to the enemy.

Meanwhile his own information was sketchy and, he feared, untrustworthy. He therefore ordered the *Enterprise* to launch an armed reconnaissance by 29 bombers and torpedo-planes. That Japanese carriers were operating to the north of the Solomons seemed to be confirmed when Fletcher's radar tracked a swarm of aircraft 100 miles to the westward, making for Guadalcanal. These, in fact, were a small striking force from the *Ryujo* which, joining up with shore-based bombers from Rabaul, were to attack Henderson Field that afternoon. Met by the forewarned Marine Wildcats, they suffered a sharp defeat, losing 21 planes against only three American.

Meanwhile Fletcher now felt confident enough to send off a striking force of 30 dive-bombers and eight of the new (Avenger) torpedo-planes from the *Saratoga*. As at the Coral

Sea, however, Fletcher had now committed the greater part of his strike strength without really knowing where the enemy's carriers were. The radio link by which he could hope to control it was a delicate, fragile connection subject to interruption by poor atmospheric conditions and congestion. Thus when messages from the *Enterprise*'s search planes reporting the various, separated groups of the Japanese Fleet began flooding the air, some confusion arose and efforts to direct the *Saratoga*'s striking force on to the most important objective, Nagumo's large carriers, were unsuccessful. The few *Enterprise* planes which found them attacked the *Shokaku* with bombs but inflicted only minor damage. The *Saratoga*'s strike found only the little *Ryujo*. Led by Lieutenant-Commander Shumway, a veteran of Midway, the dive-bombers screamed down from 14,000 feet, followed by the section led by the Air Group Commander, Commander Felt, to smother her in 1,000-lb. bomb hits. A torpedo hit by one of Lieutenant Harewood's six Avenger planes tore her open below water. The *Ryujo* was mortally wounded though it was not until 2000, after all but 100 of her crew had been taken off, that she sank. Not one of her attackers was lost.

Nevertheless, from the Japanese point of view, she had played the part assigned to her in drawing the sting of Fletcher's carriers. And, while the *Ryujo* was suffering, from the decks of the *Shokaku* and *Zuikaku*, 75 miles away to the north-east, two waves of bombers with a strong escort of Zeros were setting off. One of Nagumo's scouting planes had at last evaded the watchful Wildcats to report the position of Task Force 61. No doubt Nagumo assumed that the American fighter defences would have been depleted to escort the striking force. But twice before, at the Coral Sea and at Midway, Fletcher had seen one of his carriers succumb to the resolute attack of Japanese naval flyers. On this occasion he had sent off his bombers without fighter escort so as to hold every Wildcat on or over his ships. No less than 53 would be available when the time came.

That this could not be long delayed was apparent as the afternoon wore on. One of the several snoopers detected must surely have got a report on the air. All hands were keyed up, all preparations made when, at 1602, radar operators saw the 'blip' of a large group of aircraft appear on their screens. Both carriers at once flew off their fighters and then launched all strike aircraft remaining on board, as well as 13 dive-bombers and 12 Avengers armed with torpedoes, with orders to counter-attack the enemy ships. Then fuel lines were drained of petrol and filled with inert gas and fuel tanks isolated. Battened down, with guns manned and loaded, the American ships awaited the onslaught. The Task Force was formed up in two separate groups, each in a circular formation centred on one of the carriers, the *Enterprise* group being about ten miles north-west of the *Saratoga*'s.

Fighter control was in the hands of the fighter-direction officers of the *Enterprise*. They were able to station the Wildcats on the enemy's approach route, though the radar 'blip' soon faded from their screens and did not reappear for 15 minutes. But thereafter all was confusion. Cluttering the radar screens were friendly aircraft returning to the carriers from their search and strike missions, the anti-submarine air patrols as well as the swarm of fighters; but, above all, there was the congestion of the radio telephone circuit on which all direction depended. The mutual interference on the T.B.S. which contributed so much to the disaster of Savo Island was as nothing compared to the uninhibited chatter of excited fighter pilots with the enemy in view which swamped the efforts of the fighter direction officers to control the situation. The airmen tore furiously into combat with such enemy aircraft as they managed to intercept, but the majority became involved with the escorting Zeros, many of which they disposed of with brisk efficiency. There were a few exceptions such as Warrant-Machinist Donald Runyan who shot down three dive-bombers as well as two Zeros. Returning bombers and even planes on anti-submarine patrol also engaged the lower-flying enemy formations and shot down several. Not one torpedo-plane succeeded in breaking through to the target. Nevertheless the main body of 'Val' dive-bombers, some 30 strong, arrived over the *Enterprise* at 18,000 feet and were not sighted until, at 1641, they were seen plunging vertically down on their target.

Then a storm of gunfire broke out from every ship of the circular formation. The greatest volume came from the *North Carolina* which had been the first battleship to receive the lavish anti-aircraft armament the lessons of the war had shown to be necessary. From her decks 20 five-inch guns, four multiple, 16-barrel, 1.1-inch guns, 40 20-mm. and 26 0.5-inch machine-guns hosed a seemingly impenetrable stream of steel and explosive upwards. A number of the 'Vals' receiving direct hits, blew up. Others crashed alongside their targets, either the carrier or the battleship. But many survived long enough to release their big bombs accurately. The *Enterprise*, streaking through the water at 30 knots though she was, and swerving wildly, could not avoid them all. In quick succession three bombs hit the flight deck, two of them plunging through to lower decks before exploding. Then, suddenly, after five minutes of pandemonium, the attack was over, the gunfire died away and the last surviving enemy aircraft were flying away with Wildcats in chase. Few, indeed, were to get back to their carriers — less than ten of the 80 which had attacked.

Besides causing 170 casualties, the three hits on the *Enterprise* had wreaked heavy damage, causing flooding and starting fires. But for the precautions taken to drain fuel lines the fatal sequence that destroyed the *Lexington* at the Coral Sea and the Japanese carriers at Midway might have recurred. But much had been learnt about damage control since then and the lessons applied in constant drill and the provision of extra equipment. Within an hour, at 1749, the *Enterprise* was steaming at 24 knots into wind, landing on her aircraft.

Nevertheless an unfortunate chain of events was still to put the carrier in peril. Fire-fighting water reaching the steering-engine room at 1821 caused an electric motor to short-circuit and stop, jamming the rudder. For 38 minutes the ship lay immobilised at a time when the second strike wave from Nagumo's carriers was searching for her, being detected at one stage barely 50 miles to the westward. But the *Enterprise*'s good luck held out. After a fruitless search the 18 Japanese dive-bombers and nine torpedo-planes gave up and turned back. As soon as the *Enterprise* was able to get under way again, Task Force 61 withdrew southwards to a refuelling rendezvous. On their way they recovered the strike aircraft which had been so hastily flown off as the enemy attack was developing. The *Enterprise*'s group, ordered to seek out and finish off the *Ryujo* had found no enemy ships. The two dive-bombers and five torpedo-carrying Avengers contributed by the *Saratoga* had discovered Admiral Kondo's Advance Force. The Avengers had made a gallant but unsuccessful attack on Kondo's cruisers. The dive-bombers which had found only the seaplane carrier *Chitose*, scored such near misses that she was holed in the engine-room and only struggled back to Truk with difficulty.

At dusk Nagumo also had withdrawn his carriers and the carrier battle was over. Neither side had scored a decisive victory though Fletcher's wise deployment of his fighters over his ships at the crucial moment had once again inflicted on the Japanese losses of aircraft and trained air-crews which they could not afford; whereas the Americans, with replacement air-crews flowing in great numbers along the 'pipeline' from the flying training schools, and new carriers nearing completion in the dockyards, had suffered few casualties. Admiral Kondo tried, during the night, to redress the balance by racing southwards with the battleships and cruisers of the Advance Force in the belief that two crippled American carriers awaited the *coup de grâce* from his guns. But when his scout planes failed to find anything by midnight, he gave up and retired northwards.

Though the powerful force which, according to the plan, was supposed to be supporting him in his hazardous attempt to land troops on Guadalcanal, had thus deserted him, Rear-Admiral Tanaka, with the stubborn courage that was to earn for him the frank admiration of his enemies during the campaign, continued to press on southwards. Early on the 25th his transport force of four old converted destroyers and the ex-light cruiser *Kenryu Maru*, escorted by his flagship *Jintsu* and eight destroyers, was some 120 miles north of Henderson Field when Marine dive-bombers, led by Lieutenant-Colonel Mangrum, seeking the Japanese carriers, sighted them instead and swooped to the attack. Both the *Jintsu* and the *Kenryu Maru* took direct hits which set them on fire. Shifting his flag to a destroyer, Tanaka sent the cruiser limping back to Truk. But the transport was doomed and while the destroyer *Mutsuki* was alongside taking off her passengers and crew, eight Flying Fortresses from Espiritu Santo arrived overhead to make

123

undisturbed bombing practice on the stationary ships. Three hits sent the *Mutsuki* to the bottom, followed shortly afterwards by the *Kenryu Maru*. The grandiose Japanese attempt to reinforce their meagre garrison on Guadalcanal had finally failed and Tanaka was ordered to retire to the advance base in Shortland Island whence the night runs of the 'Tokyo Express' would be resumed.

When the flurry caused by the carrier battle of the 24th — the Battle of the Eastern Solomons as it was to be called — died away, both sides resumed their efforts to build up and supply their land forces on Guadalcanal by whatever means was open to them. The Americans, by operating their carrier force — in which the *Hornet* had come to replace the damaged *Enterprise* — to the south-east of Guadalcanal, were able to provide air cover for a regular schedule of transports from Nouméa. The Japanese were forced by the American air superiority to rely upon the fast night runs by the 'Tokyo Express'. Both sides suffered casualties, but it was the Americans who took the most severe blow through a lack of precaution against Japanese submarine attack. Occupying the same sea area between San Cristobal and Espiritu Santo for long periods while operating aircraft and at times steaming at quite slow speeds, the Carrier Task Force offered an easy target. On 31 August the *Saratoga* was torpedoed by the submarine *I-26* and suffered damage that was to put her out of action for nearly three months. Six days later the Task Force had a narrow escape when torpedoes fired by the *I-11* just missed the *Hornet* and *North Carolina*. Nevertheless the Task Force remained in the same general area and on 15 September the *Wasp* was sunk by three torpedoes from the *I-19*, the *North Carolina* and the destroyer *O'Brien* were severely damaged by others, the latter eventually sinking. The wry humour that christened the waters between San Cristobal and Espiritu Santo 'Torpedo Junction' could hardly be expected to appeal to the American Commander-in-Chief, Pacific. Criticising the handling of the Task Force he wrote:

> The torpedoing by submarines of four warships, with the loss of two of them, was a serious blow that might possibly have been avoided. Carrier task forces are not to remain in submarine waters for long periods, should shift operating areas frequently and radically, must maintain higher speed and must in other ways improve their tactics against submarine attack.

Painful as these losses were, however, they did not deprive the Americans of their air superiority over the approaches to Guadalcanal. And by the beginning of October sufficient cruisers and destroyers as well as the new battleship *Washington* had reached the South Pacific with which to challenge the Japanese surface superiority, particularly by night when, up to now, like spectres they had roamed freely up and down the Slot, only retiring at cock-crow before the threat of Allied bombs. A striking force was formed under Rear-Admiral Norman Scott composed of the eight-inch gun cruisers *San Francisco* (flagship) and *Salt Lake City*, the light cruisers *Boise* and *Helena* and the destroyers *Farenholt, Duncan, Laffrey, Buchanan* and *McCalla*. Scott had been an appalled spectator, at a distance, of the shambles off Savo Island. He had absorbed the lessons of it and passed them on to his squadron in the shape of intensive training in night encounter and a pre-arranged plan of action. He had neither the time nor the authority, however, to rectify the signal shortcomings which interfered with efficient dissemination of information and hampered control. Nevertheless, when on 7 October he led his

125

squadron out from Espiritu Santo, he felt ready to meet the Japanese on their own ground. His orders, as part of the distant cover being given to a large troop convoy for Guadalcanal, were to 'search for and destroy enemy ships and landing craft'.

The area west of Savo Island was the obvious point of interception of any Japanese units approaching to land their troop reinforcements or supplies or to make one of their frequent night bombardments of Henderson Field. Scott manoeuvred so as to remain south of Guadalcanal outside the range of enemy bombers by day, steering to pass the north-west corner of the island, Cape Esperance, an hour before midnight, while his cruisers' scout planes searched up the Slot for any approaching enemy units. During the 9th and 10th his aircraft drew blank; but the testing time was approaching, nevertheless.

For simultaneously with the American dispatch of their troop convoy, the Japanese had decided that the trickle of supplies and reinforcements being run into Guadalcanal by small fast craft was insufficient. The Japanese general commanding in the area, Lieutenant-General Harukichi Hyakutake of the 17th Army, whose troops in Guadalcanal had suffered serious defeat at the hands of the U.S. Marines on 12 September, had woken up to the vital importance of the island even compared to the capture of Port Moresby to which the majority of his troops had been committed, and to the magnitude of the task facing him. During the night of 9-10 October he was landed at Tassafaronga with several hundred troops from the light cruiser *Tatsuta* and five destroyers and assumed personal command of operations. From now on it was decided that transports would have to be used, running the gauntlet of air attack during their approach and accepting their inevitable destruction the following day, running themselves aground, if necessary, to ensure landing their cargo. As a first step, however, the seaplane carriers *Nisshin* and *Chitose* with six destroyers were to bring in troops and supplies, including heavy artillery, during the night of 11-12 October. Covering this force Rear-Admiral Goto was to bring his cruiser squadron, *Aoba*, *Kinugasa* and *Furutaka* and the destroyers *Hatsuyuki* and *Fubuki* down the Slot and, as soon as the landings had been accomplished, carry on to bombard Henderson Field.

A heavy, but ineffective, air attack on Henderson Field during the afternoon of the 11th diverted American air strength from attacking the Japanese units during their approach, but Goto's force was reported by reconnaissance planes and tracked as it ran at high speed down the Slot. Admiral Scott steered to intercept it off Cape Esperance between 2300 and midnight. When night fell he was racing north at 29 knots off the western end of Guadalcanal. The south-easterly wind was not enough to do more than ruffle the surface of the tropical sea. The night was dark and clear; but the new surface warning radar installed in the *Helena* and the gunnery radar sets in the other cruisers should make this of less than vital importance. Even earlier warning, followed by illumination, would be provided, it was hoped, by the scout seaplanes from the cruisers and at 2200 the order was given to launch them.

That signal communication was still the weak point of American naval organisation was again shown by the *Helena*'s failure to take in this order, her aircraft being eventually jettisoned as a fire hazard before action was joined. The *Salt Lake City*'s plane crashed on take off in a blaze from her accidentally ignited illumination flares. The remaining two

127

aircraft climbed away into the night; but neither were to have any influence over the coming events. The *Boise*'s plane was soon forced down by engine trouble. The flagship's aircraft discovered the Japanese landing force off Tassafaronga and reported it, but not Goto's squadron, Admiral Scott's objective. The latter, some 50 miles up the Slot, sighted the glare of the burning aircraft over the horizon ahead; but, accustomed to the exclusive occupation of these waters by their own forces by night, the Japanese took it to be some signal from the landing force and were quite unalarmed. Overconfidence and repeated demonstrations of their own superior night vision were sapping their preparedness and blunting the sharp edge of their look-outs' alertness.

Admiral Scott's disposition of his force was conditioned by two factors. Having been a helpless spectator of the calamitous events of the Battle of Savo, which he ascribed to the lack of concentration and unified control of the Allied force, he intended to keep all his ships close under his personal control. This need not have entailed the adoption of a single, continuous line ahead, which sacrificed flexibility and tied the destroyers to the less manoeuvrable heavy cruisers. But the lack of experience and training of American seamen in night encounter and the absence of a disciplined and reliable signals system made it impossible to give the destroyers freedom to operate with the independence proper for their higher manoeuvrability and powerful torpedo armament. It is probable that the design of American destroyers, with their glass-enclosed bridges, contributed largely to the apparent night-blindness so often displayed in encounters with the Japanese and which was only offset finally by the provision of efficient radar in all ships. Inevitably the captain and his watch officers tended to remain inside the 'pilot house' where were to be seen the compass binnacles and the radar scan. Ratings on look-out, no matter how conscientious, lacked the experience and practice to distinguish the first vague increase of darkness against the dim horizon that was a darkened ship.

Be that as it may, it was in a single continuous line that Scott formed his ships, with three of his destroyers in the van, the other two bringing up the rear. Goto, on the other hand, had stationed his two destroyers one on either beam of his leading cruiser.

So the two forces steered on a collision course, Goto at 26 knots down the middle of the Slot; Scott, now reduced to 20 knots, his crews at action stations, steered north-east at right angles across the Japanese front. Then at 2325 came the first contact as the *Helena*'s radar detected Goto's ships at a range of nearly 14 nautical miles. For all Scott's training effort, however, the technique of feeding combat information to the flagship to enable proper control to be exercised had not yet been mastered. For the next 15 minutes the *Helena*'s radar tracked the contact approaching at 20 knots before informing the flagship. And in the meantime Scott had decided he had gone far enough to the northeastward. At 2333, still unaware of the presence of the enemy and of his own perfect tactical position, crossing the enemy's 'T' and so able to concentrate the whole of his gunpower against a portion of the enemy's, he gave the order to reverse course. For some reason the manoeuvre ordered was neither a reversal by all ships turning together nor by the leading ship turning and the remainder following in succession, either of which would have kept Scott's force in a single body. Instead, his cruisers and the two destroyers astern wheeled in succession behind the flagship without waiting for the three destroyers in the van — *Farenholt, Duncan* and *Laffey* — who carried out an independent turn in succession, following *Farenholt*, the leader. They were then expected to increase speed so as to overtake the cruisers, passing to starboard of them on their new course, and regain station ahead. Thus, when Scott learned for the first time, at 2340, of the *Helena*'s contact, by now identified as three distinct units, the three van destroyers were passing between him and the enemy. The possibility of mistaken identity which he had tried to eliminate had arisen in its most perilous form.

To add to Scott's uncertainties, another error in combat information technique now occurred when the *Boise* also obtained radar contact with the enemy but used the code-word indicating aircraft and reported it in such a way that there was doubt whether it was the same contact as the *Helena*'s. Nor was it clear that *Helena*'s contact had been tracked in from 14 miles distance to about four and must certainly, therefore, be enemy. Scott sought confirmation by asking Captain Tobin, senior officer of the destroyers, in the *Farenholt*, 'Are you taking station ahead?' He received the reply, 'Affirmative. Coming up on your starboard side'; but, in fact, unknown to Tobin, the *Duncan* astern of him had gained contact with the enemy on her gunnery radar set. Assuming that his leader had similar information, but saying nothing, the *Duncan*'s captain had steadied on a westerly course instead of following round and was now charging off to the attack alone.

In the *Helena*, on the other hand, where the enemy had come into sight at 5,000 yards and closing fast, Captain Hoover felt constrained to ask permission to open fire. Passed in an ambiguous signal jargon, the message was misunderstood. Precious time was lost before, at 2346, the *Helena* opened fire, only to be ordered by the Admiral a minute later to cease fire because Scott believed the target to be his own van destroyers.

Before the order was complied with, however — and it was a Nelsonic disregard of the unwelcome signal that delayed this for four minutes — the battle had been virtually won. The Japanese had been caught completely unawares, their gun turrets trained fore-and-aft when the *Helena*'s first salvo erupted on and around the flagship *Aoba*, followed only seconds later by shells from the other American cruisers that savaged the *Furutaka* and set her ablaze. Goto could only imagine that he had encountered and was being engaged by his own landing force. He had time only to order a wheel to starboard before he was mortally wounded. The *Furutaka* followed the *Aoba* round and both ships as well as the destroyer *Fubuki* were exposed to the concentrated American fire. Within a few minutes the *Fubuki* had been sunk, the *Aoba* and *Furutaka* were heavily damaged and on fire, the latter to sink some time later.

As the order to cease fire percolated slowly to the American gun-crews, the gunfire died away while Scott called his destroyer squadron commander over the voice radio. 'How are you'? was the curious wording of his first question. When Tobin replied that he was 'O.K.' and steering to resume station ahead, Scott clarified his meaning by asking if his cruisers had been firing at Tobin's destroyers. The puzzled destroyer commander replied 'I don't know who you were firing at', but it was not until, at Scott's orders, the van destroyers had flashed their coloured identification lights, that the order to resume firing was given at 2351. Four minutes later Scott led his ships north-westerly in chase of the fleeing enemy.

The rear Japanese cruiser, *Kinugasa* and the destroyer *Hatsuyuki*, which, seeing what was happening to the leaders, had wisely turned to port, had escaped this storm of fire and found themselves opposed only by the *Duncan* who was now to

131

suffer for her lone act of defiance. Shells fell thickly round her from both Japanese and American guns. Hit again and again by both sides, she was quickly put out of action and left blazing. Two hours later she had to be abandoned, 48 of her crew having been killed.

In the meantime the battle settled down to a chase, north-westerly. All the American ships had selected targets and were engaging them fiercely, though not all targets were enemy. The *Duncan*, as we have seen was hit by American as well as Japanese shells. The *Farenholt*, too, was crippled by six-inch shells from the *Boise* or the *Helena*. To reduce the reigning confusion, Scott gave the order at midnight to cease fire. Of the Japanese squadron, the *Furutaka* was out of action and limping away, doomed. The *Aoba*, though heavily damaged and on fire, was still full of fight while the *Kinugasa* and *Hatsuyuki* were virtually undamaged. Scott's order was only partially obeyed and fire was soon resumed as a Japanese salvo fell in his flagship's wake, and torpedoes passing through the line were narrowly avoided by the *Boise* who turned to starboard to 'comb' the tracks.

Up to now the American cruisers had suffered hardly any damage. But now the *Boise* switched on a searchlight to illuminate a target detected to starboard by radar, and opened fire on it. It had nearly fatal consequences. The Japanese, who lacked radar, had for the first time a clear point of aim. Both the *Aoba* and the *Kinugasa* concentrated on the *Boise*. A shell penetrated her forward gun turret, exploding inside. Another, holing her below the waterline, went on to burst in the forward six-inch magazine. A tornado of blast and flame swept through the forward part of the ship, penetrating to the magazines and leaving many dead. No one remained to comply with the order to flood the magazines and the cruiser must have blown up but for the inrush of sea water that swamped the flames. Further punishment was avoided by the gallant act of Captain Ernest G. Small of the *Salt Lake City* who steered his ship to interpose her between the *Boise* and her tormentors, while the *Boise* turned away to port to fight the fires and patch up her wounds. More than 100 of her crew were dead and 35 more wounded. For a little while longer desultory fire continued to be exchanged through the darkness, with the American ships swerving out of line to avoid torpedoes. Firing ceased at 0020 and eight minutes later Scott broke off contact, leading away to the south-west, calling his ships back into line. The Japanese ships retired at their best speed up the Slot, leaving the *Hatsuyuki* to take the survivors off the foundering *Furutaka*. In spite of 40 shell hits, the *Aoba* was still capable of 20 knots, but she would require major repairs in a home dockyard. The *Kinugasa* had suffered only minor damage. They survived an air attack from Henderson Field soon after daylight and reached their advanced base on Shortland Island before noon. And while the squadrons under Goto and Scott had been locked in battle, the Japanese landing force had achieved its object by successfully landing the troops and heavy guns which would enable General Hyakutake to threaten the American hold on the all-important Henderson Field. Thus the strategic outcome of the night's activities can be said to favour the Japanese.

The melee off Cape Esperance had, it is true, ended in a minor tactical success for Admiral Scott's force. Against the loss of the *Duncan* and serious damage to the *Boise* and *Farenholt*, the Japanese had lost the *Furutaka* and *Fubuki* and the *Aoba* was heavily damaged.

Believing, however, that they had sunk four cruisers and four destroyers the Americans hailed it as an important victory, marking the end of Japanese superiority in night fighting. It gave a welcome boost to American naval morale and restored confidence in their ability to master the Japanese by night; and it also led to a belief in the wisdom of Scott's decision to keep his destroyers in line with his cruisers. Yet, in fact, following a long-range warning of the enemy's approach, and with the inestimable advantage of radar against an enemy unwontedly negligent and unwary, the final balance in favour of the Americans had not been great; and Scott's single line formation had, in fact, done nothing to prevent confusion. American night action technique and combat information organisation were still far from perfect. Efficient use was not made of the tactical advantage conferred by possession of the new surface warning radar. Had the Japanese displayed their usual night alertness and launched their deadly 'Long Lance' torpedoes in the first few minutes of battle, the outcome might have been very different. That the new confidence engendered in the American Fleet by the Battle of Cape Esperance was unjustified was soon to be painfully proved.

7. GUADALCANAL: THE SANTA CRUZ ISLANDS

The jubilation of the Pacific Fleet at the apparently victorious outcome of the Battle of Cape Esperance was not shared for long by General Vandegrift and his weary, fever-ridden Marines on Guadalcanal. The troop-convoy from Nouméa was safely brought to the anchorage on 13 October, the day after the battle, and 3,000 U.S. Army reinforcements were landed; some 90 dive-bombers and fighters were operational, making the Marines' position a potentially dangerous hornet's nest to attack. But the fighters lacked radar direction and were unable to prevent two heavy, high-flying raids that afternoon from churning up the airfield. Around 0100 that night the whole area cowered under a savage, 90-minute storm of 14-inch shells from the 16 guns of battleships *Kongo* and *Haruna* steaming in Ironbottom Sound, unopposed except for a spirited but ineffective attack by four motor torpedo boats from Tulagi. When it was over, more than half the aircraft had been put out of action; the petrol supply had mostly gone up in flames; and at noon, and again an hour later, the shaken defenders had to submit to two more air raids. Finally during the night 14-15 October Admiral Mikawa brought his two remaining cruisers, *Chokai* and *Kinugasa*, to finish the neutralisation of Henderson Field, which he did with 752 eight-inch shells.

Thus when a convoy of six transports with destroyer and fighter escort was sighted advancing down the Slot during the 14th, little could be done to oppose it and dawn of the 15th saw 4,500 Japanese reinforcements, ammunition and supplies being disembarked at Tassafaronga. Morale sank to a new low level at the sight. By getting every flyable plane into the air, partially fuelled and armed from hidden reserves which had escaped destruction, three of the transports were so damaged that they had to be beached and became total losses; nevertheless the day's end saw the number of fresh Japanese troops increased to bring the total to within 1,000 of the 23,000 fever-ridden, battle-weary Americans. The shortage of ammunition and petrol at Henderson Field was chronic, supplies only trickling through by a number of improvised means. When the Japanese cruisers *Myoko* and *Maya* took their turn during the night of 15-16 October to hurl 1,500 eight-inch shells at the field, the Marines felt their cup of bitterness was almost full. The Japanese now dominated the approaches to Guadalcanal by day as well as by night. The situation was summed up by the Commander-in-Chief Pacific, Admiral Nimitz, who recorded, 'It now appears that we are unable to control the sea in the Guadalcanal area. Thus our supply of the positions will only be done at great expense to us. The situation is not hopeless, but it is certainly critical.'

Ill-feeling grew between Vandegrift, who felt the Navy was failing in its support, and the Amphibious Commander, Admiral Turner, who considered the soldiers were being insufficiently offensive. Nimitz decided that a change of leadership, 'a more aggressive commander' was required in the South Pacific Command to restore morale. To relieve Ghormley at Nouméa came the colourful, thrusting 'Bill' Halsey who had been a carrier task force commander for the first months of the war with his flag in the *Enterprise* and had won a warm place in the hearts of the men of the fleet as a fighting admiral. His morale-boosting slogan, 'Kill Japs, Kill More Japs', became a heartening by-word in the fleet.

Halsey and his staff were still settling in at the headquarters in Nouméa when the land battle for Guadalcanal flared up, and there was little he could do in direct support of Vandegrift's force beyond the improvised trickle of supplies already set in motion under Ghormley. The South Pacific carrier strength was confined to the *Hornet* (Task Force 17) and until this was joined by the *Enterprise* which, after hasty repairs at Pearl Harbour, was hurrying on to the scene in company with the fast, new battleship *South Dakota*, there could be no question of aggressive tactics. Nevertheless a surface force (Task Force 64) under Rear-Admiral Willis A. Lee, flying his flag in the battleship *Washington*, with the cruisers *San Francisco*, *Helena* and *Atlanta* and six destroyers, was sent forward to block the 'Tokyo Express' route down the Slot by night.

The Japanese plan was for General Hyakutake's troops to advance, encircle and capture Henderson Field while Admiral Yamamoto sent the Combined Fleet south from Truk — four carriers, four battleships, 14 cruisers and more than 30 destroyers, under the command of Vice-Admiral Kondo — to hold the sea approaches, cruising to the north of the Solomons, and to fly in aircraft to occupy Henderson Field as soon as the Rising Sun flag flew over it. This was expected to be on 22 October; but meeting a gallant and dogged defence, the Japanese failed to break through the Marines' perimeter and by the 24th Yamamoto was forced to warn Hyakutake that fuel was running short and that unless the airfield was captured very soon the fleet would have to withdraw. This inspired a last desperate series of attacks and repeated assurances of imminent success; but dawn on the 26th revealed the Americans still holding out. And, indeed, the battle for Henderson Field ended triumphantly for the Marines that forenoon as the Japanese land attacks were finally, bloodily repulsed and aircraft from the field caught and sank the light cruiser *Yura* leading a bombardment unit. The Japanese fleet to the north-east of the Solomons now turned away northwards.

In the meantime, however, the *Enterprise* group (Task Force 16) under Rear-Admiral Thomas C. Kinkaid had made rendezvous with Task Force 17 on the 24th to the eastward of the New Hebrides Islands. In spite of the vastly superior Japanese fleet known to be poised northeast of the Solomons, Halsey boldly ordered Kinkaid to take the two groups northwards and sweep in a wide circle round the Santa Cruz Islands. His orders were prudently defensive, enjoining that he should then 'proceed south-westerly and east of San Cristobal to the area in the Coral Sea and be in position to intercept enemy forces approaching the Guadalcanal-Tulagi area'. Nevertheless when scouting Catalina flying boats located two Japanese carriers some 360 miles north-west of him at noon on 25th and steering south-east, Kinkaid had no doubt that aggression was expected of him. At 1330, 12 search planes were flown off, followed 50 minutes later by a striking force of 18 bombers and 11 fighters. But the Japanese had reversed course northwards and were not discovered by the carrier planes although Flying Fortresses and Catalinas attacked, unsuccessfully, with bombs and torpedoes.

During the night of the 25th-26th, Kinkaid pushed on north-westwards. Soon after midnight the enemy fleet was reported 300 miles to the north-west. Kondo was once again heading south to be in position to send aircraft to Henderson Field as soon as the Army announced its capture. When two Catalinas attacked and just failed to torpedo the carrier *Zuikaku* three hours later, the distance had closed to 200 miles. The report of this, however, did not reach Kinkaid until 0512 when, in the early dawn, he was launching from the *Enterprise* a search by eight pairs of Dauntless dive-bombers each armed with a single 500-lb. bomb. And at about this time from Halsey came the signal 'Attack — Repeat — Attack'.

The Japanese Fleet, as on previous occasions, was divided into a number of separate groups. Kondo, himself, the overall commander, was embarked in the cruiser *Atago* and had under his immediate command the so-called Advance Force comprising four heavy cruisers and the battleships *Kongo* and *Haruna* screened by a light cruiser and 12 destroyers and the new carrier *Junyo* with her own screen of two destroyers. This force was some 120 miles to the north-west of the Striking Force commanded by Vice-Admiral Nagumo which comprised a Carrier Group — *Shokaku* (flagship), *Zuikaku* and the smaller *Zuiho*, screened by the cruiser *Kumano* and eight destroyers — and a Vanguard Group under the command of Rear-Admiral Hiroaki Abe, composed of the battleships *Hiei* and *Kirishima*, the cruisers, *Tone*, *Chikuma* and *Suzuya*, screened by a light cruiser and seven destroyers, stationed some 60 miles further to the southward. The torpedo attack by the Catalinas had induced caution in Kondo's mind and at 0400 he had once again reversed the course of the whole fleet and all were now heading north.

In spite of numerous contacts with units of the Japanese fleet by flying boats during the night, Kinkaid decided to wait for reports from his own search planes before launching a striking force; and, though two of the *Enterprise* scout planes reported Abe's Vanguard Group at 0630, it was not until 0650 that another pair reported Nagumo's carriers, less than 200 miles north-west of him. It was just 0730 when the first strike of 15 dive-bombers, six Avenger torpedo-planes and eight Wildcats took off from the *Hornet*. To save time and fuel they set off as soon as formed up without waiting for the *Enterprise*'s strike group of three dive-bombers, eight Avengers and eight Wildcats which did not get off until 0800. Fifteen minutes later a second strike rose from the *Hornet* — nine dive-bombers, nine torpedo-planes and nine fighters.

Nagumo had anticipated events. A striking force, 65 planes strong, about half of them Zero fighters, was already ranged on the decks of his three carriers when final confirmation of the position of one American carrier came in at 0658 and within 12 minutes the strike was on its way. Preparations to range a second strike on deck began at once but had not gone far when suddenly, without warning there came the crescendo whistle of two dive-bombers. Not a gun opened fire, not a single Zero tried to interpose itself as they plummeted down to release their two bombs. Both exploded on the *Zuiho*'s flight-deck near the stern, punching a huge, jagged hole which effectively put her out of action for further flying operations. The pilots of the two planes, Lieutenant-Commander S. B. Strong and Ensign C. B. Irvine, had intercepted the enemy report of the first pair to locate Nagumo's squadron, Lieutenant-Commander J. R. Lee and Ensign W. E. Johnson, who had themselves been driven off by the defensive patrol, but had accounted for three Zeros before escaping into cloud. Strong and Irvine had made clever use of the broken cloud formations to arrive undetected and unopposed over the enemy and score first blood in what was to be called the Battle of the Santa Cruz Islands.

For the next two hours events piled on one another with the balance of tactical success tipping in favour of the Japanese. When their compact striking force passed their American counterparts on an opposite course, strung out in three separate groups, they could afford to detach a dozen of their swarm of Zeros to attack the small *Enterprise* group. Coming in out of the sun they caught them unawares. Three Wildcats and three Avengers were shot down and another of each type damaged and forced down at the cost of three Zeros. Meanwhile, from the *Shokaku* and *Zuikaku*, a second striking force of 44 planes had taken off at 0822. Twenty-nine more were being got ready aboard the *Junyo*.

'For what we are about to receive...' was the grisly quip of the eighteenth-century sailor as he waited for the first enemy broadside to smash cruelly into the thronged gun decks. Similar sentiments were experienced, if not voiced, in the carriers on either side as the two striking forces growled onwards towards their expectant targets. The *Enterprise*, with her up-to-date radar, had been entrusted with fighter direction for the whole U.S. force and was the first to gain contact at 0840; but fighter-direction technique was still immature and her fighter-direction officer was inexperienced. Difficulty was found in interpreting the cluttered radar picture. Wildcats of the *Hornet*'s combat air patrol who happened to sight the approaching dive-bombers were able to shoot down a number of them; but meeting them only a few miles out they could not prevent a group of about 15 breaking through to the fleet. At the same time some 20 torpedo-planes swept in low over the water, unopposed, their attack perfectly co-ordinated. Thus it was mainly on the ships' gunfire that the defence had to rely.

The *Enterprise* and her group steamed into a rain squall at 0900 before the enemy flyers had sighted them. The *Hornet*'s group, ten miles to the south-east, was therefore left to take the full force of the onslaught. The attackers met a tremendous volume of well-directed fire from the guns of the circular screen of cruisers and destroyers, as well as from the carrier herself. More than half the 'Kate' torpedo-planes were shot down before they reached the launching position. Of the 15

'Vals', 12 were fatally hit as they plunged down from 17,000 feet. But only early interception could have taken the sting out of an attack by such dedicated warriors. The squadron commander, his plane hit, deliberately crashed into the *Hornet*, wrecking the signal bridge and plunging through the flight deck where two of his bombs exploded and started a large fire. Two minutes later two torpedoes exploded amidships against her starboard side, flooding the forward engine-room and two boiler-rooms, bringing her to a halt with a heavy list. Almost simultaneously three 500-lb. bombs hit her, one exploding on impact, the other two punching through to burst in her bowels. Finally the pilot of a blazing torpedo-plane flew it suicidally into the carrier's bow, where it exploded near the forward lift. All was over in ten minutes. On board the shattered, burning *Hornet*, the crew set about a long, desperate struggle to save their ship, aided by the fire hoses of destroyers brought alongside.

Two hundred miles to the north-westward, vengeance was about to be taken, though with rather less effectiveness. The first strike wave from the *Hornet* had become split into two sections during its long flight, the six torpedo-planes and four of the fighters losing touch with the air group leader, Lieutenant-Commander Widhelm, who was with the 15 dive-bombers and their four escorting Wildcats. At 0915 Widhelm sighted the cruisers and destroyers of Kondo's Advance Force off to his port side. He was after bigger game, however. He carried on in search of carriers, but without his fighter escort, which was left beating off an attack by Kondo's combat air patrol put up by the *Junyo*, losing two of their number to the Zeros. At 0930 he sighted his objective, Nagumo's flagship *Shokaku* in company with the still burning *Zuiho*. Fighting off the Zeros sent up against them, the dive-bombers pressed on.

Widhelm's own plane was crippled but, making a forced landing, he and his gunner got safely into their dinghy whence they had a front-seat view of the events that followed.[8] Another bomber was shot down and two forced to turn back with damage; but the remainder, led by Lieutenant J. E. Vose, arrived over the *Shokaku*. Ignoring the Zeros on their tails, diving down through a curtain of vicious, black shell-bursts, they dropped four 1,000-lb. bombs squarely on to the carrier's flight deck, leaving it a tangle of twisted steel, wrecking the hangar below, where fires blazed up, and reducing her speed to 21 knots.

Had the torpedo-bombers been present to co-ordinate their attack the *Shokaku*'s career must have ended there and then. As it was she was to be out of action for nine months. But the remainder of the *Hornet*'s aircraft only succeeded in finding the Vanguard Group. Torpedoes were launched unsuccessfully at the cruiser *Suzuya*, but one dive-bomber of the second wave succeeded in scoring a hit on the cruiser *Chikuma*, heavily damaging her and sending her limping back to base. Survivors of the *Enterprise*'s striking force, split up by the Zero attack *en route*, also attacked the Vanguard Group but without any success.

So far the exchange of aerial blows between the two fleets had achieved not dissimilar results, the Japanese having two of their carriers and a cruiser put out of action, though none of them were so grievously damaged as the *Hornet*. On the other hand Japanese blind courage, coupled with a deterioration in the air-fighting skill of their carrier pilots compared to the Americans, had once again cost them carrier-trained aircrews in numbers they could not afford. They were about to double their already fearsome casualty list as the second wave of

---

[8] They were rescued two days later by a Catalina.

aircraft from the *Shokaku* and *Zuikaku* attacked. The presence of the *Enterprise* had been revealed by intercepted radio-telephone messages and it was on her that this wave concentrated, except for one 'Val' which dived unsuccessfully on the crippled *Hornet*. The remainder had been detected by the radar of the battleship *South Dakota* when still some 55 miles distant, but no fighters were directed on to them, perhaps on account of another form of threat which developed almost simultaneously. Undetected by the screen, the Japanese submarine *I-21* had worked its way into position to attack the *South Dakota*. First knowledge of her presence came at 1002 when the destroyer *Porter* picking up a 'splashed' air crew, erupted from the explosion of a torpedo in her boiler-rooms, being so wrecked that she had to be sunk by gunfire when the survivors of her crew had been taken off by the *Shaw*. Fortunately all other torpedoes of the salvo from the submarine went astray. But while attention was thus distracted the Japanese bombers were reaching their diving position unopposed.

Without waiting for the accompanying torpedo-planes, some 30 minutes behind them, they went into the attack. Only then did the guns of the *Enterprise* and her battleship and cruiser escort open up: but they did so with devastating effect. Though 23 bombs were dropped, of which two hit the *Enterprise*'s flight deck and one near miss shook her savagely, hardly a single 'Val' survived to tell the tale. The *Enterprise*'s forward lift was put permanently out of action, but the damage to her deck was repairable. More important, her speed and manoeuvrability were little affected so that, when the lagging 'Kates' streaked in low to launch torpedoes from either side, she was able to comb the tracks of some and outrun others. Intercepted by Wildcats, the torpedo-planes lost ten of their number to them and five more fell to the ships' guns, leaving only nine able to deliver their attack on the carrier and one which deliberately crashed into the destroyer *Smith*, causing nearly 50 casualties and wrecking her forecastle.

Extravagant as the price paid by the Japanese airmen had been, the situation of Kinkaid's Task Force was an unenviable one at this moment. Out of sight of the *Enterprise* to the west, the *Hornet* lay a motionless wreck which the cruiser *Northampton* was making strenuous but as yet unsuccessful attempts to take in tow. Under an overcast sky which favoured surprise air attack, the crew of the *Enterprise* were struggling to repair her flight deck so that the swarm of American aircraft with fuel running low could be taken aboard: and all unsuspected, a fresh striking force of 29 planes from the *Junyo* was approaching. At 1121 about 20 of them suddenly broke out of the overcast in shallow dives. They did not achieve anything and eight of them were shot down. Seven minutes later the remainder struck at the *South Dakota* and the light cruiser *San Juan*. The battleship took a bomb on her forward turret but the armoured roof was not penetrated and damage was slight. The *San Juan* was equally lucky. The armour-piercing bomb which hit her exploded underneath after passing clean through her thin plates. Both ships for a time careered menacingly through the circular formation temporarily out of control, but no collisions occurred and they were soon back in station little the worse.

The *Enterprise* was now able to recover the majority of the waiting planes though a few were forced down into the sea as their fuel ran out. Nevertheless Kinkaid's air-power, offensive and defensive, was for the time being virtually eliminated, and facing a greatly superior enemy surface force, he could do nothing but retire from the battle, abandoning the *Hornet* to her fate. Kondo, with two of his carriers — *Zuikaku* and *Junyo* — undamaged, though bereft of all but a handful of their aircraft, was hurrying to renew the attack, hoping to be able to bring his battleships and cruisers into action after nightfall. Meanwhile what remaining aircraft could be flown were launched from the Japanese carriers to disrupt the efforts being made to salvage the *Hornet*.

By 1330 the *Northampton* had succeeded in getting the carrier in tow and at a painful three knots headed southwards while all but a handful of the *Hornet*'s crew were transferred to destroyers. The two ships had not gone far when at 1515 six enemy torpedo-planes streaked in low over the water. The cruiser just had time to slip the tow and gather speed with which to avoid the torpedoes; but the carrier, lying stopped and helpless, took one on her starboard side which further tore her already riven hull. Water flooding into her after engine room increased her list to 14 degrees. The *Hornet* was clearly doomed. Preparations were being made finally to abandon her when at 1540 the guns of her protective cruisers and destroyers opened up a furious barrage in the face of which a few dive-bombing 'Vals' failed to score any hits. But ten minutes later six bombers making a level attack on the easy target hit her flight deck with one bomb. Yet the *Hornet* was still afloat when another small group of dive-bombers dropped a final bomb at 1702 which penetrated to her hangar. It was time to sink her and retire. The inefficiency of American torpedoes of that date was demonstrated when, out of 16 torpedoes fired by two destroyers, only eight ran correctly to hit. The resultant explosions failed to sink the ship. So did more than 400 rounds of five-inch shell pumped into her, though they set her ablaze from bow to stern. The Japanese Vanguard Group was hurrying forward through the darkness attracted by the glare.

The American destroyers could not stay to complete the destruction; but enough had been done to prevent the *Hornet* falling into enemy hands. When Admiral Abe came up with her, he could no more than order the *coup de grâce* by four 'Long Lance' torpedoes.

The Battle of the Santa Cruz Islands was over. For although Admiral Kondo lingered in the battle area until the following afternoon, Kinkaid had withdrawn, his fleet no longer battleworthy. Thus, superficially, the Japanese had won a tactical victory over the weaker, hastily gathered American carrier task force, and it might have been thought that Japanese domination of the sea approaches to Guadalcanal would now seal the fate of the beleaguered American expeditionary force on the island. But in fact the slaughter inflicted on the Japanese carrier aircrews had left Yamamoto with only sufficient to operate the two small carriers *Junyo* and *Hiyo*, less than 100 planes in all, too few to have the commanding influence hitherto held by the big carriers. The *Enterprise*, on the other hand, was being hastily repaired at Nouméa. In the meantime both sides planned to run reinforcements through to Guadalcanal covered by shore-based air-power and naval surface forces.

In both these elements the Japanese were numerically superior in striking power, but the Americans had the advantage of possession of the only airfield at the crucial point. From it, about 50 fighters and a similar number of strike planes still exercised local air superiority by day. That a clash was impending there could be no doubt. At Truk, Rabaul and the Shortlands Island bases the Japanese were gathering transports which it would be 'Tenacious Tanaka's' task to deliver to Guadalcanal. At Espiritu Santo and Nouméa Rear-Admiral Turner was similarly engaged, loading troops and supplies in seven large transports which would be escorted by cruisers and destroyers under Rear-Admiral Daniel Callaghan, flying his flag in the cruiser *San Francisco*.

The American convoys were to be ready first, but even earlier the Japanese had renewed their night runs down the Slot, no less than 65 destroyers and two cruisers delivering troops and supplies between 2 and 10 November. Turner's Amphibious Force arrived off Henderson Field on 11th and 12th and began feverishly unloading supplies and disembarking troops while the escorting cruisers and destroyers steamed to and fro to seaward, their radars searching the skies, sonar beams probing underwater for submarines. Air attack began on the 11th with a dive-bombing attack mounted from the *Hiyo* operating to the north of the Solomons and was followed by heavy bomb and torpedo raids from Rabaul. With the aid of warnings from the faithful coast watchers the enemy were each time met by fighters from Henderson Field and a daunting barrage of gunfire. The transports escaped serious damage.

But during the 12th information began to come in of strong Japanese surface units steering to converge on Guadalcanal that night. Analysis of the various reports resulted in an estimate of two battleships, several cruisers and a dozen destroyers. A grim situation was facing the Amphibious Force. Turner's transports could and did retire to safety; but Henderson Field and its defenders could not be left defenceless against the storm of high explosive shell that the guns of the Japanese battleships, cruisers and destroyers could hurl at them. The *Enterprise*, with repair parties still at work on board her trying to get her damaged lift working, accompanied by the new fast battleships *Washington* and *South Dakota*, was racing north from Nouméa, but this force could not be in the area until the following day. Having seen the transports safely away, therefore, Admiral Callaghan gathered his force together, the two heavy cruisers *San Francisco* and *Portland*, each mounting nine eight-inch guns, the light cruisers *Helena* (15 six-inch), *Juneau* and *Atlanta* (16 five-inch) and eight destroyers, and turned back into Ironbottom Sound to challenge the approaching enemy.

8. THE BATTLES OF GUADALCANAL AND TASSAFARONGA

The Japanese force, steaming through the night for Guadalcanal, though not quite as alarming as Admiral Turner estimated, was not to be despised. When it concentrated to the north of Santa Isabel on the afternoon of 12 November, it comprised two battleships, *Hiei* (flagship of Vice-Admiral Hiroaki Abe) and *Kirishima*, the light cruiser *Nagara* and 14 destroyers. Numerically impressive, indeed; but its effectiveness for a sea fight was reduced by the fact that the Japanese ships had been specially supplied for the occasion with thin-shelled, impact-fused bombardment projectiles. Ponderous, unhandy battleships, also, were not the most suitable craft for the close work of night action. On the other hand they had the advantage of flashless cordite whereas their opponents had still to fight at night blinded by their own gunfire; and they had the 'Long Lances', deadly efficient weapons as compared with the unreliable American torpedoes.

Against all this, Callaghan had the inestimable advantage of effective, modern surface warning radar in several of his ships. Could this be efficiently harnessed to defeat the night fighting skill of the Japanese? The victor of a night action was likely to be the side which got its blow in first, a feature to which radar should certainly decisively contribute. Unfortunately, this 'magic eye' was still an innovation and its use not fully appreciated by some senior officers. Rear-Admiral Scott was serving in Callaghan's force, his flag flying in the *Atlanta*. In spite of his experience during the Battle of Cape Esperance, in which the need for the Senior Officer to have radar under his own eye had been painfully demonstrated, Callaghan had been allocated — or had chosen — for his flagship the *San Francisco*, which did not have it.

A quite unwarranted estimate of the extent of Scott's success on that occasion had also encouraged confidence in the single line ahead formation which was also the simplest for a gathering of ships unfamiliar with each other, liable to signal confusion and, judging by previous experiences, subject to a distressing poverty of night vision. Callaghan now decided to imitate it. That his much larger force would be even more unmanageable in single line was presumably accepted. Any idea of allowing his experienced destroyers freedom to act independently to bring their powerful torpedo armament into play was ruled out.

Thus it was in single line ahead that the destroyers *Cushing*, *Laffey*, *Sterett* and *O'Bannon* (in that order) led the *Atlanta*, *San Francisco*, *Portland*, *Helena* and *Juneau*, with the destroyers *Aaron Ward*, *Barton*, *Monssen* and *Fletcher* bringing up the rear. With all ships closed up in correct station the line was more than three-and-a-half nautical miles long, liable to 'snake' or to 'concertina' and calling for a concentration on station keeping at the expense of a keen look-out. Perhaps feeling that the uncertainties of night encounter defied anticipation, the admiral issued no battle plan, nor did he pass any appreciation of the situation to his subordinates, most of whom had no combat experience and had not previously operated together.

Such was the force that filed slowly westwards past Lunga Point a mile or so off-shore through the dark, moonless, overcast night of 12-13 November 1942, with only a gentle following wind scarcely ruffling the black waters of Ironbottom Sound. The rear ship was still abreast the Point at 0124 when, over the T.B.S. circuit, came a voice message from the *Helena* reporting two groups of ships bearing north-west at ranges of 27,000 and 32,000 yards between Savo Island and Guadalcanal. On the same circuit the Admiral now began to manoeuvre his squadron, first altering course in succession to 310 degrees — directly towards the reported contact. By 0130 the *Helena* had had time to develop a plot and she reported that the contact was steering 105 degrees at 23 knots. A further wheel to starboard to a course of north and an increase of speed to 20 knots set the van of Callaghan's line steering across the contact's bow. There could be no doubt now that it was an enemy force approaching at high speed.

Admiral Abe's squadron — for such it was — had entered the Slot passing between Santa Isabel and Florida and had steered to leave Savo Island to port. He had formed six of his destroyers and the light cruiser *Nagara* into an orthodox arrow-head screen round his two battleships steaming in column with the *Hiei* leading. Five other destroyers had been stationed farther ahead, three on the starboard bow and two on the port as an outer defence against any attack by the motor torpedo boats known to be based on Tulagi. Three destroyers were detached to patrol west of Guadalcanal to guard against any interference by American forces that might approach by that route.

A thick tropical rain squall into which the force had run north-west of Savo, however, had caused the Admiral to reverse course for a time until it passed; in the process the three destroyers to starboard had fallen out of station and were now far back on the port quarter. No inkling of Callaghan's presence had come to Abe, but in the Japanese ships there was no lack of alertness.

From the T.B.S. loud-speakers on the bridges of the American ships an almost continuous succession of messages, orders and acknowledgments was flowing, including repeated urgent demands from the flagship for radar information from the *Helena*, as the opposing squadrons raced forward on collision courses. In the midst of this confused chatter the moment for ordering fire to be opened with guns or torpedoes on the unsuspecting enemy passed with no action taken. Then, at 0141, the leading American destroyer *Cushing*, and the two Japanese outriders, *Yudachi* and *Marusami*, crossing ahead of her at 3,000 yards, came simultaneously in sight of each other. The *Cushing* swung hastily to port to avoid collision and to bring her torpedo tubes to bear, while the alarm was passed by radio.

In the American van all was at once confusion as the ships astern of the *Cushing*, caught unawares by her unexpected turn, tried to follow round in her wake, but succeeded only in achieving a pile-up. The voice radio traffic degenerated into a frustrating babble. The Admiral was so bemused by it that the *Atlanta*'s turn to port ahead of his flagship took him by surprise and he had to ask her what she was doing. The reply from Captain Jenkins that he was 'avoiding our own destroyers' did little to enlighten him. In the *Cushing* the divisional commander, Commander Stokes, was asking permission to fire torpedoes but by the time he received it the enemy had vanished into the darkness. At last at 0145 Callaghan gave the preliminary order 'Stand by to open fire'. With no knowledge of what he had encountered, the order to open fire could not yet be given. For five more minutes action waited, while the leading Japanese units were passing on both sides of the bunched American line. Then the calm was ended by the sudden glare of searchlight beams stabbing out and settling on the *Atlanta* and a hail of shells fired at point-blank range smothering her, one of them killing Admiral Scott and nearly all of his staff on the bridge. Only then was the order received from the American flagship 'Odd-numbered ships commence firing to starboard, even-numbered to port'.

On the Japanese side, lacking radar, surprise had initially been complete, but there had been less confusion and no hesitation as they found enemy ships inside their formation. Torpedoes were quickly on their way and before the hapless *Atlanta* had fired more than a few salvoes at the Japanese destroyers on either bow, she was brought to a standstill by the devastating explosion of a 'Long Lance' warhead. From now onwards the battle resolved itself into a confused melee as ships loomed briefly out of the darkness, or were silhouetted against the light of star shells or searchlight beams, were taken under gun and torpedo fire, reciprocated and vanished into the murk and smoke, the main feature being the deadly effectiveness of the Japanese torpedo compared to that of their opponents, owing principally to the poor quality of the American weapon.

The van destroyers of the American line found themselves almost at once in the middle of the Japanese formation. The *Cushing* had exchanged only a few salvoes with one of the enemy destroyer screen, though she received crippling hits in the process, when the menacing bulk of the *Hiei* loomed up. Manoeuvring his almost immobilised ship with difficulty, her captain, Lieutenant-Commander Parker, launched six torpedoes at the battleship, but without effect. Immediately afterwards the *Cushing* was illuminated and taken under such effective gunfire that she was torn apart and left sinking. Her division mates, *Laffey*, *Sterett* and *O'Bannon*, also came up against the Japanese flagship. All turned their guns and torpedoes on her and though their five-inch shells had individually little effect on her armoured bulk, and their torpedoes failed either to hit or to explode, the combined effect was enough to cause

Abe to order a retirement. But in return they suffered heavily, the *Laffey* being sunk by a combination of gunfire and a torpedo which blew off her stern, while the *Sterett* received a salvo on her port quarter which disabled her steering gear and, meeting an enemy destroyer at close range while in this condition, was further damaged, set afire and driven out of the action. Only the *O'Bannon*, coolly extricated from the shambles, escaped unhurt.

The *Hiei* and *Kirishima* turned away to port. The latter had hardly been fired at and was undamaged and soon drew away out of the action. Abe's flagship, on the other hand, had been the main target for the American ships and was already partially crippled when the eight-inch cruisers brought her under fire, both the *San Francisco* and the *Portland* hitting her heavily. She circled slowly in a parlous condition on to a westerly retirement course, still able to hit out fiercely at any targets that came in sight. Two Japanese destroyers also suffered, the *Akatsuki* being sunk and the *Yudachi* wrecked and immobilised. Meanwhile, however, tragedy had engulfed the American cruisers.

Soon after the *Atlanta* had been so swiftly eliminated, the *San Francisco* had gone into action with an enemy ship which she illuminated with starshell. Satisfied after seven salvoes that she had dealt out severe punishment, when a fresh target had presented itself — a 'small cruiser or large destroyer' at close range — she had shifted fire to it. Out of two full salvoes of eight-inch guns, almost every shell had hit and the target had been set ablaze from end to end.

At this moment the Japanese battleships had come in sight. The *San Francisco*'s guns had again been given a fresh target and had begun to fire at the *Hiei* when the horrified Admiral Callaghan, evidently believing, probably justifiably, that the 'small cruiser or large destroyer' had in fact been the crippled *Atlanta*, and that others of his ships were making the same mistake, at 0155 had given the order to cease fire. Captain DuBose of the *Portland* promptly queried the order. The confirmation he received was almost the last word spoken by the Admiral. The *San Francisco*, her guns silent, starkly illuminated in the glare of searchlights, was set upon by the 14-inch guns of the *Kirishima* as well as by two other ships at point-blank range. Under the hail of shells, her bridge structure disintegrated. Admiral Callaghan, his flag-captain and staff were all killed.

Little attention was paid elsewhere to the cease-fire order. The wild melee continued, the *Hiei* on the one side, the *San Francisco* and *Atlanta* on the other taking the brunt of the gunfire. It was the 'Long Lance' torpedoes that tipped the balance sharply in favour of the Japanese. The *Atlanta* and the *Laffey* had already been put out of action by them. Now the *Portland* took one in the stern which left her helplessly circling. The *Helena*, next in the line, twisting this way and that to keep clear of the circling *Portland*, of the shattered *San Francisco* and of the burning, immobile wreck that was the *Atlanta*, fired briefly at a number of unidentified targets as they swung across her sights. She bore a charmed life and suffered no serious damage; but she could not be expected to make good shooting under the circumstances. The *Juneau* had the same difficulty but less luck, for a torpedo explosion tore open her forward engine-room, leaving her stopped, out of action, and in danger of sinking.

The four destroyers bringing up the rear fought a similarly chance-guided action with vaguely identified targets while turning, stopping or going astern to avoid collision with ships ahead.

The flotilla leader, *Aaron Ward*, after engaging several ships, one of which appeared to blow up and sink, was herself hit again and again and withdrew from the fight with heavy damage, including a flooded engine-room, that soon brought her to a standstill. The *Barton*, next astern, also had to stop to avoid collision, and before she could get under way again was rent asunder by two torpedoes and sent to the bottom with almost all her crew. The *Monssen* suffered a spectacular, horrifying catastrophe. She had gone spiritedly into action, launching one salvo of five torpedoes at the Japanese battleships and another at something smaller when her captain, believing he was about to be taken under fire by his own side, switched on his fighting lights. Japanese ships on both sides, a clearly identifiable target at last presented to them, concentrated a hurricane of shellfire on the destroyer. Rent by 37 shell hits the *Monssen* was set uncontrollably ablaze. Ready-use ammunition erupted from time to time as the flames reached it. There was nothing for the crew to do but to take to the life-rafts, whence they watched their ship burn, finally to blow up at around noon. The *Fletcher*, rear ship of the line, in sharp contrast to her flotilla mates, emerged from the fight without a scratch. Guided by the new radar with which she was fitted, she was extricated from the dangerous area round the burning *Monssen*, *Cushing* and *Atlanta*, circled round the melee and came in to launch ten carefully aimed torpedoes. That none found a target, or if they did, did not explode, was the usual fate for American torpedoes at that time.

The opposing forces disengaged and the firing died away soon after 0215. Only one Japanese ship, the destroyer *Akatsuki* had gone down. The *Hiei* had accumulated damage from scores of shell hits which sent her limping erratically away, barely under control, to the northward of Savo Island.

The *Yudachi* was left burning and abandoned by her crew who had been taken off by the destroyer *Samidare*. Three other destroyers with varying degrees of damage, but none fatal, made up the sum of the Japanese casualties. Behind them they left scenes of grim horror. Survivors from the sunken *Laffey* and *Barton*, the abandoned *Cushing* and *Monssen* tended their wounded shipmates on life-rafts as best they could until daylight brought rescue by craft from Guadalcanal. A number of wounded found to be still aboard the burning *Monssen* were saved in the nick of time.

Dawn broke over an Ironbottom Sound littered with other crippled ships. The *Portland*, her torn and twisted stern plates making her uncontrollable, steamed in circles, but had escaped serious damage otherwise. The *Aaron Ward* lay riddled and helpless. But it was the *Atlanta*, shattered by American as well as Japanese shells, torn open under water by torpedoes and with nearly half her crew killed, that made the most pitiful sight. Nevertheless her crew struggled on to save her and at 0939 she was taken in tow by a tug from Guadalcanal which brought her by 1400 to anchor off Lunga Point. But it was to no avail. She was clearly doomed and that evening her end was hastened by scuttling charges. The tug transferred her attentions to the *Portland* and with her aid the cruiser was brought, soon after midnight, into Tulagi harbour, as was the *Aaron Ward*.

The remainder of the American squadron, the *San Francisco*, upper works almost as ravaged as the *Atlanta*'s but her armoured hull not penetrated by the Japanese bombardment shells, the *Juneau* precariously afloat but able to steam, the *Sterett*, her damage partially repaired, and the unscathed *O'Bannon* and *Fletcher*, had been led off the scene by the *Helena*. By dawn they had worked up to 18 knots and were zigzagging through Indispensable Strait *en route* for Espiritu Santo. But last bitter dregs remained in the cup for the American squadron. Part of the Japanese plan had involved the deployment of nine submarines in the approaches to Guadalcanal. At 0950 the *Sterett* believed she had made sonar contact with one of them. If so, the threat was fended off by the depth-charges the destroyer dropped. But an hour later the submarine *I-26* was undetected as she launched a salvo of torpedoes aimed at the *San Francisco* who was following 1,000 yards astern of the *Helena*. The torpedoes streaked harmlessly past the big cruiser. But 1,000 yards on her beam was the *Juneau*. No means of sounding the alarm had survived the *San Francisco*'s battering. Horrified watchers on her deck looked on helplessly as one of the torpedoes drew the white line of its track across the intervening water straight for the *Juneau*'s side. It exploded abreast her bridge with such devastating force that the ship disintegrated and vanished, leaving nothing but a tall pillar of smoke, and amazingly, more than 100 survivors struggling in the water to mark her passing. With further attacks possible on his vulnerable ships, the senior officer cleared the area at his best speed, keeping his destroyers to screen them. The *Juneau*'s survivors were left to their fate. Tragically, a message passed to a patrolling bomber, asking for rescue craft to be sent, never reached headquarters. Only ten of the *Juneau*'s crew remained alive when flying boats eventually reached the scene. The rest had died of their wounds, of thirst, or had been taken by sharks. The *Juneau*'s end marked the lowest ebb in American fortunes in the Battle of Guadalcanal. From now on the balance of success was to tip in their favour.

As the sun rose over the disputed waters of Ironbottom Sound and the Slot, mastery over them passed once again into the hands of American aviators. At first light Marine bombers took off from Henderson Field and attacked the *Wei*, limping slowly away north of Savo, escorted by the three destroyers which had been left on patrol and which had taken no part in the battle. Hastening up from the south was Admiral Kinkaid's Task Force 16 centred on the *Enterprise*. Her damage had been made good at Nouméa except for her forward aircraft lift on which technicians were still furiously working. This, of course, greatly restricted the tempo of her flying operations. At dawn a scouting force of ten planes had taken off from her deck to search the Slot. When they drew a blank, therefore, Kinkaid decided to send some of his aircraft to operate from Henderson Field. Nine torpedo-carrying Avengers and six Wildcats were launched with orders to land there after searching for any enemy ships to attack. They found the crippled *Hiei* still only ten miles north of Savo Island — a rich, alluring target.

The torpedo-planes, led by Lieutenant John F. Sutherland, made the most of it, dividing into two sections that broke through low cloud at 1020 to launch simultaneous attacks on either bow. They were still armed with the torpedoes of unpredictable and indifferent performance that had handicapped them since the beginning of the war, but two hits were scored, one of which wrecked the battleship's rudder, leaving her steaming in circles. Three hours later, having refuelled and rearmed at Henderson Field and accompanied by eight Marine Corps dive-bombers, they were back again. The *Hiei* was by now quite unmanoeuvrable. Four of the torpedoes ran true. Two bounced off without exploding but two detonated correctly, bringing the battleship to a halt, a target for successive strikes by shore-based bombers. Though she seemed unsinkable by bombs, her persevering crew finally gave up hope of saving her. They were taken off by the attendant destroyers that evening and she was scuttled — the first battleship to be lost by the Japanese.

Meanwhile great precautions for a final show-down in the struggle for Guadalcanal had been going on. The loss of the *Hiei* had not caused the stubborn Japanese to abandon their plans to bombard Henderson Field and to land reinforcements. From the Shortland Island base, early on the 13th, Admiral Mikawa had sailed in his flagship the *Chokai* with the *Kinugasa, Suzuya* and *Maya* — all heavy cruisers with eight-inch guns — the light cruisers *Isuzo* and *Tenrya* and six destroyers. Routed well to the north of Choiseul and Santa Isabel they had turned south in time to arrive off Savo Island at midnight, passing between Santa Isabel and Florida.

There was sufficient evidence from long-range reconnaissance aircraft for Admiral Halsey to appreciate that, with nightfall, Japanese surface forces would be back to harass the long-suffering defenders of Henderson Field. He did not intend to leave them unchallenged and during the afternoon he ordered Kinkaid to be prepared to detach his two battleships, *Washington* (flagship of Rear-Admiral Willis A. Lee) and *South Dakota* with four destroyers (Task Force 64). But Kinkaid was operating far to the south of Guadalcanal and though he promptly turned north with his whole force he was still some 350 miles from Savo Island when the order to detach Lee reached him. Task Force 64 parted company but could not reach the scene of action before daylight.

Thus when Mikawa arrived and sent forward the cruisers *Suzuya* and *Maya* with the *Tenryu* and four destroyers to deliver the bombardment, while with the remainder of his force he patrolled in support to the westward, he met no opposition but that of two motor torpedo boats which gallantly but unsuccessfully attacked. For more than half-an-hour, under the light of flares from spotting aircraft, eight-inch shells screamed in from seaward to burst on the airfield. Eighteen aircraft were destroyed and 32 damaged; but the airstrip remained operational and, at dawn, aircraft took off to seek revenge.

Mikawa's force had retired westward passing north of Russell Island and south of New Georgia. By 0700 on 14 November search planes had discovered him. A force of six Avengers, seven Dauntless dive-bombers and seven fighters was quickly on its way. At 0800 they swooped to the attack. A torpedo holed the *Kinugasa*, bombs hit and set her on fire. Other bombs damaged the *Izuso*. The planes returned to base without loss.

More trouble was on its way to Mikawa. Two hundred miles to the southward, the *Enterprise* had sent out planes searching for him, and a strike of 17 dive-bombers was already airborne when their contact report was received. Two of the scouts dropped their bombs on the *Kinugasa* causing further damage and, when the striking force arrived, it took little to finish her off and send her to the bottom, while both the *Chokai* and the *Maya* were damaged. But in the meantime a more important target had been discovered. Proceeding boldly down the middle of the Slot was a convoy of 11 transports encircled by a screen of 11 destroyers. Overhead was a combat patrol of Zeros.

At the masthead of the leading destroyer, *Hayashio*, flew a Rear-Admiral's flag, that of the indomitable Raizo Tanaka. His famous flagship, *Jintsu*, was still under repair from the damage she had received during the Battle of the Eastern Solomons.

No doubt the inclusion of this expedition of slow, vulnerable ships in the Japanese plan was made on the assumption that by the morning of the 14th Henderson Field would have been neutralised by bombardment and that no American carrier could be operational; in which case American local air superiority would have been sufficiently reduced for the convoy to be fought through under the umbrella of Zero fighters provided by the light carriers *Hiyo* and *Junyo* operating to the north of the Solomons. As early as 0830, when two dive-bombers from the *Enterprise* attacked, one of them being shot down by the Zeros, it must have become clear that the assumption was false. Before midday the first mass attack, by seven torpedo planes and 18 dive-bombers from Henderson Field, which crippled several of the transports, told Tanaka of the desperate ordeal ahead of him.

Perhaps any other Japanese flag officer would, at this stage, have given up the hopeless attempt and turned back. But Tanaka had on previous occasions displayed a stubborn courage, refusing to be deterred by losses. Pride or dedicated self-sacrifice now drove him on. Gathering his destroyers in a tight ring round his transports he held his easterly course and awaited the onslaught. From Henderson Field and from the *Enterprise*, dive-bombers with fighter escort arrived at brief intervals to scream down on the transports. From Espiritu Santo, Fortresses came to make high altitude bombing runs. The defending Zeros proved no match for the Wildcats, a sure sign of the deteriorated standard of Japanese fighter pilots since the opening weeks of war.

Relentlessly Tanaka drove his ever-diminishing convoy forward, transferring to destroyers the troops from those set ablaze, immobilised or sunk. By nightfall only four transports remained with him. But darkness brought relief from ceaseless air attack. With these four he pressed on. Behind him the night was lit by the flames of burning ships. In the course of the entire day the Americans had lost only five planes. But now, with the fall of darkness, the airmen perforce rested from their destructive activities. Domination of the Slot and Ironbottom

Sound was left open to dispute by the surface forces which were approaching from north and south. From the north, since 1000 that morning, 14 November, a Japanese squadron led by Vice-Admiral Kondo had been steering to enter the Slot, passing east of Santa Isabel, bent on delivering the bombardment which had been frustrated by the battle of two nights earlier. Undamaged survivors from that battle had joined Kondo, flying his flag in the heavy cruiser *Atago* to form a powerful Emergency Bombardment group. The *Atago*, her sister *Takao* and the battleship *Kirishima* had a close screen of the light cruiser *Nagara* and six destroyers, while the light cruiser *Sendai*, flagship of Rear-Admiral Hashimoto, and three more destroyers steamed ahead as an advanced screen. It made a thorny object for submarine attack so that when the U.S.S. *Trout* fell in with it north of Santa Isabel during the afternoon, her torpedoes, fired from outside the screen, failed to score. Her urgent signal, however, reporting the encounter, gave vital warning to Rear-Admiral Lee who, with his Task Force 64, had been hovering during the day 100 miles south of Guadalcanal. With his two battleships and the destroyers *Walke*, *Benham*, *Preston* and *Gwin* he promptly headed north in challenge and by the evening was rounding the western end of Guadalcanal.

Lee was by reputation a highly efficient officer. He knew, none better, the value of team training to a squadron going into battle, particularly by night. He had been, indeed, director of fleet training until three months ago. He cannot therefore have had great confidence in the unfamiliar, hastily gathered force under his flag on this occasion. The two battleships, *Washington* and *South Dakota*, had not previously worked together. His four destroyers all came from different divisions. Like Scott and Callaghan before him, he ordered the formation most easily maintained and which would minimise the chances of mistaken identity — single line ahead with his destroyers leading the two battleships. By 2150 Lee had rounded Savo Island and was steering south-eastwards into the fateful waters of Ironbottom Sound glinting placidly under the light of a quarter moon sinking towards the western horizon where it was due to set at 0100. Unbeknown to him, he had barely slipped in before Kondo's outriders, some seven miles behind him and undetected by radar amongst the confusing land echoes. Over the voice radio he called for any information held by Guadalcanal headquarters. Not having been allocated a voice radio call-sign, he had to try to identify himself by using his own name. The suspicious operator ashore was not convinced and it was not until after some quaint exchanges, in which Lee injected the nickname 'Ching Lee' by which General Vandegrift had known him in his Naval Academy days, that his identity was established, at 2230, only to hear that no new information was available.

In fact twenty minutes earlier, from the bridge of the *Sendai*, leading Kondo's advanced screen, his ships had been sighted, silhouetted against the moonlight. Passing a warning to Kondo, Hashimoto had detached the destroyers *Ayanami* and *Uranami* to circle Savo to the westward while he himself shadowed from astern. Kondo at once issued typically intricate battle orders, sending the *Nagara* and four destroyers of his close screen ahead to follow the *Ayanami* and *Uranami* in support, while he himself came along behind with the remaining destroyer of his close screen. It was a multiple division of his forces that only a Japanese, sublimely confident in his superiority as a night-fighter, could have contemplated. It was to come within a fraction of spectacular success, only confounded at the last moment by his opponent's radar advantage.

At 2252, having reached the middle of Ironbottom Sound north of Lunga Point and found it clear, Lee's squadron altered round in succession to a course of west to pass south of Savo. By 2300 the turn had been completed and the line of ships had settled down on the new course: and now, for the first time, Lee discovered he had a 'tail'.

The *Washington*'s radar detected the *Sendai* and her accompanying destroyer north-north-west, nine miles. For 12 minutes the contact was tracked. The range had closed to about seven miles before the *Sendai* came dimly into view through the gun director telescopes of *Washington* and *South Dakota*. In both ships the triple 16-inch gun turrets swivelled silently round. Inside the armoured gun houses, massive machinery slid silkily to thrust the huge shells and their cordite charges into the breeches; the breech-blocks closed; the long, dully gleaming gun barrels rose, checked and steadied following the movements of the director sights. 'Gun-ready' lamps flicked on. Only the pull of a trigger was now needed to blast the shells on their way. At 2316 the Admiral gave the order 'Commence firing when ready'. With a blinding flash and a head-splitting concussion the great guns opened fire.

Hashimoto turned away at once at high speed behind a smoke screen; but when, after a few salvoes, Lee's ships ceased firing, he swung back, steering south down the eastern shore of Savo to take his part in the encounter about to take place. Lee, indeed had found more immediate matters to engage his attention. At 2322 the *Walke* at the head of his line had opened fire to starboard, being soon joined by the *Benham*, *Preston* and *Gwin* astern of her.

The two destroyers that Hashimoto had detached from his advanced screen, *Ayanami* and *Uranami*, had circled Savo to the westward and were now steering into Ironbottom Sound to the northward of Lee. It was these that the *Walke*'s look-outs had sighted and the three leading American destroyers had engaged, a fierce gun duel developing in which both sides suffered. Close behind the *Ayanami* and *Uranami* came the *Nagara* and four destroyers detached from Kondo's close screen. On them the *Gwin* trained her guns. Then the *Washington* added the fire of the five-inch guns of her secondary armament, selecting targets from the uncertain picture presented by her radar, which was confused by the several contacts merging with the backdrop of Savo Island. The *South Dakota* suffered an electric failure which put her radar sets temporarily out of action. Having come to rely on these electronic aids, her gun control organisation found itself helpless. Her guns were impotent and silent.

In the glare and confusion of the gun battle, just which ship was firing at which was impossible to determine. One thing was certain. The Japanese fire, returned with interest in reply to that of the American destroyers, was infinitely the more effective. The duel had only lasted eight minutes when the *Walke* crippled by shell-bursts, fell out of the line. The *Preston* was soon afterwards stopped by shells which burst in her boiler-room and was then reduced to a sinking wreck by a concentration of fire by several enemy ships. The *Gwin* suffered a little less, but one engine room was wrecked and a shell, which burst on her upper deck aft, stripped the safety stops of her torpedo tubes allowing the torpedoes to slide harmlessly overboard.

In reply only one Japanese ship, the *Ayanami* was seriously damaged; and while the American destroyers, reluctant to expend their torpedoes on destroyer targets, held on to them until too late, the Japanese had no such inhibitions. At 2338 the 'Long Lances' began to arrive. One tore the forecastle of the *Walke* leaving her ablaze and sinking. Another shattered the bow of the *Benham*, up to this time little damaged by gunfire. Within 13 minutes of the beginning of the destroyer action, all four American ships were out of action. The *Preston* was abandoned at 2336 and sank soon afterwards. The *Walke* went down six minutes later.

Meanwhile Kondo with his three heavy ships and two destroyers had been keeping to the west of Savo Island, clear of the melee, his object still to deliver his bombardment as soon as the enemy opposition had been brushed aside. But at 2355 came a startling signal from the *Nagara* giving him the first intimation that enemy battleships were present. He at once turned to enter the fight.

The *Nagara* and her four destroyers, after launching the torpedoes which hit the *Walke* and *Benham*, had reversed course to retire westwards. Out of the darkness had loomed the massive bulk of a battleship on a roughly parallel course. It was the *South Dakota* which had sheered out of line to starboard to avoid the crippled destroyers. 'Blind' as a result of her radar failure, she had at once lost touch in the darkness with the flagship, which had turned the other way, and she now blundered on into view of the *Nagara*'s force. As the light cruiser and her four destroyers swung away, 34 torpedoes sped from them towards the blind monster. Incredibly, not one hit their target. The battleship sailed on. Suddenly, into the eyes of her bridge personnel and her gun directors, flashed the blinding glare of searchlight beams.

It was Kondo's destroyers which were illuminating her for his heavy ships. Shells from 14-inch and eight-inch guns began to smash destructively into her superstructure. Torpedoes streaked past, but once again failed to hit. All she could do in reply was to fire at the searchlights. The *South Dakota* was threatened with the same fate that had befallen the *Hiei* two nights earlier. But in the nick of time came relief. The *Washington* had not suffered the *South Dakota*'s defects. Her radar system was functioning smoothly and, as she had drawn clear of the melee south of Savo, an accurate picture of the situation was obtained. The biggest target had been tracked for several minutes and the information fed into the control system of her 16-inch guns, trained, loaded and ready. Fears that the target might be the straying *South Dakota* were swept away as she was seen on a different bearing in the light of the searchlights. At a range of 8,400 yards the *Washington* opened fire with both 16-inch and five-inch batteries.

At last the American radar advantage paid its dividend. Caught completely by surprise, the *Kirishima* was smothered; nine 16-inch and some 40 five-inch shells reduced her to a burning, rudderless wreck in seven searing minutes. The *South Dakota*, much damaged in her upper-works, a turret out of action, on fire in several places but luckily not crippled, took the opportunity to retire to the west of Guadalcanal followed by the damaged *Gwin* and *Benham*. The *Washington* was now on her own, facing the formidable Japanese force which still mustered two heavy cruisers, two light cruisers and eight destroyers, none of which had been much damaged. Nevertheless, to interpose himself between the enemy and his own cripples, Admiral Lee put a bold face on it and steered north-west parallel to the enemy. But Kondo had had enough. His planned bombardment had been frustrated and at 0030 he turned away north to retire to Truk, leaving the *Sendai* and four destroyers to stand by the *Kirishima*.

Lee now reversed course to regain contact with the survivors of his force. The moment was luckily chosen, for it coincided with the launching of torpedoes by two Japanese destroyers sent forward by Tanaka to fend off any attack on his transports, still steering doggedly for Guadalcanal. But for the reversal of course they must surely have hit the *Washington*. As it was, several exploded in her wake.

So the two-day naval Battle of Guadalcanal drew to a close. Once again it had revealed a marked Japanese superiority in night-fighting. This is easily understood if it is remembered that the Japanese crews were an elite of highly trained experienced seamen and were opposed by crews heavily diluted by virtual amateurs called up from all over the United States to man the many new ships emerging from American yards to form the biggest Navy the world had ever seen. Such a state of affairs was not to be wondered at. A peace-loving nation of huge industrial and scientific potential had been forced unwillingly and unready into war with a martial race long determined on and intensively prepared for it. Ships and guns and weapons could be more quickly constructed than efficient crews to man them could be trained. The vital need to halt Japanese plans of conquest had led to American crews being sent into the battle line with the barest minimum of training, relying upon superior equipment, particularly electronic, to counter-balance this defect. Unfortunately, so far, Japanese equipment in the shape of torpedoes and searchlights had also proved superior to that of the Americans. Only in respect of radar did the Americans have an advantage and even here it had been found that there was no substitute for human skill and training to make good use of the technical advantage.

But at last in this battle something of what could be achieved by a properly trained gun control team using radar had been demonstrated. Under the critical eye of Rear-Admiral Lee, himself a master of radar technique, the *Washington*, commanded by Captain Glenn Davis, had reached a high standard of skill. Except for a period early in the battle when a plethora of contacts, further complicated by the proximity of land, had confused the radar team, Lee had had a clear picture of the situation and at the crucial moment the guns of the battleship had been turned with devastating accuracy and with shattering effect on the principal enemy target.

Henderson Field had been saved from what might have been decisive destruction by bombardment. The cost in American lives and material had been heavy, nevertheless. The *South Dakota*, with nearly 100 casualties, was out of the war for some months to come while her damage was repaired in a home yard. The *Walke* and *Preston* had joined the rusting wrecks on the floor of Ironbottom Sound. About half their crews had died. The *Benham*, limping precariously under escort of the *Gwin*, had soon to be abandoned and sunk. On the Japanese side, the loss of the *Kirishima* as a result of the brief, pulverising cannonade by the *Washington* more than matched the American losses. She and the destroyer *Ayanami* were scuttled and their crews taken off by Japanese destroyers before daylight could bring out the vengeful flyers from Henderson Field.

The airmen did not lack for targets, nevertheless. While Ironbottom Sound had been reverberating with the thunder of battle, 'Tenacious' Tanaka had continued doggedly to shepherd his four remaining transports towards Guadalcanal. At first light they arrived off Tassafaronga. To ensure getting their troops and as much as possible of their stores ashore before the dive-bombers sent them to the bottom, they were run aground on the landing beaches. The stage was set for a scene of horrifying butchery. Naval and Marine fighters and bombers swarmed out to strafe and to drop incendiaries and high explosive on the helpless transports, setting them on fire and touching off explosions amongst ammunition dumps, wreaking fearful slaughter amongst their crews and the unloading parties. They were joined by the destroyer *Meade* which smothered them with five-inch shells and 40 mm. machine-gun fire to complete the shambles. The *Meade* then proceeded to pick up some 260 survivors of the *Walke* and *Preston* from their life-rafts. Tanaka, for the loss of 11 of Japan's irreplaceable and rapidly diminishing merchant fleet, had managed to add only 2,000 demoralised soldiers, 250 cases of ammunition and 1,500 bags of rice to General Hyukatake's resources. The naval Battle of Guadalcanal finally decided the fate of the island. For another ten weeks the Japanese were to continue a stubborn defence, but the outcome of the struggle was never again in doubt. The U.S. Navy was shortly to suffer another signal defeat by night in the waters of Tassafaronga but this would not restore the Japanese Army's supply route. Starvation, disease and lack of ammunition sapped the fighting spirit of its soldiers. Their fanatical determination to die rather than surrender only delayed the end.

The naval Battle of Guadalcanal marked the turning point in the war in the Pacific. It coincided remarkably with an equally clear-cut turn of the tide in the European theatre where the defeat of Rommel's Army at El Alamein at the end of October 1942 and the successful Allied landings in Morocco early in November had evoked Winston Churchill's announcement of 'the end of the beginning', while at Stalingrad the Red Army was poised for their decisive victory. In the South-West Pacific, too, the struggle for New Guinea had turned at last in the Allies' favour in November with the Japanese troops forced back across the Owen Stanley Mountains from Port Moresby by the Australians, while American and Australian troops were landed on the north shore near Buna. By the end of January

1943, hard fighting, of which Australian troops bore the brunt, would have wrested the whole of Papua from Japanese hands.

Not yet, however, did the Japanese abandon hope of winning back Guadalcanal. The loss of their two battleships and the hammering taken by Mikawa put an end to efforts to bring naval bombardment to bear on the struggle and Yamamoto withdrew his heavy units to Truk, preserving them against the day when he might be able to bring on a decisive fleet action. Heavy air losses had confirmed the Allied air supremacy over the Solomons. No longer could Tanaka contemplate running slow transports down the Slot and he now fell back to Rabaul to lick his wounds.

In spite of their heavy losses in the two-day naval battle, the Americans could justly claim a victory, for during the next ten days, while the Japanese troops on Guadalcanal remained unsupported and unsupplied, the Americans were able to bring in two fresh regiments of Marines and an infantry division to relieve the Marines of the 1st Division, weary and fever-weakened after 15 weeks of continuous, desperate fighting in the swamps and jungles. The air strength on Henderson Field, now comprising a main bomber runway and two shorter fighter strips, reached a new high level with 127 aircraft, including eight Flying Fortresses. The security of Guadalcanal was assured and, as can be more clearly appreciated now than then, the final outcome of the Pacific War determined. Nevertheless the U.S. Navy was to suffer more defeats before the Solomons campaign was over.

Confidence was running high in the South Pacific Force. At last, it seemed, the measure of the Japanese surface forces had been taken. Radar technique had been mastered and the tactical lessons of the past absorbed. Rear-Admiral Thomas Kinkaid, to whom Halsey gave command of the newly formed

173

striking force of cruisers and destroyers (Task Force 67), organised it into two cruiser groups, in each of which there would be at least one ship equipped with the latest surface warning radar, and a destroyer group which in a night encounter would be thrown forward 30 degrees on the engaged bow where, using their radar, they would be able to launch a surprise torpedo attack. Kinkaid's orders were that the cruisers, keeping outside 12,000 yards from the enemy, should withhold their gunfire until these torpedoes were reaching their targets. Then the cruisers' float planes would drop flares to augment the starshell illumination of the enemy. With this plan he felt confident of beating the Japanese at their own game. For the first time an attempt was to be made to use destroyers effectively. Perhaps if Kinkaid had remained to implement it himself, his plan might have succeeded; but the day after he promulgated it he was relieved by the newly arrived Rear-Admiral Carleton H. Wright and though his successor readily adopted it, he lacked the ability to execute it. In the event, radar advantage and a paper plan were once again to weigh less in the scales than experience, training and initiative.

Tanaka's withdrawal to Rabaul was temporary only. By 27 November he had advanced again to Buin at the southern end of Bougainville with the 2nd Destroyer Flotilla, his flag flying in the *Naganami*. That stubborn fighter had not yet acknowledged defeat. He was to achieve one last, spectacular victory. Unable to run slow transports down the Slot or even to let his destroyers linger long enough off the landing beach at Tassafaronga to disembark supplies and so expose themselves to air attack at dawn as they retired, Tanaka planned to load his flotilla of eight destroyers with stores contained in buoyant drums, which would be jettisoned off the beach to be gathered in by Japanese boats after daylight.

174

Tanaka's arrival at Buin was duly reported by a coast-watcher: so was his disappearance on the morning of 30 November. By that time, while Tanaka was leading his flotilla eastwards to the north of Choiseul and Santa Isabel prior to turning south to enter Indispensable Strait, Rear-Admiral Wright, in the heavy cruiser *Minneapolis*, was steering at high speed to intercept him with Task Force 67. At the same time an American troop convoy was returning from Guadalcanal and when it met Task Force 67 in the Lengo Channel, two destroyers from its escort were detached to join Admiral Wright.

It was 2225, a dark, overcast night with visibility about two miles, when Task Force 67 cleared the Lengo Channel and steered into the black, glassy waters of Ironbottom Sound at 20 knots. The cruisers were in line ahead, 1,000 yards apart, in the order *Minneapolis*, *New Orleans*, *Pensacola*, *Honolulu* (flagship of Rear-Admiral Tisdale) and *Northampton*. The destroyers *Fletcher*, *Perkins*, *Maury* and *Drayton* (in that order) in line ahead, were stationed 20 degrees on the port bow, two miles separating the *Drayton* from the flagship. Prolonging the cruiser line astern, came the two newcomers, the destroyers *Lamson* and *Lardner*. Already one of the element's of Kinkaid's operation plan was being neglected; for he had laid down that destroyer pickets should be stationed five miles ahead of the van destroyers to provide early warning. At 2238 the force altered 40 degrees to port, all ships turning together, on to a course of 280 degrees, heading for Tassafaronga, formed in a 'line of bearing'.

At this time Tanaka's flotilla was passing to the westward of Savo Island, steering south, preparing to alter course parallel to the shore line of Guadalcanal and, reducing to 12 knots, to jettison the supply-drums.

175

Following the *Naganami* in line were the *Makinami, Oyashio, Kuroshio, Kagero, Kawakaze* and *Suzukaze*. Stationed three miles on the flagship's port bow as a picket, was the *Takanami*. The flotilla was organised in three divisions: Transport Unit No. 1 composed of the four ships immediately astern of the flagship; Transport Unit No. 2, the two rear ships; and Patrol Unit *Nakanami* and *Takanami*, carrying no supplies and so, unlike the remainder, ready for instant combat. By 2306 the Japanese had rounded Savo Island and on a course parallel to the shore were approaching the dropping position. In the ships of the Transport Units, sailors were busy unlashing the drums which, stacked on deck, obstructed the torpedo tubes. No hint of the presence of an enemy to dispute control of Ironbottom Sound had reached Tanaka. But his opponent already knew of Tanaka's approach. On the radar screen of the *Minneapolis*, a pinpoint of light had appeared, the first intimation of the enemy at a range of 11½ nautical miles directly ahead. Admiral Wright at once ordered a turn, 40 degrees to starboard, all ships turning together, which put his cruisers and rear destroyers in line ahead again, with the van destroyers, also in line ahead, 20 degrees on their port bow. This was approximately the disposition laid down in Kinkaid's plan; but when, during the next eight minutes, the radar contact resolved itself into a line of ships on a south-easterly course, Wright ordered a wheel 20 degrees to port, parallel to the enemy's track, at 2314. This put his whole force into a single line ahead, the same simple formation that had been adopted by Scott and Callaghan on the previous unhappy night encounters. Two elements of Kinkaid's plan had thus been discarded — early warning by an advanced picket and stationing of destroyers on the engaged bow to give their torpedoes a short run to the target.

The advantage conferred by radar was slipping fast through Wright's fingers as the opposing forces ran on opposite courses at a combined speed of 32 knots. Quick decisions, or a willingness to let his destroyers off the leash could still, nevertheless, have grasped the fruit of surprise. For by 2316, Commander Cole, leading the van destroyers in the *Fletcher*, had tracked the unsuspecting enemy on his radar into a position 7,000 yards on his port bow, and he now asked by T.B.S. for the necessary permission to launch torpedoes. For four vital minutes the Admiral hesitated. He was doubtful whether his destroyers were within effective range, probably justifiably, as the main body of the enemy was some 2,000 yards beyond the target at 7,000 yards which was the solitary *Takanami*. Meanwhile the bearing of the enemy was veering rapidly aft. The range was increasing, and the position of torpedo advantage had been lost. If fired now, the torpedoes would have to make a long stern chase to reach the target during which sharp-eyed look-outs would have time to sight their tracks and the Japanese destroyers to turn to evade them. Only by releasing his van destroyers to close the enemy before launching torpedoes could Wright have ensured an effective attack. But this was either beyond the capability and training standards of the recently collected Task Force or the Admiral feared confusion and mistaken identities such as had occurred on previous occasions. A simple permission to fire torpedoes was tardily passed.

Even now, however, success might have been achieved if the third stipulation of Kinkaid's plan, that gunfire should not be opened until the torpedoes had had time to reach the enemy line, had been followed. From the *Fletcher*, ten torpedoes were launched; from the *Perkins* eight. The *Maury*, equipped only with air-warning radar, had no data with which to solve the

177

firing angle problem and withheld fire, while the *Drayton*, similarly uncertain, fired only two. In the Japanese destroyers there was still no inkling of the presence of an enemy to interfere with the business of clearing away and launching the supply drums. The explosion of torpedoes against their thin steel hulls might have been the first intimation.

Instead, the lightning flash of heavy gunfire on the port beam suddenly sounded the alarm. For the American torpedoes had hardly started on their long run to the target when Admiral Wright gave the order to his ships to engage with gunfire. The eight-inch guns of the *Minneapolis* and *New Orleans* opened fire at once on the nearest radar contact, the *Takanami*.

Caught completely by surprise, the Japanese might have been excused if they had fallen temporarily into confusion. But these were the seasoned veterans of Tanaka's own 2nd Flotilla. They had trained and operated under his inspiring leadership and critical eye throughout the campaign, some since the Java Sea Battle in the opening days of the war. Tanaka had only to give one brief, familiar order to set on foot the often practised manoeuvres of reversing course, divisional leaders together, the remainder following them round and firing torpedoes independently. They had no radar, but the brilliant flashes of the enemy's gunfire gave them all the information they needed. In the shock of surprise and, in the rear divisions, caught with obstructed torpedo tubes, the neat, parade ground countermarch of practice occasions was too much to expect and, in fact, the various sections took their own line, turning to port or starboard as convenient. They knew what was expected of them, however, and used their initiative. The *Takanami*, closest to the enemy, loosed her torpedoes before turning to starboard amidst a concentration of fire from several of the

American ships which quickly smothered her and brought her to a standstill in a sinking condition. Tanaka's flagship similarly turned to starboard and then loosed her torpedoes. The division of four ships astern of her, however, continued on the south-westerly course for a time while feverish efforts to disencumber their torpedo tubes were being made. Two of them, *Kuroshio* and *Oyashio*, fired their torpedoes before turning to starboard. In the process they lost touch with the *Makinami* and *Kagero* who waited until course had been reversed, when they steered to reduce the range before launching. In the Japanese rear, the *Kawakaze* and *Suzukaze* had been the first to fire, turning at once to port on receipt of the order to attack.

While this had been going on, the American ships had been getting haltingly into gun action with the aid of starshell and radar. Lacking flashless ammunition, their blinded control teams could see little of their fall of shot. They blazed away hopefully; but except for the luckless *Takanami*, pounded to a wreck, the Japanese ships remained undamaged; and while the flash of the American guns provided the Japanese with illumination and aiming marks for their torpedoes, Tanaka's guns remained silent, his ships only intermittently visible.

Meanwhile Japanese torpedoes were streaking through the water towards the long American line, still moving ahead on a steady course, offering a perfect target. At 2327 the 'Long Lances' struck home with two savage explosions against the flagship, *Minneapolis*, one devastating a boiler-room, the other wrecking her forecastle, leaving it hanging down below the water. Flames which leapt up forward were as suddenly extinguished as two columns of water as high as the masthead collapsed in a torrent on deck. As the flagship's speed fell suddenly away, the *New Orleans*, astern of her, swerved sharply to starboard to avoid collision. She was still swinging when she also took a torpedo hit forward and in the vast combined explosion of its warhead and the cruiser's forward magazine, her whole fore part, as far aft as her No. 2 turret, broke off. The wreckage bumped its way down the ship's port side, tearing holes in the side plating as it sank.

The *Pensacola* now sheered out to port long enough to avoid the wrecks and then resumed the west-north-westerly course. It was a fatal move, taking her on athwart the track of the Japanese torpedoes. At 2339 the next salvo of torpedoes arrived, one of them hitting squarely amidships, wreaking fearful damage, flooding the after engine-room, inflicting very heavy casualties and leaving the ship stopped and blazing. Meanwhile the two rear ships had turned away to starboard. The *Honolulu*, zig-zagging north-westward at 30 knots, escaped; but the *Northampton*, after circling to the northward and so avoiding these first torpedo salvoes, came back to a westerly course only to meet the same fate as the *Pensacola* at 2348, two torpedoes reducing her to a flaming wreck. The four American destroyers in the van, unable to distinguish any target, had sped away off the scene to the north-west and with the *Honolulu*, circled round Savo Island. They left utter confusion behind them, with the two rear American destroyers being taken under fire by bemused gunners in the shattered cruisers. Tanaka's flotilla, except for the sinking *Takanami*, sped scatheless away up the Slot. While the *Honolulu* spent the remainder of the calamitous night patrolling Ironbottom Sound in groping search of the vanished enemy, in the other cruisers men laboured to save their shattered ships. In the *Northampton*, all efforts were in vain. Ninety minutes after being torpedoed, she was listing at 23 degrees and her abandonment was begun, the destroyers *Fletcher* and *Drayton* coming to rescue her crew. The list steadily increased. When Captain Kitts went over the side with the last survivors, she was lying over at 35 degrees. Soon after 0300 the *Northampton* sank to the wreck-strewn floor of Ironbottom Sound. Fifty-eight of her crew of 830 had died. In the three other torpedoed cruisers, heroic conduct, engineering skill and good seamanship combined to save them. Each of them was got haltingly under way and reached Tulagi where, with the rudimentary resources of the motor-torpedo-boat base, all were amazingly made seaworthy enough to reach repair yards.

Tassafaronga was the last major surface action of the campaign for Guadalcanal. It must be conceded that American night-fighting capability had progressed not at all since the disastrous opening battle of Savo Island three and a half months' earlier. This is not to be wondered at, however. More American ships had been equipped, to be sure, with the excellent S.G. surface warning radar, giving them an immense initial advantage over the Japanese ships which still had only the human eye to rely upon. Lessons of previous encounters had been absorbed and new tactics devised. Ultimately, though, it was upon the quality of the men involved that the issue depended. The hastily trained, inexperienced crews of American ships gathered into improvised task forces at short notice were no match for Japanese professional veterans led by the stout-hearted Raizo Tanaka.

9. KULA GULF — EMPRESS AUGUSTA BAY

The sight of the flames licking round the four torpedoed American cruisers off Tassafaronga no doubt brought balm to the Samurai soul of Raizo Tanaka. Vengeance in full measure had been taken for the annihilation of his transport convoy two weeks earlier. It did not, however, affect the fate of Guadalcanal. This had been sealed by Yamamoto's decision not to risk either transports or heavy fleet units again in support of the troops ashore. During December 1942 Tanaka's destroyers, about ten at a time, made three dashes down the Slot, running the gauntlet of air attack during daylight, and opposed by motor torpedo boats based on Tulagi off the landing beaches after dark. Air attacks damaged two of his ships. Motor torpedo boats sank another and on one occasion forced Tanaka to retire with his supplies still on board. Results were neither adequate to maintain the troops ashore nor worth the steady attrition of Japanese destroyer strength. At the end of December the Japanese finally abandoned plans to recapture Guadalcanal and on 4 January the Imperial General Staff gave orders for the troops to be evacuated. Defensive positions were, instead, to be set up in New Georgia where, cleverly concealed amongst palmgroves, an airfield was under construction at Munda.

By this time Admiral Halsey's South Pacific Force had been strongly reinforced, bringing it up to two fleet carriers (*Saratoga* and *Enterprise*), three modern and four older battleships, 11 cruisers and 37 destroyers. In the face of this naval and air superiority, the problem for the Japanese of evacuating some

12,000 troops from Guadalcanal was a knotty one. For once, however, American intelligence failed to discover Japanese intentions. When, during January 1943, the 'Tokyo Express' made three runs to Guadalcanal, it was assumed that these were a continuation of efforts to build up Japanese strength on the island, whereas in fact they were preparations for a secret evacuation. Then, on 1 February, the Japanese put their well-concealed plan into operation. While the Japanese fleet put to sea from Truk and steered threateningly towards the Solomons to concentrate Halsey's attention on it, 20 destroyers came down the Slot on 1 February. Fighter cover, provided by a carrier air group disembarked at Buin, kept their casualties from air attack down to one destroyer damaged. In a fierce fight with American motor torpedo boats, three of their attackers were sunk, but the destroyer *Makinami*, running foul of a newly-laid minefield off the beaches, was also lost. The remainder, unknown to the Americans, duly evacuated their quota of troops. On the 4th, a cruiser and 22 destroyers repeated the operation. Overhead a long air battle raged in which 17 Japanese and ten American aircraft were shot down. Two destroyers were damaged by dive-bombers, but the remainder got through. Three days later a final expedition by 18 destroyers fought its way through attack by Henderson Field dive-bombers, at the cost of two destroyers damaged, to embark the last Japanese soldiers from Guadalcanal. Some 12,000 in all had been lifted from under the noses of the Americans, a success surely attributable to American inability to challenge the enemy by night. Only when the American forces on the island completed an encircling move on the afternoon of 9 February, and found nothing in their laboriously laid trap, was it realised.

While this withdrawal was taking place in the Eastern Solomons, the Japanese had been transferring their main efforts to strengthening their positions in the New Georgia group of the Central Solomons and to counter-attacking in New Guinea. In the Central Solomons area, during the next four months, the Americans prepared to capture New Georgia and advance up the island chain. An air base was established in the Russell Islands and the Japanese build-up of their bases at Munda on New Georgia Island and Vila on Kolombangara Island was harassed by naval and air bombardment and offensive mining operations. During this time the chief struggles were taking place around Northern New Guinea.

Early in January 1943 the Japanese had been able to run reinforcements into New Guinea. A thorn in the flesh to them since the beginning of the war had been the isolated, inland base of Wau with its primitive airfield, where a band of gold miners, reinforced by a small Australian unit known as the Kanga Force, had defied all efforts to eliminate them. On 30 January the Japanese launched an attack on it, only to be once again repulsed with heavy losses. Exasperated by this set-back, they now decided to bring in a whole division from Rabaul, and on 28 February some 7,000 troops were embarked in seven transports, a collier and eight destroyers. Taking a route to the north of New Britain, the convoy passed through the Vitiaz Strait between New Britain and New Guinea during the night 1-2 March. Bad weather had given it protection so far, but on the morning of the 2nd, aircraft of the Allied Air Forces, South-West Pacific Command began a series of attacks which continued intermittently for the next 36 hours by the end of which, for the loss of only five Allied aircraft, the whole convoy and four of the destroyers had been sunk, together with more than 2,000 Japanese troops.

A situation similar to that which had prevailed in the Guadalcanal area now developed around Northern New Guinea with the Japanese reduced to running supplies in destroyers and submarines. With such slim resources, offensive operations came to a halt. The ambitious plans the Japanese had held earlier were finally discarded in favour of a defensive strategy with the object of holding a perimeter in the Pacific stretching from the Aleutians, through Wake, the Marshall and Gilbert Islands, to the Bismarcks and New Guinea. The offensive had passed into the hands of the Allies. The only question was what form it should take. General MacArthur's grand strategy had never wavered from a determination to fight his way back along the island chain to the Philippines and onward to the Japanese homeland. As early as 9 January 1943 he had been asked by the American Chiefs of Staff to submit plans for the capture of Rabaul. His reply was that this operation could only be undertaken with a long period of preparation and buildup of trained amphibious forces. A period of virtual stalemate ensued through the first six months of 1943, therefore, in which the most notable activity was the Japanese effort to re-establish air superiority over the South-West Pacific, and with it, to hit at Allied bases and disrupt preparations for their next offensive.

For this purpose Admiral Yamamoto at the end of March concentrated in the area naval air groups from the fleet carriers to the number of 96 Zero fighters, 65 dive-bombers and some torpedo-planes to reinforce the land-based air force of 86 fighters, 27 dive-bombers and 72 twin-engined bombers of the 11th Air Fleet already stationed there. With this force he opened his air offensive on 1 April with a fighter sweep down the Slot. The results of the great air battle which developed over the Russell Islands according to the account brought back by his returning airmen were highly encouraging. In fact, however, for the loss of 18 Zeros they had only shot down six American fighters. On 7 April Yamamoto's air armada struck at the concentration of Allied shipping in the Guadalcanal area with 67 'Val' dive-bombers, escorted by more than 100 Zeros. The dive-bombers managed to sink the U.S. destroyer *Aaron Ward*, the American tanker *Kanawha* and the antisubmarine trawler *Moa* of the Royal New Zealand Navy at a cost of 12 of their own number shot down, while the swarms of fighters fought a fierce battle above. Nine Zeros were destroyed and a great many damaged. Of the seven Marine fighters shot down, only one pilot was lost.

Yamamoto's offensive was not achieving its object. Optimistic reports from his aviators, however, continued to mask the fact and on 11 April the Allied anchorage at Oro Bay near Buna in New Guinea was attacked. For the loss of six aircraft shot down, one merchantman was sunk, another had to be beached and the minesweeper H.M.A.S. *Pirie* was damaged. No Allied planes were lost. The huge force of 131 fighters and 43 bombers that struck at Port Moresby on the following day had even less success. Finally on 24 April nearly 200 Japanese aircraft attacked the Allied base at Milne Bay at the eastern tip of Papua where they sank one merchantman and damaged two others. By this time Yamamoto believed that one cruiser, two destroyers, and 175 planes belonging to the Allies had been accounted for. Well satisfied, he called off his offensive. His carrier air groups, sorely depleted, were withdrawn to Truk. The Commander-in-Chief of the Combined Fleet was not to live to know the extent of his failure. On 18 April the aircraft in which he was travelling from Rabaul to Buin was ambushed and shot down by fighters of the U.S. Army Air Force from Henderson Field.

Allied preparations to resume their advance up the island chain continued. But a major change in Pacific strategy was about to be made. It was becoming clear that General MacArthur's island-hopping strategy would involve a long, hard slogging fight against well-trained garrisons fanatically determined to resist to the death. It would require large numbers of trained soldiers which could not be provided so long as the Allies held to their intention of concentrating first on the defeat of Germany and diverting only sufficient resources to the Pacific to hold the enemy in check. On the other hand, this strategy did not call for large U.S. naval forces in the Atlantic, and the Pacific Fleet was now expanding very fast. From the clanging shipyards of the United States, four fast fleet carriers of the new *Essex* class (the first of no less than 24 projected), with a complement of 90 aircraft each, and five light fleet carriers, each carrying some 40 aircraft, would soon join the *Enterprise* and *Saratoga* to make an immense concentration of naval air-power. Air support for MacArthur's operations could be supplied by Army and Marine flyers based ashore. The main portion of the Pacific Fleet would therefore be available to carry out a strategic plan which had always appealed to the U.S. Chiefs of Staff — a thrust across the Central Pacific through the island groups of Micronesia into the heart of Japan's defensive system. In March 1943 the Central Pacific Force of Admiral Nimitz's Pacific Fleet was created and put under the command of Vice-Admiral R. A. Spruance, the victor of Midway. During the spring and summer of 1943 it was built up into the most powerful fleet the world had ever seen, with three Task Forces — Task Force 50, a fast carrier force centred round 11 aircraft carriers, six battleships and six heavy cruisers; Task Force 54, an Amphibious Assault Force; and Task Force 57 which combined operational control of all shore-based aircraft, naval and army, within the area of operations with that of the Mobile Service Squadron, composed of repair ships, a destroyer tender, tugs, etc., to supply advance base services. During the same time, intensive training of the largely inexperienced personnel manning the myriad ships and craft took place and tactical trials were made of the carrier group organisation in which carriers and fast battleships combined. By September the force was ready to begin the process of softening up Japanese bases in Micronesia by massive air-strikes. From that time onwards the centre of interest, from a naval point of view, would move away from the South-West Pacific where, under General MacArthur's command, the slow, difficult advance towards the Philippines would be primarily a military and not a naval task.

In the interval, however, the Allied naval forces in the South-West Pacific had still to dispute control of the waters round the New Georgia group of islands in fierce clashes with their opponents. Following the loss of Guadalcanal, the Japanese continued stubbornly to reinforce and supply by every available means their advanced air bases of Munda at the south-western corner of New Georgia and Vila, on Kolombangara Island, across the Kula Gulf. While planning to invade New Georgia as the next move up the island chain towards Rabaul, Admiral Halsey sought means to neutralise these bases.

Bombardment was the first to be tried. In the first, dark hour of 6 March, the cruisers *Montpelier* (flagship of Rear-Admiral A. S. Merrill), *Cleveland* and *Denver*, screened by the destroyers *Waller*, *Conway* and *Cony*, entered the Kula Gulf from the north to bombard Vila. At the same time four destroyers were approaching Munda from the south. As Merrill's force neared

188

the bombardment position, radar detected two ships between it and the target. They were two Japanese destroyers, *Minegumo* and *Murasame*, retiring northwards up the gulf after running supplies into Vila. The American radar advantage was now to give a devastating demonstration of its effectiveness. At the order to open fire, a stream of six-inch shells from all three cruisers smothered the leading destroyer, *Murasame*, in a forest of tall columns of water in the midst of which flames leapt up from direct hits. Then came a huge explosion as one of a salvo of five torpedoes fired by the *Waller* hit the Japanese destroyer amidships, breaking her in two to send her to the bottom, leaving a sheet of flaming oil fuel on the surface. Gunfire was now shifted to the *Minegumo* with the same radar-controlled accuracy. Within three minutes, she, too, was sinking. Then Merrill's cruisers turned their guns on the Vila air base and for 16 minutes pounded it savagely before setting course, well satisfied, for base. At the same time Munda was ploughed up by the five-inch guns of the destroyer force.

Bombardments proved to have a very temporary effect, the damage being quickly repaired. More effective were the minefields laid by aircraft and destroyers off Munda, Vila and Buin. Three of Tanaka's crack 2nd Flotilla, *Oyashio*, *Kuroshio* and *Kagero* were sunk and another badly damaged as a result of the minelaying off Vila; a large transport was sunk, the light cruiser *Yubari* and the destroyer *Kazegumo* crippled by mines off Buin.

Meanwhile preparations for the invasion of New Georgia had been going ahead. Japanese aircraft from Rabaul in huge numbers attempted to dislocate them, only to be repulsed with heavy losses amounting, on occasions, to virtual annihilation at the hands of Marine and Army fighters from Henderson Field. By 30 June all was ready and Rear-Admiral Turner's

Amphibious Task Force 31 began operations by quickly capturing Rendova Island. The struggle for New Georgia itself was to be long and hard-fought, however, Munda not falling into American hands until 5 August. The last Japanese resistance in the island was overcome on the 23rd. During the campaign, the Japanese strove to support their bases at Vila and Munda by means of night runs of the 'Tokyo Express'. Warned by coast watchers of their departure from Buin, Halsey repeatedly threw his Support Groups of cruisers and destroyers athwart their path. Thrice they met to match night-fighting abilities again.

The first encounter, to be known as the Battle of Kula Gulf, took place on the night 5-6 July 1943. On the previous night, the Support Group commanded by Rear-Admiral Ainsworth, three cruisers and four destroyers had escorted a convoy of destroyer-transports taking 2,600 troops to occupy Rice Anchorage on the western coast of New Georgia. While the landings were taking place, they had bombarded Vila on Kolombangara and Bairoko Harbour on the New Georgia shore opposite it. Two Japanese destroyers which had made a supply run to Vila were nearly trapped as the American force steamed into Kula Gulf; but by hugging the western shore of the Gulf, they escaped detection. A 'Long Lance' torpedo, one of a salvo launched as they fled, hit and sank the destroyer *Strong*. The mystified Americans presumed it must have come from a submarine. Ainsworth had barely arrived back off Tulagi on the afternoon of 5 July when orders reached him to get back with all speed to Kula Gulf. A large Japanese supply run for Vila was on its way. It comprised two Transport Units of three and four destroyers respectively, carrying troops and supplies, and a fighting Support Unit of three unhampered destroyers, *Niizuki*, *Suzukaze* and *Tanikaze*. Rear-Admiral

190

Teruo Akiyama commanded the force, his flag flying in the *Niizuki*. Racing up the Slot to meet him were the six-inch cruisers *Honolulu* (flagship of Rear-Admiral Ainsworth), *Helena* and *St Louis* and the destroyers *Nicholas*, *O'Bannon*, *Radford* and *Jenkins*.

Weight of metal and technical equipment gave an apparent overwhelming advantage to the Americans. The cruisers' six-inch guns, 15 in each ship in triple turrets, had such a high rate of fire that traditional control by 'laddering' on to the target was too deliberate a method and had been discarded in favour of opening with continuous rapid fire with the range and bearing provided by radar. All ships, furthermore, had the excellent S.G. surface warning radar. On the Japanese side, seven of the ten ships were cluttered with troops and stores. Only the flagship, *Niizuki*, possessed a radar set. But the absence of such technical aids encouraged the vigilance of look-outs and bridge personnel and kept gun- and torpedo-tube crews ready for instant action with no warning. The same taut efficiency that had brought victory at Savo Island and Esperance Bay held good in Akiyama's ships. Balancing the overwhelming gun superiority of the American ships were the fast, long-range 24-inch torpedoes, eight in the tubes in each ship, others stowed on deck as 'reloads'. In spite of their record since the beginning of the war, the existence of these deadly weapons was still unknown to the Allies.

Akiyama was the first to arrive in Kula Gulf. Running down the eastern shore of Kolombangara Island at 21 knots, he had detached the 1st Transport Unit of three destroyers for Vila and at 0118 with the remainder in line ahead, had reversed course. As he steered northwards, Ainsworth's force rounded the north-eastern corner of New Georgia and steered across the mouth of the Gulf at 25 knots. At 0140 they made radar contact at 12½ miles. Calling his destroyer screen into the line of battle, *Nicholas* and *O'Bannon* in the van, *Jenkins* and *Radford* in the rear, Ainsworth executed a turn to port, all ships together to close the range, altering back into line ahead at 0149 when the range was 11,000 yards.

In the *Niizuki*, Akiyama had just detached the 2nd Transport Unit, *Amagiri*, *Hatsuyuki*, *Nagatsuki* and *Satsuki* for Vila when, at 0147, look-outs sighted the black bulk of the cruisers against the clear northern horizon. Calling the Transport Unit to rejoin him, he increased to 30 knots and with his fighting unit of three, raced forward into action. For the next eight minutes as Ainsworth's force steered across the enemy's front, his cruisers' loaded guns were being laid on the enemy, the range and bearing being supplied by the radar. Some delay was caused when the Admiral first selected the departing Transport Unit as target but then shifted to the *Niizuki* when it became clear that the former was steering away at high speed. At last, at 0157, when the *Niizuki* was 6,800 yards on the port beam, the cruisers' guns roared out in rapid fire. With deadly accuracy, a storm of six-inch shells struck on and around the Japanese flagship, the first few salvoes tearing her apart to leave her shattered and sinking.

Devastating as was this radar-controlled fire at short range, it was ill-directed in that nearly all of it was concentrated on the leading ship, leaving the *Suzukaze* and *Tanikaze* only lightly damaged. With cool competence, they launched their 16 torpedoes at the easy target offered by Ainsworth's long single line, and then retired westwards behind a smoke-screen to reload their tubes. In comparison the American destroyers, tied, as usual, to the cruisers, had waited for an order from the flagship to fire torpedoes. By the time battle was joined, no suitable targets remained for their comparatively slow torpedoes, though at various times later in the battle they launched them with little prospect of success at retreating enemy ships, at the sinking hulk of the *Niizuki* or, in one case, at a phantom target.

While the Japanese 'Long Lances' streaked through the water at 49 knots, Admiral Ainsworth, deceived by the smoke and explosions round the *Niizuki*, decided that the whole of Akiyama's unit had been knocked out and he ordered a reversal of course, ships turning in succession. But the American line had been steering a steady course and speed for 14 minutes — long enough to make the perfect target for torpedoes. The flagship was leading round to starboard when the *Helena*, next in line and about to follow, was struck by three of them in quick succession. The first explosion shattered her fore part, tearing it off as far aft as No. 2 turret. The next two hit amidships. Her hull torn wide open, within six minutes the *Helena* had sunk, leaving only the amputated bow floating.

Though the *St Louis* had to sheer sharply to starboard to avoid the riven hulk and had to cut across the bows of the *Honolulu*, nothing of the calamity to the *Helena* was known to Admiral Ainsworth whose attention was now drawn to the radar plot of the Japanese 2nd Transport Unit, by this time coming north in answer to Akiyama's recall. This put the Americans steering across ahead of the enemy line, an ideal gunnery situation. At a range of 11,600 yards the *Honolulu*'s guns began to spout their awe-inspiring stream of six-inch shells at the leading destroyer, *Amagiri*. But the slim, end-on target escaped serious damage, swerving away to starboard behind a smoke-screen. The next in line, the *Hatsuyuki*, steaming full into the storm of falling shells, had a miraculous escape. Three shells hit her, but none exploded. Even so, she suffered considerable damage and, turning away to port, she limped away southward. The last two destroyers, reversing course at once, avoided any damage. All four thereupon, with bold effrontery, made for Vila to complete their transport mission and land their troops. Contact with them faded from Ainsworth's radar screens and he now turned back westerly. He found no enemy in that direction. The *Suzukaze* and *Tanikaze* had retreated well to the west, beyond the range of Ainsworth's radar, to reload their torpedoes preparatory to re-entering the fray. The remainder of the Japanese force, except the sunken *Niizuki*, were busy unloading troops and supplies off Vila. At 0307 Ainsworth turned back to the eastward and, when no contact with the enemy had been made by 0330, he ordered the *Nicholas* and *Radford* to rescue survivors from the *Helena* while the remainder set course for base.

There were skirmishes yet to come, however, before the Battle of Kula Gulf was over. By 0315, after difficulties and delays caused by the damage they had received, the *Suzukaze* and *Tanikaze* had reloaded their torpedo tubes. At 0400, the *Radford* and *Nicholas*, picking up survivors from the *Helena*, saw them appear on their radar screens and they set off to meet them. The Japanese, however, sighting nothing soon turned away again and rescue operations were resumed. Ainsworth, who had turned back on hearing the destroyers' enemy report, also resumed his retirement. All the while, at the bottom of the Kula Gulf, the destroyers of the Transport Units had been unloading in anxious haste, but undisturbed.

First to complete was the 2nd Transport Unit. Getting under way again, the *Nagatsuki* ran aground. Efforts by the *Satsuki* to tow her off were unsuccessful and she had to be left to her fate. The *Satsuki* and *Hatsuyuki* departed by way of Blackett Strait, south of Kolombangara and avoided further action. The *Amagiri*, on the other hand, set course up the Kula Gulf, and at

0515 came across the *Niizuki*'s survivors. She had stopped to rescue them when the *Nicholas* and *Radford* detected her on their radar screens and once again interrupted rescue operations. Seeing them almost simultaneously, the *Amagiri* had likewise to abandon rescue work — in her case permanently, and after picking up only a handful of survivors. As she ran north-westward out of the Gulf, both *Nicholas* and *Radford* were able at last to fire torpedoes at a likely target; but they had no luck, their torpedoes closely missing. The *Amagiri*, too, fired torpedoes, also ineffectively. A gun duel then began, in which the Japanese was hit amidships whereupon she fled the scene behind a smoke-screen.

All through the night, while battle flashed and rumbled on the northern horizon, the 1st Transport Unit, *Mochizuki*, *Mikazuki* and *Hamakaze* had lain off Vila disembarking troops and stores. At about 0500, the latter two had got under way and, threading Blackett Strait, had taken the unopposed route home to the west of Kolombangara. The unit commander in the *Mochizuki* was delayed, however, and dawn was near when he finally set out. He chose the route up Kula Gulf and once again the *Radford* and *Nicholas* had to give up rescue work to go into action. A brief gun duel ensued in which the Japanese suffered minor damage before escaping behind smoke. The Battle of Kula Gulf was at last over. With the *Helena* had gone 168 officers and men. On the Japanese side, Admiral Akiyama was among the 300 dead. Nevertheless his supply mission had been brilliantly accomplished and a greatly superior American force defeated. Ainsworth, unaware of what had been taking place off Vila during the night, had gathered an impression from the smoke and flame of night battle and the picture presented by his radar plot that he had achieved much more than the destruction of one Japanese destroyer. Until the facts came to be known later, the Battle of Kula Gulf was counted an American victory. His brother Task Force commander in the area, Rear-Admiral Merrill, meeting him off Tulagi a few days later, signalled, 'I'm afraid you've spoiled the hunting by taking too much game on your last hunt'. Ainsworth's ill-found satisfaction was about to be shattered in a disastrous return fight in the same disputed waters off Kolombangara.

His hard-worked Task Force had returned to Tulagi on 12 July after another night run to the Kula Gulf, escorting a group of destroyer-transports. There was to be little rest for his ships, however. At Halsey's headquarters it had been learnt that the indomitable Japanese were once again sending a fast supply unit of four destroyer-transports to Vila. Escorting it were the destroyers *Mikazuki*, *Yukikaze*, *Hamakaze*, *Kiyonami* and *Yugure* led by Tanaka's famous flagship *Jintsu*, returned to the fray after repairs to her battle injuries. But it was not Tanaka's flag which flew at her masthead. He had been superseded by Rear-Admiral Shunji Izaki. This force had sailed from Rabaul at 0500 that morning. To meet him in the Kula Gulf, Ainsworth's Task Force 18 left Tulagi at 1700. Following his flagship *Honolulu* were the light cruiser H.M.N.Z.S. *Leander*, slow and lightly armed compared to the American ships, and the *St Louis*. Two destroyer squadrons accompanied them. Destroyer Squadron 21, commanded by Captain McInerney, comprised the four ships which had taken part in the Battle of Kula Gulf, reinforced by the *Taylor*. Destroyer Squadron 12, commanded by Captain Ryan, consisted of the *Ralph Talbot*, *Buchanan*, *Maury* and *Gwin*. Night fell as they pounded up the Slot, a night dark but clear except for occasional rain squalls. Night-flying Catalina flying boats were scouting along the route from Rabaul and, at 0036, one of them located the *Jintsu* and her five destroyers north of the island of Vella Lavella racing at 30 knots on a south-easterly course for the Kula Gulf. They were 26 miles ahead of Ainsworth and should soon appear on the palely glowing radar scans. Though the American admiral now ordered his force into the usual single line ahead, with Destroyer Squadron 21 in the van, Destroyer Squadron 12 bringing up the rear — a line some six miles long, steering 275 degrees at 26 knots — he was not going to restrict himself to the rigid, unimaginative tactics of previous occasions. He was prepared to unleash his destroyers at an early stage to attack with torpedoes. On the other hand, still ignorant of the performance of the Japanese torpedoes, or that they carried spares with which to reload their tubes, he had no adequate plan to counter them.

For his part Admiral Izaki was not steering blindly into a radar-controlled ambush as his predecessors had had to do. The *Jintsu* had brought with her a new electronic device which could detect and measure the direction of radar transmissions at twice the range at which the radar could detect her. By this time Izaki had gathered enough information to plot the movements of the approaching Allied force. Sending away his destroyer transports to deliver the troops and supplies at Sandfly Harbour on the west coast of Kolombangara, he steered for the enemy, the destroyer *Mikazuki* ahead of the *Jintsu*, the other four astern. For all his initial advantage, however, there was bound to be a period between the moment he was detected by his opponent's radar, which occurred at 0100, and the moment he reached the effective firing range of his torpedoes, during which he was exposed to radar-controlled gunfire to which he could make no reply. Ainsworth's battle plan, on the other hand, which called for gunfire to be withheld until the range was down to between 8,000 and 10,000 yards, could not take advantage of this situation. From 0100 to 0112 the two forces charged towards each other at a combined speed of nearly 58 knots. At 0108 Ainsworth ordered his destroyers to attack with torpedoes. The van destroyers which had already turned to starboard to close the range, fired theirs a minute or so afterwards at a range of 8,150 yards; the rear destroyers launched between 0112 and 0118 at 11,000 yards. The fast Japanese torpedoes were already on their way, however, having been fired at 0108 when the *Mikazuki* led the line round to port.

At last, at 0112, the range of the enemy from the *Honolulu* was down to 10,000 yards. Ainsworth gave the order to his cruisers to turn 30 degrees to port together to bring all guns to bear and to commence firing. The *Jintsu*, larger than her companions, stood out most conspicuously on the radar screens and was taken as target for all the 38 six-inch guns which hurled their shells at her in a continuous stream. Under such a concentration of fire she could not survive long. Within five minutes she was stopped, a torn and twisted hulk. Now Ainsworth ordered his force to reverse course 180 degrees to a north-easterly heading of 065 degrees, all ships turning together. The *Leander*, sandwiched between the two American cruisers, had a wider turning circle than they. Furthermore, the executive signal for the turn was passed on voice radio which faded at the crucial moment and was missed by the *Leander* and four of the rear destroyers. In the darkness, made more obscure by the thick smoke of battle, confusion reigned during the next few minutes and there were some narrow escapes from collision. While the ships manoeuvred clear of that danger, another was streaking through the water at 49 knots, towards them. By good fortune, however, only one of the Japanese torpedoes found a billet, hitting the *Leander* which had just steadied on the new course. One boiler-room was torn open to the sea, another had to be shut down and evacuated. Twenty-eight men were killed. She was no longer in the battle and could only limp away to Tulagi, escorted by two of Ainsworth's destroyers. At almost the same moment one of the torpedoes fired by Ainsworth's van destroyers hit the immobilised *Jintsu* amidships. In spite of the fearful punishment she had taken, the stout little ship even now stayed afloat until a torpedo from a later American salvo completed her destruction at 0145. There were very few survivors. Of the Japanese destroyers, the leader, *Mikazuki*, lost touch with the remainder after standing by the sinking flagship until driven off by the gunfire of the two American cruisers and the van destroyers, which continued to hammer the *Jintsu* with guns and torpedoes until she sank. In the general hurly burly, during which the Americans gathered the impression from flashes and explosions in the black night, and from the radar picture, that several of the Japanese ships had been destroyed, the *Mikazuki* disappeared from the scene and took no further part in the events to follow. The other four Japanese destroyers, after emptying their torpedo tubes at the enemy in the first few minutes of the battle, had turned away to the north-westward. There, under cover of a rain squall, they set about reloading. A Catalina overhead tracked them as they retired. On receiving its report, Ainsworth led round in pursuit and by 0142 the *Honolulu* was steering north-west at 30 knots followed by the *St Louis* and the rear destroyers.

By this time the Japanese destroyers had completed their reload and were returning to the fight. At 0156, the *Honolulu*'s radar detected them 11½ miles fine on the port bow, but there was doubt as to their identity. A minute later the Japanese sighted their opponents who continued to steer a steady course, offering a perfect target. At 0205 a swarm of the big torpedoes was sent on its way. In the *Honolulu* all was still uncertainty. The positions of the American destroyers of the van were doubtful. Amidst the almost continuous chatter flooding the T.B.S., each had to be contacted and questioned. Seven minutes were occupied with this and with establishing a plot of the radar contact and discussing inconclusively if it was friend or foe. Still unsure, at 0203, the Admiral ordered starshell fire to illuminate the target. The first flare blossoming in the sky exposed the Japanese destroyers turning at high speed having just fired their torpedoes. Doubts resolved, the Admiral gave the order for a 60-degree turn to starboard to bring all guns to bear and then to commence firing.

It was too late. Before the guns could fire, the *St Louis'* bow was rent by the explosion of a warhead. The *Honolulu*, tracks sighted all around, turned frantically in an effort to avoid them; but one torpedo, hitting right forward, demolished her bow; another in her wake plunged squarely into her square stern — and failed to explode! Ahead of the *Honolulu*, the destroyer *Gwin* erupted in violent flame as she was hit in her engine-room. In six catastrophic minutes the Japanese had once again demonstrated their superb night-fighting skill and enterprise. Their destroyers retired from the scene quite unscathed. Ainsworth was comforted by the mistaken belief, as in the battle of the previous week, that five enemy ships had been destroyed during this Battle of Kolombangara, while all his own cruisers were able to limp back to Tulagi under their own steam. Only the *Gwin* was sunk.

It was as well for the morale of Halsey's South-West Pacific force that the true results of the succession of night actions were not known until long after. Nevertheless, for all the Japanese tactical victories, the story of Guadalcanal was repeating itself at Munda and Vila. The trickle of supplies and reinforcements that could be run into these bases by the 'Tokyo Express' was insufficient to hold them; and the Japanese could not afford the slow but steady attrition of their naval forces which was the price they had to pay, whereas the American Fleet was by this time receiving reinforcements of new ships at such a rate that they could look upon destroyers and even cruisers as 'expendable'. It can be argued, indeed, that the very superiority in ships held by the Americans constituted a handicap to them. Against small, easily manoeuvrable units of destroyers they pitted, time after time, large unwieldy gatherings of cruisers and destroyers, the former, with their highly sophisticated gun armament, requiring a high degree of training for which they had had insufficient opportunity. Concentrating on bringing their impressive gun power to bear, they neglected to give their destroyers a reasonable chance to meet the enemy with similar weapons. What might otherwise have happened in Ironbottom Sound and in the Kula Gulf was demonstrated on the night of 6-7 August in the Vella Gulf to the west of Kolombangara.

The battle came about, as on previous occasions, as a result of news of a 'Tokyo Express' heading for the Vella Gulf to land troops on the west coast of Kolombangara. But on this occasion no cruisers were available and Rear-Admiral Wilkinson, who had relieved Rear-Admiral Turner in command of the Amphibious Force, sent what he had — six destroyers under Commander F. Moosbrugger. This force entered the Vella Gulf from the south at 2200 and by 2230 was steering north up the west coast of Kolombangara at 25 knots in two divisions in line ahead. Division 12, Moosbrugger's own, was in the order *Dunlap*, *Craven*, *Maury*. Two miles to starboard, and lying back 60 degrees abaft the beam of

Division 12, was Commander R. W. Simpson's Division 15, *Lang*, *Sterett* and *Stack*.

The enemy force of four destroyers, *Shigure*, *Hagikaze*, *Arashi* and *Kawakaze*, the last three carrying troops and supplies, steering to enter the Gulf from the north, had been reported by aircraft. Contact was expected any time after 2300. The American crews were at battle stations and nerves were taut when course was altered at 2323 to the north-eastward parallel to the shore line of Kolombangara. Ten minutes later came the expected radar contact. It quickly resolved itself into four ships approaching at 25 knots and Moosbrugger led his division on to a course of 335 degrees, parallel with the enemy's track, and prepared to fire torpedoes. Simpson's division conformed, but was free to act independently.

In the Japanese flotilla which had no radar, there was no inkling of an enemy's presence. The American destroyers merged with the dark bulk of Kolombangara behind them until suddenly at 2342 white streaks were seen and taken for the wakes of motor torpedo boats. At once all was confusion in the Japanese ships, in which a most unwonted lack of preparedness prevailed. In any case it was too late for any action to be taken. The white streaks were the high, frothing stern waves of Moosbrugger's division turning 90 degrees away to starboard after firing torpedoes. And now, in quick succession, the three rear Japanese destroyers were rent by fiery explosions and stopped, dead in the water. Only the *Shigure* escaped and, after firing eight torpedoes, turned away and then, under cover of smoke, retired northwards to reload her tubes. Had the 15th Division continued slavishly to follow the 12th, they must have run foul of this salvo. But they were not tied to conforming with an Admiral's motions as on previous occasions. As the other division fired its torpedoes,

Simpson led his round to port, across the enemy's line of advance, and added to the destruction with the fire of his five-inch guns. The *Kawakaze*, in which a magazine had been detonated, soon sank. *Arashi* and *Hagikaze* kept up a feeble and erratic fire until hammered to a wreck. *Arashi* was finally dispatched by torpedoes from the 15th Division and *Hagikaze* blew up and sank under the concentrated gunfire of the six American ships. The Japanese flotilla commander, returning in the *Shigure* unnoticed, with tubes reloaded, chose the part of discretion and fled to report the catastrophe at Rabaul.

The Battle of Vella Gulf was little more than a skirmish. But the initiative allowed to a subordinate unit and the intelligence with which it was seized marked a real improvement in American night-fighting tactics, though the Japanese ships engaged contributed largely to their own defeat by their unusual lack of alertness. On the next occasion that similar forces met, with the odds reversed, three U.S. destroyers meeting six Japanese in another skirmish known as the Battle of Vella Lavella, results were less encouraging, two of the American destroyers and one Japanese being torpedoed.

One more major night battle was to take place in the South-West Pacific before the main naval confrontation shifted to the vast spaces of the Central Pacific where the opposing fleets fought at ranges of hundreds of miles with dive-bombers and torpedo-planes delivering the blows instead of guns and torpedo tubes. In October 1943, with the New Georgia group of islands at last in Allied hands, it was decided to seize a beachhead at Empress Augusta Bay on the west coast of Bougainville Island where forward airfields could be established in fighter range of Rabaul. The initial landings were successfully accomplished on 1 November but vital stores still remained to be disembarked from some of the transports when night fell. From Rabaul had sailed that afternoon a Japanese force of cruisers and destroyers bent on breaking up the American amphibious force. To oppose it, Wilkinson ordered out Rear-Admiral Merrill's Task Force 39 of four cruisers and eight destroyers. At 0230 the two forces met in battle some 20 miles to seaward of the beachhead.

The Japanese force, shadowed and reported by aircraft as it steered for Empress Augusta Bay, was centred on the two heavy cruisers, *Myoko* (flagship of Rear-Admiral Omori) and *Haguro*. Screening them to port were the light cruiser *Sendai* with three destroyers *Shigure*, *Samidare* and *Shiratsuyu* following her in single line ahead. Similarly disposed to starboard were the light cruiser *Agano* and destroyers *Naganami*, *Hatsukaze* and *Wakatsuki*. Merrill, in his flagship *Montpelier*, followed by the *Cleveland*, *Columbia* and *Denver* — new six-inch cruisers all — steered north to throw his force 'across the entrance to Empress Augusta Bay and to prevent the entry therein of a single enemy ship'. His cruisers were stationed 1,000 yards apart. Ahead and astern, separated by 3,000 yards from the nearest cruiser, were respectively Captain Arleigh Burke's Destroyer Division 45 — *Charles F. Ausburne*, *Dyson*, *Stanly* and *Claxton* — and Commander Austin's Destroyer Division 46 — *Spence*, *Thatcher*, *Converse* and *Foote*.

The formation was reminiscent of those earlier fateful occasions when the American force went into battle in one long, unhandy line. But, in fact, the situation was very different. Merrill had absorbed the lessons from those battles. His destroyer divisions were to be loosed to close the enemy and attack with torpedoes, acting independently from the moment of release. Furthermore, Merrill had at last learnt the impressive characteristics of the Japanese torpedo. He intended to engage at long range, between 16,000 and 20,000 yards and his guns would stay silent until his own destroyers' torpedoes had had time to reach their target. Furthermore he had learnt the fatal consequences of offering a steady target to the enemy's torpedoes. So when radar contact with the enemy was established at 0230 at nearly 18 miles range, Captain Burke's Division 45 in the van turned at once and steered to attack the nearest of the three enemy columns, the port screening line led by the *Sendai*. At 0239, in conformity with his plan to keep between the enemy and Empress Augusta Bay, Merrill reversed course to south, his cruisers turning together. His rear destroyers, which, at the same time were released to attack the enemy's southern group, reversed course in succession, following their leader, the *Spence*, except for the rear ship of the line, the *Foote*. Mistaking the order she turned immediately and was quickly separated from the remainder. The misunderstanding was to bring her fatal consequences.

By 0246 the reversal of course had been completed. To the north-west Burke's destroyers were in the act of firing their torpedoes at the *Sendai*. Commander Austin had turned west to lead his division into the attack. And now, for the first time, the alarm was sounded in the Japanese force as a flare from a scouting aircraft blossomed in the sky above Merrill's cruisers. Omori's heavy cruisers were still too distant to see anything of their opponents, although from the *Sendai* they were in sight. Nevertheless Omori at once ordered the leaders of his columns to lead round to starboard to form line of battle. The alteration was quickly apparent on Merrill's radar screens. He had been withholding gunfire in accordance with his plan until the torpedoes of Division 45 reached their target. But now he could wait no longer, particularly as the turn frustrated Burke's torpedo attack. From his four cruisers burst the head-splitting drum-roll of rapid fire from 60 six-inch guns, all directed at the nearest and clearest radar contact, the *Sendai*. She was able to get off a few salvoes, accurate enough to cause Merrill to lay a defensive barrier of smoke; but within a minute or two she was smothered, set on fire and knocked out of action. The water round her was such a maelstrom of leaping shell splashes that the destroyers following her manoeuvred frantically to avoid it and two of them, *Samidare* and *Shiratsuyu* collided and were damaged. The third destroyer, *Shigure*, circled and steered away south to join the cruisers.

Merrill's ships, altering 20 degrees to starboard together at 0215 to maintain the chosen gun range of 19,000 yards, now shifted fire to the Japanese cruisers. The storm of shells, of which the 'overs' were falling amongst the ships of the *Agano*'s column, had a similar effect as on the *Sendai*'s column, destroyers turning hastily this way and that to get clear. In the course of it, the *Hatsukaze* tried to cut too close across the bows of the cruiser *Myoko*, which crashed into her. A large section of the destroyer's bow was torn away, leaving her crippled to limp slowly away north-westward. In spite of the impressive volume of the American cruisers' fire, however, it was achieving little. In the 30 minutes of gunfire that followed, the *Myoko* and *Haguro* received only minor damage, though the latter was hit by six shells, four of which failed to explode, and her speed was temporarily reduced. The Japanese cruisers relying upon starshell for illumination, did no better, getting only three eight-inch shells home on the *Denver*, all of which failed to detonate, but reducing her speed to 25 knots. The ineffectiveness of the shooting on both sides was probably attributable to the comparatively long range for night action, and it is noteworthy that the hits on the *Denver* and the *Haguro* occurred when the range had fallen to less than 14,000 yards.

206

Another reason was the complex pattern of manoeuvres begun by Merrill at 0301 when, after steering in a generally southerly direction for 20 minutes, he altered course to north and thereafter marched, countermarched and side-stepped by simultaneous turns of his ships for the next 50 minutes to complicate the torpedo attack problem for the enemy.

At 0337, Admiral Omori decided to break off the action. He had been under the impression throughout that he was up against as many as seven cruisers and 12 destroyers. When, in the confusion caused by battle smoke and the normal obscurity of night action, he thought he had sunk two American cruisers, he felt justified in retiring. Together with the survivors of the *Agano*'s column and the *Shigure* he turned away to the northwest and ceased firing. The main action then came to an end.

Meanwhile, both American destroyer divisions had been operating independently. While Burke's Division 45, which had become split up during their torpedo attack, were reconcentrating, Austin's Division 46, having mislaid the wayward *Foote*, had steered to close the enemy. The *Foote*, making to rejoin, had the ill-luck to be hit by one of the torpedoes fired by the *Sendai*'s column at the beginning of the action. With her stern blown off, she lay, a helpless hulk, until taken in tow the following day by a tug. Austin at this time was distracted by finding himself in his own cruisers' line of fire. Some hasty manoeuvring brought his 'flagship' *Spence* with a rending thump alongside the *Thatcher*, next in line, but without serious damage. A shell hit on the water line of the *Spence*, soon afterwards, increased the confusion during which the perfect position for firing torpedoes at the Japanese cruisers, which Austin had attained, was neglected through doubts of their identity. The two forces raced past each other on opposite courses.

The *Spence* now steered for what seemed likely contacts to the northward and found the crippled *Sendai*. *Spence* and *Converse* fired eight torpedoes at her at 0328 and all three destroyers then set off in pursuit of the *Samidare* and *Shiratsuyu* which, since their collision earlier, had been standing by their shattered flagship but now fled north-westwards. By this time Division 45 had reformed and they, too, came north-westward, giving the *Sendai* her quietus as they passed her. Much confused fighting and manoeuvring occupied the last, dark hour of the night. Division 46 exchanged gun salvoes with *Samidare* and *Shiratsuyu* to little purpose, and launched 19 torpedoes fruitlessly at their fleeing enemy. Then the *Spence*, water contaminating her fuel as a result of the shell hit, lost speed and fell out of line, circling to the westward where she came under fire for a time from Division 45. She then ran across the crippled *Hatsukaze* but was so short of ammunition by this time that Austin had to call on Burke to give her the *coup de grâce*. As dawn was breaking, all American destroyers turned back in response to Merrill's recall. The night Battle of Empress Augusta Bay was over.

It was the last major clash between naval surface forces in the South-West Pacific. It might have been otherwise; for hurrying to Rabaul from Truk, bent on wiping out the American amphibious force at Empress Augusta Bay, were six heavy cruisers of the Japanese 2nd Fleet under Vice-Admiral Kurita. With no equivalent force available, Admiral Halsey turned to his carrier Task Group (*Saratoga* and *Princeton*) to redress the balance. Flying off from a position 235 miles south-east of Rabaul, 22 dive-bombers, 23 torpedo-planes with an escort of 52 fighters, struck the enemy cruiser force as it was refuelling in the harbour. Five cruisers were damaged and the whole force retired to Truk. Control of the waters round the

Bismarck Archipelago passed into the hands of Allied aircraft. Under their umbrella MacArthur would fight his way up the island chain on the long road back to the Philippines to fulfil his promise 'I will return'. The centre of naval interest now moved to the Central Pacific.

10. THE BATTLE OF THE PHILIPPINE SEA

General Douglas MacArthur, writing his Memoirs long after the war, professed to be still puzzled and indignant at the lack of naval and air support given to his campaign amongst the islands of the South-West Pacific. One can sympathise with his frustration as he fought his way back to the Philippines with what he considered inadequate troops and shore-based air-power while his naval colleague Nimitz was accumulating an immense naval and amphibious force, including 19 carriers, on board which were some 900 aircraft.

Nevertheless the course of events was to show that the decision taken by the Joint Chiefs of Staff in May 1943 to employ this great access of naval power in a drive through the Central Pacific directly at the heart of the Japanese defence system, was the correct one. At the conclusion of the long struggle for the Solomons in November 1943, the much depleted and exhausted Japanese naval air groups had returned to their carriers which then retired to home waters to rehabilitate and re-equip. After the debacle at Rabaul in November, when carriers lent to Halsey from the Pacific Fleet crippled the majority of Kurita's cruiser force, the waters of the Solomon Sea became an Allied lake.

North of the Bismarcks, however, the Japanese Combined Fleet based on Truk, though bereft of its carriers, still dominated the seas through possession of its many island air bases in Micronesia. Not only did this pose a constant threat to the flank of MacArthur's north-westward thrust, but it constituted a bar to the Allied plan to attain a position in the

Western Pacific from which Japan could be forced to surrender through air action or invasion. At the same time these scattered air bases, on which were distributed the aircraft of the shore-based 22nd Air Flotilla, were exposed to overwhelming surprise attack by the American carrier task forces, arriving unheralded and vanishing again into the immensity of the ocean.

Here was the proper objective for carrier forces, allowing them to exploit surprise and mobility, both of which would have been sacrificed if they had been committed to operations in the confined waters of the East Indian island chain. So a new fashion in naval warfare was introduced. With the aid of an immense logistic effort enabling the huge fleet to operate for long periods without benefit of permanent bases, the vast spaces of the Pacific Ocean were made to serve a useful purpose instead of presenting a problem. From out of the blue would come sudden, massive air-strikes not only at the main objective but at any bases from which air reinforcements could come to the support of the point of attack. Then, following more air raids and heavy bombardment by cruisers and battleships to soften up the ground defences, the amphibious assault would go in. The first objectives were to be Tarawa and Makin in the Gilbert Islands, D-day for the landings being set at 20 November 1943.

The organisation of the U.S. 5th Fleet (as the Central Pacific Force was now known) for this operation was the model for all future amphibious assaults in the Central Pacific. The amphibious element under the command of Rear-Admiral Richmond K. Turner, was divided into a Northern Attack Force (T. F. 52) which was assembled and trained in Hawaii and a Southern attack force (T. F. 53) which was mounted from New Zealand and at Efate. The objective of Task Force

52 was Makin, while Task Force 53's troops would assault Tarawa. Each of these attack forces was self-contained with its own squadron of three escort carriers, a squadron of battleships, a squadron of cruisers and some 14 destroyers for close escort of the transports and for bombardment purposes. Covering the attack forces was the Fast Carrier Force (T. F. 50) organised in four task groups amongst which six large and five light carriers were divided, each group with its screen of fast battleships or cruisers and destroyers. In place of the outdated Devastator torpedo-bombers, the air groups were now equipped with the greatly superior Avengers carrying, at last, efficient torpedoes or a heavy bomb load. The Wildcat fighters which had put up such a gallant fight against the superior performance of the Zero, had been superseded by the Hellcat which was more than a match for the Japanese plane. Task Force 57, providing land-based air support with flying boats and heavy bombers (including more than 100 Liberators) all under the naval operational command of Rear-Admiral John H. Hoover, resembled the Japanese organisation which had so brilliantly supported the southward drive in the early months of the war. The whole vast armada of some 200 ships and more than 1,000 aircraft was under the Commander 5th Fleet, Vice-Admiral R. A. Spruance. Early in November it was ready. On the 10th the Northern Attack Force left Hawaii. Two days later the Southern Attack Force sailed out of Efate. On the 20th, Makin and Tarawa were simultaneously assaulted. The former was lightly held and fortified and, though the small garrison resisted with such dogged determination that it took two days to eliminate it, the issue was never in doubt. Tarawa, on the other hand, had been built up into a veritable fortress. Desperate fighting over three days, with casualties to the U.S. Marines of 913 killed and 2,037 wounded, eventually captured

it, however, when the last man of the 4,690 strong Japanese garrison had been killed. To complete the occupation of the Gilberts, Abemama Atoll, south-west of Tarawa was occupied on the 26th against minor opposition. The Japanese Combined Fleet at Truk, its cruiser force out of action since the carrier air attack on Rabaul two weeks earlier, and lacking the whole of its ship-borne air strength, could make no move to interfere. Submarines were sent to harry the attack forces, however, and one of them, the *I-175*, torpedoed the escort carrier *Liscombe Bay*. Her store of aircraft bombs exploded and she sank with a loss of more than 700 officers and men. Shore-based torpedo-planes from the Japanese air bases on Nauru Island and the Marshalls sought out the carrier groups and the Northern Attack Force. The Southern Carrier Group (T. G. 50.3) was surprised by a wing of some 20 torpedo planes and the *Independence* was torpedoed but managed to reach Funafuti on one propeller. The transports of the Northern Attack Force, attacked at dusk on the 25th, escaped damage by skilful manoeuvring.

With the Gilberts secured and the Tarawa airfield in their hands, the Americans were ready for the next move — to the Marshalls. Admiral Nimitz's plan was a bold one. The Japanese air bases on the southern and eastern atolls, Jaluit, Mili, Maloelap and Wotje, would be neutralised by massive air strikes and by-passed by the attack forces which would attack and occupy the group of islands comprising Kwajalein Atoll. At the same time the undefended Majuro Atoll whose lagoon would make an excellent advanced base for the fleet, would be occupied.

The operation began on 29 January 1944 when Admiral Hoover's shore-based air force from Tarawa and the Ellice Islands pounded Jaluit and Mili. Maloelap and Wotje were each struck by the aircraft of one carrier group, while the remaining two carrier groups concentrated on Kwajalein itself. That night Eniwetok to the west, from which Japanese reinforcements could come, was subjected to a hail of 16-inch and eight-inch shells from battleships and cruisers. With the dawn came carrier planes to complete the destruction. The pounding of Kwajalein, Maloelap and Mili went on all through the 30 January and on the 31st the assault went in with 53,000 troops, half of them soldiers and half marines. By 4 February all was over. For the loss of 177 killed and a thousand wounded, the whole Marshalls group except Eniwetok had been captured. For Wotje, Maloelap, Mili and Jaluit were simply kept neutralised from now on by occasional air raids, mounted to give the carrier air groups combat experience. Eniwetok, 350 miles north-west of Kwajalein, could not be so ignored. It lay on the direct route to Nimitz's next objective, the Marianas. To allow the Eniwetok Expeditionary Force, carrying some 10,000 troops, to assault unhindered, it was necessary to neutralise the air bases on Ponape and Truk in the Carolines, and Saipan and Tinian in the Marianas. Ponape was made the target for the shore-based air forces in the Gilberts. The great mobility of fast carrier forces was made use of to strike at Truk and the Marianas, 600 miles apart. While one carrier group went with the Expeditionary Force, the other three steered first for Truk. For two days the naval base was pounded almost without a break. Besides putting 270 aircraft out of action, two cruisers, four destroyers, 19 transports and five tankers were sunk. While Eniwetok was being assaulted and captured, two of the carrier groups, after refuelling and replenishing at Kwajalein, made for the Marianas where a large force of bombers on Guam, Saipan and Tinian, freshly arrived from Japan, was destroyed before it could interfere.

With the capture of the Marshalls, the main Japanese defensive perimeter had come under threat. The two-day pounding of Truk by the Pacific Fleet which made that fleet base untenable and forced Yamamoto's successor, Admiral Koga, to withdraw to Palau, made the first breach in the perimeter. The exposure of the inability of Japan's naval air force, that once incomparable fighting instrument, to defend Truk, advertised her ultimate defeat beyond doubt. In two years of incessant fighting, 8,000 naval aircraft had been destroyed. Of the experienced pilots with which Japan had gone to war, very few remained. Like other consequences of a long war, such losses had not been prepared for. Frenzied efforts to man the front-line aircraft had resulted in such a drop in fighting skill that casualties became progressively heavier until neither in quantity nor in quality could the losses be made up. Saburo Sakai, the 'ace' Zero pilot, one of the few to survive, who was shot down at the end of 1942 over the Solomons with the loss of an eye and other crippling wounds, and relegated to instructing, has described in his book, *Samurai*, the state of affairs at this time when he was a flying instructor at Omura in Japan:

> I found it hard to believe, when I saw the new trainees staggering along the runway, bumping their way into the air. The Navy was frantic for pilots, and the school was expanded almost every month, with correspondingly lower entrance requirements. Men who could never have dreamed even of getting near a fighter plane before the war were now thrown into battle.
>
> Everything was urgent! We were told to rush the men through, to forget the fine points, just to teach them how to fly and shoot. One after the other, singly, in twos and threes, the training planes smashed into the ground, skidded wildly through the air. For long and tedious months, I tried to build

215

fighter pilots from the men they thrust at us at Omura. It was a hopeless task. Our facilities were too meagre, the demand too great, the students too many....

The withdrawal of the Combined Fleet from Truk, first to Palau and soon afterwards to Singapore, was forced not only by the devastating blow struck by the U.S. 5th Fleet but also by the attacks on Japanese supply convoys of the Pacific Fleet submarine force, which had been rapidly increasing in both weight and efficiency as a result of the flow of new submarines from the shipyards and of their equipment, at last, with a reliable torpedo. The Combined Fleet was thus forced back on a base closer to its source of oil supply in Sumatra and Borneo. The neutralisation of Truk, however, though it was a setback fraught with omens of ultimate defeat for Japan, did not bring the war close home. The Japanese did not feel bound to defend it at all costs. The next American objective, the Marianas, was a different matter. The capture of Saipan would not only cut across Japan's line of communication with the southern regions; it would also provide a base for the strategic bombing of the homeland. The enemy would be at the gates. The threat would have to be met with the full force of the Combined Fleet.

Both sides prepared for the clash that was bound to come. The Japanese Fleet was reorganised under its new Commander-in-Chief, Admiral Soemu Toyoda, who had replaced Koga on 31 March, when the latter's aircraft disappeared when taking him from Palau to set up a shore headquarters at Davao in Mindanao. Toyoda also decided to exercise command over his far-flung fleet from the shore, delegating sea-going command to Vice-Admiral Jisaburo Ozawa who had relieved Nagumo of his command of the Carrier Force in November 1942.

The fleet which Ozawa commanded, renamed the Mobile Fleet, was organised in three forces. The Van Force, under Vice-Admiral Takeo Kurita, included the greater part of the battleship strength, *Yamato, Musashi, Haruna* and *Kongo* as well as four heavy cruisers, a light cruiser and nine destroyers, spreading an armoured shield and a bristling array of gun defences round a carrier squadron composed of three light carriers, *Chitose, Chiyoda* and *Zuiho* which operated 30 aircraft each. Force A, under Ozawa himself, with his flag in the new large carrier *Taiho*, accompanied by the *Shokaku* and *Zuikaku* provided the main air strength with 207 aircraft. Two cruisers, a light cruiser and nine destroyers formed the screen. Force B, commanded by Rear-Admiral Joshima, was grouped round the light carrier *Ryuho* and two large but comparatively slow (25 knots) carriers *Junyo* and *Hiyo*. Between them, they operated 135 aircraft. The battleship *Nagato*, a cruiser and ten destroyers completed the force.

Opposing this fleet was the spearhead of Admiral Spruance's 5th Fleet, Task Force 58, commanded by Vice-Admiral Marc Mitscher, with seven large and eight light carriers operating a total of 900 aircraft, divided into four carrier task groups, each with a powerful screen of cruisers and destroyers and a further task group known as the 'Battle Line' under Vice-Admiral Willis A. Lee composed of the fast and powerful new battleships *Washington, North Carolina, Iowa, New Jersey, South Dakota, Alabama, Indiana*, four cruisers and 13 destroyers.

The American superiority was overwhelming even without taking into account the warships of Task Force 51, Vice-Admiral Turner's Expeditionary Force — five older battleships, 11 cruisers and 12 escort carriers operating more than 300 aircraft. The Japanese counted on bringing on a battle in an area in which their shore-based air-power, distributed amongst the Carolines, the Southern Philippines and the Marianas, could intervene to redress the balance. They remained blithely confident of the outcome of such a battle, blinding themselves to the neutralising effect of the ceaseless air-strikes delivered by American carrier-borne and shore-based air-power and to the calamitous lowering of the quality of their aviators by this time. Toyoda's operation plan known as 'A-Go' to be set in motion as soon as the Americans committed themselves to their next advance, issued on 3 May 1944, laid down that 'a decisive battle with full strength will be opened at a favourable opportunity'. It visualised 'at least one third of the enemy task force carrier units' being destroyed by the shore-based air forces 'prior to the decisive battle'. In preparation, the Mobile Fleet was concentrated at an anchorage at Tawi Tawi in the Sulu Archipelago.

On the Allied side, while Admiral Turner's Expeditionary Force was organising and training, General MacArthur's forces in the South-West Pacific had been continuing their advance along the north coast of New Guinea.

By the end of February 1944, landings on New Britain and the occupation of the Admiralty Islands had put a ring round the bases of Rabaul and Kavieng which made them useless to the Japanese. They could now be safely by-passed and allowed to wither on the vine. When Madang on the New Guinea coast fell without serious opposition into Allied hands at the end of April, MacArthur decided on a long leap forward to Hollandia in Dutch New Guinea. Nimitz sent Task Force 58 in full strength to support the operation. Massive strikes by the carrier air groups neutralised Palau, Yap and Woleai at the beginning of April while the U.S. Army Air Forces reduced the Hollandia air base to rubble. Then on 21 April the Task Force joined in the preinvasion bombardments and on the following day the troops were put ashore. In four days the Hollandia area was in Allied hands. Another jump forward to Wakde on 17 April was followed by landings on the island of Biak. Here the Japanese, recognising the serious threat to the Southern Philippines that the loss of Biak would mean, fought long and desperately. In support of the defences, and with half an eye on the possibility of luring the American Fleet southwards, Admiral Ozawa despatched a squadron from the Mobile Fleet centred round the *Yamato* and *Musashi*, commanded by Rear-Admiral Ugaki. It reached Batjan in the Moluccas on 11 June; but before it could intervene in the struggle for Biak, events elsewhere were to lead to its hasty recall. By 2 July Biak was finally in Allied hands and MacArthur was ready for the final phase of his journey back to the Philippines. Before this, however, an event of dramatic grandeur had altered the whole shape of the campaign. The opposing carrier fleets had met in the greatest air battle of the war, and American troops were swarming ashore to capture the Marianas.

This operation had been organised, like that which had previously captured the Marshalls, with a Northern Attack Force under Vice-Admiral Richmond Turner, who was also in overall command of the expedition, assembling at Hawaii, training and embarking 71,000 troops to assault Saipan, and a Southern Attack Force under Rear-Admiral R. L. Connolly bringing 56,500 troops from Guadalcanal and Tulagi to assault Guam. The Northern Attack Force sailed from Hawaii between 25-30 May and concentrated at Eniwetok on 8 June, Connolly's force arriving on the same day at Kwajalein. D-day for Saipan was to be 15 June. The date for Guam was kept flexible, depending upon how things went. While the huge troop convoys with their protective destroyer screens and escort carriers were moving forward to the assault, Army air forces from the Marshalls were neutralising Japanese bases in the Carolines; Rear-Admiral Mitscher's carrier task force was already in action, softening up the defences and fighting for air supremacy over the Marianas. The carriers of Task Force 58 were divided into four self-contained task groups, each with its escort of cruisers and destroyers:

T.G. 58.1 *Hornet, Yorktown, Belleau Wood, Bataan*
T.G. 58.2 *Bunker Hill, Wasp, Monterey, Cabot*
T.G. 58.3 *Enterprise, Lexington, Princeton, San Jacinto*
T.G. 58.4 *Essex, Langley, Cowpens.*

In addition there was Lee's 'Battle Line', Task Group 58.7.[9]

During the past 12 months this vast force had been growing in size and efficiency. Action experience had been gained by a score of air-strikes on Japanese-held bases, from Wake in the north to Rabaul and Hollandia in the south. Operational efficiency had been raised to a pitch that would have been scarcely imaginable at the time of Midway and now the whole vast array of 15 carriers, seven battleships, 13 cruisers and 58 destroyers covering hundreds of square miles was manoeuvred as one to turn into wind to fly aircraft on and off. Aircraft direction, too, had achieved a scientifically controlled certainty far from the hit-and-miss muddles of the earlier carrier battles.

Operations began with a fighter sweep over the islands by 208 Hellcats on the afternoon of 11 June. For the loss of 11 fighters and six pilots, 36 enemy aircraft were destroyed on Guam, Saipan and Tinian. During the next day one group concentrated on Guam while the remainder struck Saipan and Tinian. On the evening of the 12th two groups (58.1 and 58.4) broke away and raced 650 miles north to attack Chichi Jima

---

[9] For full details see Appendix I

and Iwo Jima on 15th and 16th, whence Japanese air reinforcements from Japan could come.

By the end of the 13th, air supremacy over Saipan and Guam had been secured and, while bombers from the carriers roamed at will seeking targets, the battleships of Lee's force, as well as those of the Expeditionary Force, moved in to pound the defences with 16-inch and 14-inch shells. All was ready for the D-day assault.

But meanwhile, in his flagship, the cruiser *Indianapolis*, the Fleet Commander, Admiral Spruance, had been receiving vital information. The Japanese Fleet was on the move. The carrier airstrikes had led Admiral Toyoda on the 13th to alert the fleet to prepare for Operation 'A-Go'. From Batjan, Admiral Ugaki was urgently recalled. Two days later, at the news of landings in Saipan, the order to begin the operation went out.

Though the Marianas area in which Ozawa was ordered to give battle was not the location hoped for by Toyoda in his plan, it was still within range of the island air bases of Guam, Rota and Yap and of air reinforcements from Japan, staged through Iwo Jima. Not realising to what extent these had been neutralised, Ozawa counted on the help of some 500 aircraft in the battle to come.

On receipt of Toyoda's order on the 15th, the Mobile Fleet, which had been fuelling in the Guimaras Strait between the Philippine Islands of Negros and Panay, got under way and steering north through the Visayan Sea, made for the San Bernadino Strait. The decisive nature of the clash that was coming was acknowledged by the message from the Commander-in-Chief passed to every ship, a replica of that which Admiral Togo had made on the eve of the Battle of Tsu-Shima. 'The fate of the Empire rests on this one battle. Every man is expected to do his utmost.' That evening the fleet steamed out into the Philippine Sea and shaped its course for a rendezvous with Ugaki's detachment coming up from Batjan. It did not pass unseen. In its wake, the submarine *Flying Fish* foamed to the surface to send an urgent radio report. Away to the south-eastward, an hour later, the submarine *Seahorse* added the news of Ugaki's two monsters coming north to their rendezvous.

Off Saipan, Admiral Spruance calculated distances and weighed the possibilities. The Northern Attack Force was already fully committed to the assault on Saipan. It would be highly vulnerable to any attack and Spruance dared not move far to the west to challenge Ozawa lest the Japanese should outflank him during darkness and fall on Turner's forces in his rear. In his mind was a recollection of the favourite Japanese gambit of tempting the enemy to expend his attack on a decoy. He would therefore await the enemy's advance. On the other hand the enemy could not reach the area until the 19th. Spruance therefore allowed his two detached task groups to complete their interdiction strikes on Iwo Jima and Chichi Jima and ordered a general rendezvous for the evening of the 18th in a position 180 miles to the west of Tinian. From Turner's command he called eight cruisers and 21 destroyers of the five support groups to join his flag and augment the already vast Task Force 58.

Nearest to the enemy was stationed the Battle Line, Vice-Admiral Willis Lee still flying his flag in the *Washington* in which he had saved the day at the naval Battle of Guadalcanal. Twelve miles to the north of this force, Task Group 58.4, with its three carriers, was stationed to give it air cover. The deployment of this shield drawn up in proud array can only be ascribed to a vestigial belief in the role of the dying queen of naval warfare, the battleship. It would be on Mitscher's 900 aircraft that the outcome of the coming fight would depend. The likelihood of the 18-inch and 16-inch guns of the opposing battleships exchanging broadsides was remote. Fifteen miles to the eastward of the battle line, the three other carrier task groups stationed themselves in the order, from north to south, 58.1, 58.5 and 58.2. Meanwhile Spruance waited impatiently for further news of his adversary.

Since the reports from the *Flying Fish* and *Seahorse* three days earlier he had had only one contact report — from the submarine *Cavalla*, which, on the evening of the 17th had sighted 15 or more large warships some 700 miles west of Guam, steering east at 20 knots. This was part of Ozawa's fleet which had duly made rendezvous the previous day with Ugaki and with their attendant tankers and had spent all the daylight hours of the 17th refuelling. American shore-based air search had failed to make contact. Scouting carrier planes had turned back, at the limit of their fuel range, 60 miles short of the Japanese Fleet. Spruance was handicapped by American shortcomings in the one aerial technique in which the Japanese were still superior — naval reconnaissance. So far as ship-borne aviation was concerned, this can be attributed to the greater range of Japanese carrier aircraft and the abandonment by the Americans of catapult-launched float-planes in their battleships and cruisers. At the same time, the fact that American multi-engined aircraft were usually manned by Army Air Force crews trained primarily for bombing operations may have affected the efficiency of their maritime reconnaissance. Ozawa was better served. A search by seven planes from his carriers during the afternoon of the 18th gave him a rough picture of his enemy's disposition, though individual aircraft only sighted portions of Spruance's vast array which covered an area some 700 square miles in extent. The two fleets were

223

420 miles apart and Ozawa, deciding that he would keep it so, to take advantage of the greater range of his aircraft compared to his opponents', turned away to the southward. This move frustrated the intentions of his subordinate carrier admiral, Rear-Admiral Obayashi, commanding the carrier squadron of the Van Force. Being out of touch with his force commander, he had decided on his own initiative to launch a strike of 67 planes. Taking off at 1637, they would have arrived over Task Force 58 as the sun was setting and might have achieved surprise and a notable success. But on receipt of the Commander-in-Chief's order, Obayashi recalled them. Ozawa was planning to launch a more massive, concentrated attack the following morning. During the night he disposed his fleet in battle array so that when he altered course north-east for the enemy at 0300 the following morning, Kurita's powerful Van Force was 100 miles ahead of the remainder, its three carriers, each with its circular screen, steaming abreast of one another, some 12 miles apart. The object of this was partly to offer a heavily armed and armoured force as a shield to absorb the enemy's blows (the decoy motif again), and partly to make the best use of the scout planes in the battleships and cruisers. Forces A and B, each in a circular formation with three carriers in the centre, were more lightly screened, an arrangement fraught with fatal consequences.

Still ignorant of Ozawa's position and anxious lest the enemy should slip past him during the night to fall upon the all-important Expeditionary Force which it was his primary duty to defend, Spruance had turned eastward at nightfall. At 2200 had come a significant report from Pearl Harbour. Direction-finding stations had 'fixed' an enemy force transmitting in a position 350 miles to the west-south-west of his position. How much reliance could he put on a source of uncertain reliability?

It did not, in any case, necessarily fix the whole of the enemy's force: it could even be a variation of the Japanese use of decoys intended to lure him away from Saipan. His speculations were coloured by the belief that, earlier, a message from the submarine *Stingray*, patrolling 175 miles to the east-south-east of the 'fix', had been jammed by the enemy. Admiral Mitscher, unaffected by responsibility for the safety of the Expeditionary Force, urged Spruance to reverse course so that he could be in position to launch a strike at dawn. The Fleet Commander was not to be persuaded. He held his course eastward until daylight, a decision that was in due course to come in for criticism.

Under the circumstances such criticism is of doubtful validity. At the same time it is fascinating to speculate what difference it would have made if another message made during the night had reached him. The crew of a naval flying-boat searching 600 miles west of Saipan had seen their radar screen glow with a mass of pinpoints of light indicating no less than 40 ships in two groups. Urgent reports were radioed and were repeated when no acknowledgment was received; finally the pilot flew back to base to deliver his message. Not until 0900 did it reach Spruance, too late to have any value. A search during the night by 15 radar-equipped Avengers from the *Enterprise* had extended to within 40 miles of Ozawa's Van Force, but had brought no contact. At dawn more search planes fanned out westwards, again without results, although visibility was extreme.

Nevertheless, though deprived of knowledge of the enemy's position, the American 5th Fleet was alert and ready. Hellcats of the combat air patrols climbed aloft at first light into a cloudless blue sky over a sea barely rippled by a light south-easterly breeze. Those of the southern carrier group were quickly in action, directed on to two dive-bombers coming from the direction of Guam, an early reminder that Ozawa's fleet was not the only enemy to be faced. And, indeed, the situation was as visualised in the A-Go plan, with the American Fleet caught between the hammer of Ozawa's carrier force and the anvil of Japanese island-based air-power. Unfortunately for Toyoda's strategy, however, the latter was only a shadow of what it was expected to be. Preliminary strikes by the U.S. carrier forces and Army bombers had destroyed much of it. More was held back at Yap and in the Palaus which the Japanese expected to be attacked. A handful flown to Guam from Truk only brought the operational air strength there up to 50. Nevertheless Spruance could not afford to ignore them and the first air battle of the day developed over Orote Field on Guam as the combat air patrol from the carrier *Belleau Wood* swooped on aircraft taking off. Soon afterwards more Japanese aircraft were detected approaching Guam from the south-west. From each of the task groups, flights of Hellcats were sent to intercept, and in the whirling dog-fights that developed more than 30 Japanese planes were shot down. Shore-based air-power was achieving nothing more than to engage the attentions of Mitscher's fighters; and of these he had plenty and to spare.

Meanwhile the tempo of events in the opposite direction had been quickening. At 0445 the first of 16 Japanese scout seaplanes had been catapulted from Kurita's battleships and cruisers and flown off in the direction of the coming dawn. Half-an-hour later his carriers had turned briefly into wind to launch 14 more search planes. The course of the latter group took them directly towards Admiral Lee's battleship group but they got no further than his outlying picket destroyers which they reported. Half their number were shot down by planes from the *Langley*. The first group of search planes were sent too far to the north and failed to make contact until one of them, on its homeward flight, sighted Task Group 58.4 on the southern horizon at 0730. An hour later the first Japanese strike composed of 45 Zero fighter-bombers, eight torpedo-planes and 16 Zero fighters from the van carriers had formed up and set out. A few minutes before 0900, Ozawa's own Force A also turned into wind and from the decks of the three big carriers 53 dive-bombers, 27 torpedo-planes and 48 Zeros began taking off. That Fortune had by now abandoned the Japanese, transferring her favours to the side with the 'big battalions', was to be made apparent in the events of the next few hours. Four U.S. submarines, *Albacore*, *Finback*, *Fang* and *Stingray* had been stationed in an area through which it had been calculated that the Japanese Fleet must pass. At 0816, Commander Blanchard of the *Albacore*, who had been forced by a patrolling plane to submerge, sighted through his periscope the top hamper of a cruiser, the masthead of numerous other ships and the flat silhouette of an aircraft carrier coming over the horizon. Astute foresight by Nimitz's submarine force commander, Admiral Lockwood, must take credit for the encounter; but in the trackless spaces of the ocean, luck plays a large part in such an event.

Blanchard lost no time in shaping course to intercept this target but he had hardly started to do so when another carrier came in sight presenting a simpler attack problem, and Blanchard transferred his attentions to her. Planes taking off from her deck restricted her to a steady course and speed. Blanchard waited with easy confidence for the moment to fire. A last minute failure of the torpedo deflection computer caused only a moment's alarm. The human eye could make all the calculations necessary and six torpedoes sped away, spreading fanwise, for Ozawa's proud new flagship the *Taiho*. There now occurred a moment of tragic drama. A Japanese pilot, Sakio Komatsu, had just taken off. He saw the track of a torpedo streaking through the water for the carrier and without hesitation dived his plane on to it, torpedo and plane blowing up together. His sublime act of sacrifice was in vain. Another torpedo hit the *Taiho*. The damage it caused seemed far from lethal, however, and the carrier steamed on at a scarcely reduced speed. That a fatal sequence of events had begun was not contemplated. Air operations continued unchecked and the 42 planes she was contributing to the second strike were safely launched. Joining up with the remainder, they set off, their course taking them over the Van Force. Nervous gunners there opened fire and before they could be stopped had shot down two planes and damaged eight more which had to return to their carrier.

By this time the first strike force was well on its way and, at 1000, radar in Lee's battle fleet detected them at more than 150 miles. Mitscher at once recalled the Hellcats fighting over Guam and at 1023 his entire carrier force turned, as one, into wind, and began launching every available fighter. Bombers, for which no target had as yet been located, were flown off to keep the decks free for the fighters. They were kept in the air, orbiting clear of the air battle, allowing the carriers to concentrate on keeping a maximum fighter force in the air, launching reliefs for those Hellcats needing replenishment of fuel or ammunition which were landed-on, hastily serviced and sent back aloft. In the day-long aerial fight that was about to open, some 300 Hellcats were to be engaged intercepting the enemy attackers; others were to be occupied interdicting Orote Field on Guam. Spruance's criticised 'defensive' tactics were thus to enable a death-blow to be struck at Japanese naval air-power and at the same time seal the fate of the Imperial Navy as effectively as any air-strikes on its ships might have done.

The first Japanese striking force was still 45 miles short of the nearest American task force — Lee's battleships — when the first excited cry of 'Tally-ho' from intercepting fighters was heard over the radio. It came from the leader of a formation of 11 Hellcats from the *Essex*, Lieutenant-Commander Brewer. At 18,000 feet a wild melee ensued in which the rugged, highly manoeuvrable Hellcats, in the hands of experienced, well-trained airmen fought Zeros in which, for the sake of high performance, no armour protection or self-sealing petrol tanks had been included, flown by airmen whose patriotic fervour could not compensate for lack of flying hours and fighting skill. Of the 69 aircraft making up this first strike, 42 were shot down. Not one succeeded in breaking through to attack the American ships. By 1100 the remnants were straggling back to their carriers.

Radar screens were not clear of enemy contacts for long. The swarm of aircraft composing Ozawa's second strike was detected at a range of 115 miles at 1107. More Hellcats streamed off the decks of Mitscher's carriers and climbed away to meet them 45 miles beyond Lee's Task Group. Once again from the heights came tumbling down a host of broken, burning aircraft — Zeros, 'Jill' torpedo-planes and 'Judy' dive-bombers. Over a wide area the blue sea was stained with ugly patches of oil, smoking wreckage and floating debris. About 20 survivors, out of more than 100 intercepted, drove doggedly on to be met by a barrier of high explosive from battleships, cruisers and destroyers. A torpedo-plane crashed into the *Indiana* on her waterline, but the torpedo did not explode. Only a handful of 'Jills' and 'Judies' broke through to attack the carriers beyond. The and the *Bunker Hill* suffered minor damage and a few casualties from near bomb misses. A torpedo exploded in the *Enterprise*'s wake. This was the sum total of the raid's achievements. By 1200 it was all over.

At about the time that the 30 survivors out of the 128 aircraft which had set out from Force A were turning disconsolately for home, the luckless Ozawa was suffering a painful shock. At 1220, as his carriers were steaming into wind, recovering planes, the *Shokaku* shuddered under the explosion of three torpedoes. They came from the submarine *Cavalla*. Though she had been forced to lose touch with Ozawa's fleet sighted on the evening of the 17th, through having to surface to signal her report, she had chased after it through the night at top speed. Force A's manoeuvres to operate aircraft had brought it straight for the submarine which had only had to dive and wait for it to steam overhead as planes were being recovered. Lieutenant-Commander Kossler had had no difficulty in working his way through the meagre screen to launch six torpedoes at close range. Pouring smoke from petrol fires and shaken by further explosions, the *Shokaku*'s speed fell away. For the next three hours the fires were fought and intermittently mastered only to be renewed as leaking petrol fumes spread through the ship. Then came a final monstrous explosion and the veteran carrier was torn asunder and sank.

Even as the *Shokaku* going down, Ozawa's flagship, the *Taiho*, was also reaching the end of her brief career. Since being torpedoed six hours earlier, she had continued to operate and had apparently suffered little damage. But the explosion had ruptured the petrol system. To clear the fumes the order was unwisely given to turn on the forced ventilation system throughout the ship. Instead of clearing them, this spread the explosive gases to every compartment. The inevitable eruption occurred at 1532, tearing holes in the ship's side and bottom, distorting the flight-deck and setting her ablaze. The *Taiho* was doomed. Ozawa and his staff were transferred to the cruiser *Haguro* but only about 500 of her crew of 2,150 had been taken off when, after a further heavy explosion, she capsized and sank.

In the midst of these upheavals, the disasters overtaking his airstrikes were not immediately known to Ozawa. Two more had been launched during the forenoon. Of the first of these, out of 47 aircraft from Force B, half had failed to find the enemy and had turned back. The remainder were detected by the most northerly Carrier Task Group at 1300 coming in from the north. Though intercepted by double their own number of Hellcats and losing seven, shot down, a number broke through, dropped their bombs ineffectively and escaped.

The next striking force, 82 planes strong, despatched from Force B and the *Zuikaku* were directed too far south owing to a navigational error by a scout plane. A group of them caught sight of the southern Carrier Task Group and made an ineffective attack, nearly all being shot down for their pains. However, 49 sighted nothing and made for Orote Field, Guam. It was a fatal decision. For most of the day Orote Field had been under intermittent attack by American bomber squadrons flown off during the forenoon to leave the carrier decks clear for the fighters. By now the runways had been made unusable. Crash landings would be the fate of any aircraft seeking refuge there. Few of the straying strike force were to be able to do so, however. As they approached the island they were set upon by 27 Hellcats from the *Cowpens*, *Hornet* and *Essex*, which shot down no less than 30 of them. The last of Ozawa's raids for the day had gone down in ruin. Of 373 planes which had taken off from his ships during the day, only 130 had returned. Counting the 50 aircraft based on

Guam and operational losses, the total destroyed during the day amounted to about 315. The Americans had lost only 23 aircraft shot down and six operationally. No wonder their exulting sailors and airmen dubbed it 'The Great Marianas Turkey Shoot'. The Japanese losses were irreplaceable and never again would they be able to man or equip an effective carrier force. Spruance's tactics of letting the enemy come to him had been decisively successful.

Nevertheless there was a natural feeling of disappointment in the 5th Fleet and at Pearl Harbour that the Japanese Fleet had escaped. The full magnitude of the *Albacore*'s and *Cavalla*'s exploits was not yet known. The doctrine, propounded by the naval historian, Mahan, that the enemy's fleet must be the main objective, was perhaps too literally accepted. In the new. air age, carriers are only as important as the aircraft they can operate; but the consuming desire naturally persisted, to destroy the villains of the Pearl Harbour treachery.

Spruance, poorly served by shore-based reconnaissance, had had no information of the enemy's position since the *Cavalla*'s report at 1215. Task Force 58 turned westward at 24 knots as soon as the last planes had been gathered in and Spruance signalled to Mitscher:

> Desire to attack enemy tomorrow if we know his position with sufficient accuracy. If our patrol planes give us required information tonight no searches should be necessary. If not, we must continue searches tomorrow to ensure adequate protection of Saipan.

But Ozawa, too, had turned away north-westward towards a rendezvous with his fuelling force, so that at dawn he was still some 400 miles distant. An early morning search launched at 0530 on 20 June thus failed to reach him. Fortunately for

American hopes, however, Ozawa was to linger on the field of battle, offering himself a target for the counter-attack.

By transferring his flag to the cruiser *Haguro* with her limited signal communications facilities, he had so reduced his sources of information that he was unaware of the appalling air losses he had suffered. Not realising that Guam had been neutralised, he imagined that many of his missing planes had landed there and that with the aid of its shore-based air forces he would be able to renew his attacks on the American Fleet as soon as he had replenished his fuel tanks. From what could be gathered from aviators who had survived the massacre of the 19th, Task Force 58 had already suffered heavily, with at least four carriers sunk and great numbers of aircraft shot down.

Kurita, his battleship Admiral, was sceptical and, early on the 20th, advised retirement to Japan; but Ozawa would have none of it. Fuelling was to begin as soon as possible; but in this, too, Ozawa's isolation in the *Haguro* dislocated the organisation so that it was not until midday that a programme was issued. Before it could be implemented, however, there were indications of the enemy's approach. From the cruiser *Atago* at 1615 came news of an intercepted signal by an American plane reporting contact with the enemy fleet. Orders for fuelling were cancelled and retirement to the north-west ordered. By this time Ozawa had at last been able to shift his flag to the *Zuikaku* where he learnt that only some 100 operational planes remained to him. He remained undismayed. Let him get refuelled and he would return to the attack, he insisted. But his hopes were about to be finally shattered.

While the Japanese Fleet lingered at the fuelling rendezvous in confusion owing to the lack of a controlling hand, Task Force 58 was cutting down the intervening distance. When the afternoon search flew off at 1330, it had only 300 miles to go to discover Ozawa's force. It fell to Lieutenant R. S. Nelson piloting an Avenger from the *Enterprise* to signal the long-awaited enemy report at 1605. It was desperately late in the day. A striking force launched at once could not get back to the carriers before dark. Many of the American pilots were trained only for daylight operations. Not only would their landings on deck be extremely hazardous, but with the prevailing easterly winds the carriers would be steaming away from the enemy through the landing operations: stragglers and cripples would splash in the sea short of them. Mitscher, who had been unhappy at Spruance's prudent tactics during the previous night, took the bold decision to risk all to give one massive blow while the opportunity offered. Within half-an-hour of Nelson's report, 77 dive-bombers, 54 torpedo-planes with an escort of 85 fighters had roared off his carriers' decks and climbed away towards the sun, already low in the western sky.

At 1825, patrolling Japanese airmen sighted the approaching swarm and 15 minutes later the Americans sighted the first group of enemy ships. This was the force of six tankers and their screen of destroyers, left astern when Ozawa at last realised the wisdom of beating a hasty retreat. A section of dive-bombers broke away from the American formation to attack them, damaging two that were subsequently scuttled. Thirty miles beyond them, spread in an arc from north-west to west was the fleet in its three divisions. Ozawa's own Force A, reduced now to the *Zuikaku* and the screening cruisers and destroyers was the most northerly, with Force B some 20 miles south-west of it. Ten miles southward again was the Van Force with the giant battleships and numerous heavy cruisers in tight circles round the carriers. The sun was just setting as the main body of American aircraft swarmed over the three groups, brushing aside the thin screen of Zeros that rose to meet them, to concentrate on the carriers. Through a spectacular curtain of multi-coloured tracers and vicious shell bursts, dive-bombers screamed down and torpedo-planes swooped low over the water while the Hellcats and Zeros fought high above them. In 20 minutes it was all over and the American planes were streaming back towards the darkening western horizon, 300 miles of empty ocean and, for many of them, their first night deck landing ahead of them. Behind them they left the carrier *Hiyo* torpedoed and sinking. The *Zuikaku* had taken a number of bomb hits. Fires that engulfed her were mastered only just in time for the order to abandon ship to be countermanded. The carrier *Chiyoda*'s flight-deck was a mangled wreck and she was on fire. A bomb on the battleship *Haruna* had flooded a magazine. The cruiser *Maya* was fighting a fire.

It was not a remarkable score for 131 strike aircraft, of which 14 were shot down. It goes further to confirm the correctness, whether deliberate or not, of Spruance's tactics. The Hellcat fighter was a master weapon in his hand. By standing on the defensive on the 19th he brought it into play in overwhelming numbers. By the time his strike aircraft went in he could afford to give them massive fighter escort and though their achievements were disappointing, their losses were light, while Ozawa's defending planes again suffered severely. Out of the 100 with which Ozawa had started the day only 35 remained to him as he fled through the night to Okinawa.

Meanwhile darkness had fallen over Mitscher's carrier groups, a darkness made complete by a layer of heavy cloud that had spread itself overhead at sundown. On the radar screens the long, straggling line of homing planes appeared. Disregarding any risk from enemy bombers or submarines, Mitscher ordered every form of illumination to be used, star shells overhead, flight-deck floodlights, navigation lights and signal lamps flashing identifying call signs. At 2045 the first homecoming aircraft were droning overhead, pilots seeking their own carriers before entering the circuit and dipping down to a perilous landing. Many crashed on deck. Others ditched as their engines spluttered and died, as the last of the petrol drained from their tanks. Many more landed on carriers other than their own. By 2252 all were down. Eighty planes had splashed or crashed but few of their crews were lost or seriously hurt. When rescue operations during the night and following day were completed, only 16 pilots and 33 air-crew were missing.

The Battle of the Philippine Sea was over. For though Spruance loosed Admiral Lee's battleship force in chase they had no chance of catching the fleeing enemy, nor had Ozawa left any cripples behind to be snapped up. After a long day's search on 21 June, Spruance called off the hunt and turned to resume direct support of the landing operations on Saipan. It was the last classic carrier battle to be fought and was a clear-cut, decisive victory for the Americans. The humiliated Ozawa offered his resignation, but Toyoda refused to accept it. Yet in the American Fleet deep disappointment was felt amongst the carrier Admirals and even Spruance came to think he had missed a great opportunity by holding back during the night of 18-19 June and so failing to knock the last Japanese carriers out of the war. Those carriers, it is true, were to intervene once again at a crucial moment; with no trained aviators to operate from them, they would be in fact only an empty threat, but in the true Japanese heroic tradition they would still play an effective part in self-immolation.

11. LEYTE: SIBUYAN SEA AND SURIGAO STRAIT

With the retirement of the defeated Japanese Fleet from the Battle of the Philippine Sea, the way was open for Admiral Turner's Expeditionary Force to proceed with the capture of the Marianas, free from serious outside interference. The dogged gallantry with which small units of Japanese aircraft flew up from Truk, Palau and Iwo Jima, to make night attacks on ships of the assault force off Saipan until that island was finally secured could only be classified as nuisance raids, though one of them succeeded in torpedoing and damaging the battleship *Maryland*. Saburo Sakai who had by this time, in spite of his single eye, been sent to Iwo Jima leading a wing of half-fledged fighter pilots, has described his sentiments as he watched the Japanese bombers take off from the island on their forlorn hopes. Remembering his brave days in New Guinea when he had shot down so many Allied planes, 'which pounded Lae, day and night, without fighter escort, hurling their defiance in the teeth of dozens of Zero fighter planes', he now saw the reverse of the coin.

But it was worse [he groans]; in the early months of 1942 the American twin-engine bombers had a fighting chance. With the 'Bettys' it was different. Let a fighter plane catch a 'Betty' in its sights for a second or two, let an anti-aircraft shell spill its hot fragments into the fuselage, and the odds were that there would be no more bomber, but a roaring mass of flames disintegrating into the water....

The hours between each take-off and the return of the surviving bombers seemed interminable. Our pilots carried

237

out their bombing runs with the utmost gallantry and scored some hits. But what did it mean? These were only fleabites!

And every night perhaps one or two planes limped back to Iwo Jima with fuselage and wings holed, the crews desperately tired, their eyes haggard from watching their friends going down, one after the other, even before they were within attack range. The few pilots who returned to the island told us of fighters coming in after them in almost total darkness and finding their planes unerringly in the gloom, of tracers bursting bright as day when all the guns on the American ships opened up at them. Brilliant explosions, cobwebs of spitting tracers which seemed to be impenetrable walls of fire blocking their path as they swung into their bombing runs.

In a few days there were hardly any of the twin-engined Mitsubishi bombers left on the island. Then Iwo threw in its torpedo-bombers, single-engined planes ['Jills'] which attempted zero-level torpedo attacks. They fared little better than the larger planes.

To prevent air reinforcements coming from Japan, Task Group 58.1 (carriers *Hornet*, *Yorktown*, *Belleau Wood* and *Bataan*) returned to Iwo Jima on 24 June. A force of 51 Hellcat fighter-bombers launched to attack grounded aircraft, was intercepted by 80 Zeros of the 27th Air Flotilla. Leading a section of them was Saburo Sakai who gives a stirring account of his first encounter with the redoubtable Grumman fighter plane. He himself got safely back from the wild air battle that ensued during which, it seemed to him, Hellcats and Zeros were tumbling down in flames in about equal numbers. 'But the day's toll was staggering', he admits. 'Nearly 40 — almost half of all our fighters — had been shot down.' And American losses had in fact been very few.

Meanwhile, on Saipan, against a frenzied defence organised by the Japanese commanders, General Saito and Admiral

Nagumo, amongst the jumbled mass of coral rock and the cave-studded hills and cliffs of the island, the attackers made slow and painful progress. Not until 9 July, after Saito and Nagumo had shot themselves, and a horrifying mass suicide had been staged by a number of Japanese civilian inhabitants, men, women and children, who hurled themselves over a cliff, was Saipan officially secured and even then for some weeks afterwards isolated knots of Japanese soldiers, resisting to the death, had to be hunted out of caves. Tinian and Guam, assaulted after being subjected to a smothering aerial and gunfire bombardment — for 13 days continuously in the case of the latter — were secured less expensively though the defence was no less frantically stubborn.

Both to the Japanese and the Americans the capture of Saipan was the grand climacteric of the Pacific War. To the former, it represented the first breach in Japan's vital defences and made it impossible to disguise any longer that ultimate defeat was certain. General Tojo and his Cabinet resigned. The new Government, under General Koiso would have welcomed peace but knew not how to bring it about, nor, with the Japanese attitude to surrender, dared they propose it.

For the Allies it opened shining prospects of bringing about a rapid end to the Pacific War. It also brought to a head the sharp difference of opinion between General MacArthur on the one side and the American Joint Chiefs of Staff on the other. MacArthur's eye had never wavered from his goal of the Philippines since the tragic day on which he had left Corregidor to set up his command in Australia. In his thoughts were always the American and Filipino troops he had been forced to abandon to the dreadful Death March and the inhumanity of their captors. To the Filipino people, too, he felt an absolute obligation to liberate them at the earliest possible moment from the cruel subjection by the Japanese to which their loyalty to the United States had condemned them. For Douglas MacArthur the road to Japan led only through the Philippines. The Chiefs of Staff, in particular the Commander-in-Chief U.S. Fleet, Admiral King, and the Commander-in-Chief Pacific Fleet, Admiral Nimitz, thought they saw a better route from Saipan to Formosa, by-passing the Philippines. The deadlock between the two strategies was resolved by President Roosevelt after hearing MacArthur and Nimitz personally, during a visit to Hawaii in July 1944. The result was tabled at the 'Octagon' Conference at Quebec which opened on 11 September. Both MacArthur's South-West Pacific forces and Nimitz's Central Pacific forces would advance, the former up the island chain via Morotai, Salebaboe and Mindanao to Leyte, the latter to capture Peleliu, in the Palaus, Yap and Ulithi. Both forces would then combine to occupy either Luzon or Formosa, and Amoy on the China coast.

No firm decision had been reached when there came an electrifying message to the Chiefs of Staff from the Pacific. There, command of Admiral Spruance's mighty 5th Fleet had been taken over by Admiral Halsey under a scheme whereby command would alternate between the two, one retiring to Pearl Harbour with his staff to rest and to plan his next operation while the other embarked with his own staff to direct current activities. While Halsey was in command, the fleet, though composed of the same ships, became the 3rd Fleet, with the Carrier Task Force, still under Marc Mitscher, as Task Force 38. Starting on 28 August, Task Force 38 had sailed from Eniwetok to deliver a series of softening-up strikes in support of MacArthur's advance to Morotai and the Central Pacific forces' capture of the Palaus and Yap. Swarming over Japanese air bases in Mindanao, the carrier planes had found the opposition negligible. After two days Halsey had shifted the attacks to the central Philippine Islands only to find the same conditions. With the Japanese shore-based air-power so apparently emasculated, MacArthur's customary progress by forward moves limited to the supporting range of his own land-based air force could be boldly replaced by one long leap from New Guinea to Leyte. It could be supported by the air strength of Task Force 38 and reinforced by the Central Pacific troops earmarked to occupy the Palaus and Yap, which Halsey suggested was unnecessary. The planned stepping-stones of the Talaud Islands and Mindanao could be bypassed.

Halsey's suggestion appealed greatly to the Chiefs of Staff assembled at Quebec, seeking for means to speed up the Pacific War. Except for the capture of the Palaus, the by-passing of which was too great a risk, and against which operations were already under way, the plan was put to MacArthur with a target date for landing on Leyte, 20 October. It meant committing his whole army to a sea-borne advance past enemy bases and an assault some 1,500 miles from the starting point relying solely upon ship-borne air cover; but MacArthur accepted immediately.

When the decision was taken, MacArthur's 7th Amphibious Force was already on its way to Morotai, while Nimitz's two attack forces were approaching the Palaus and Yap. The Eastern Attack Force, assigned to the assault of Yap, was at once diverted to Manus to join MacArthur's South-West Pacific Command. Morotai was taken by surprise against negligible opposition. In the Palaus, the objective was the little island of Peleliu on which was the airfield. The Japanese garrison had extended the many natural caves in the limestone ridge overlooking the airfield until it was honeycombed with interconnecting passages, making it almost impregnable. The defenders fought with such dogged determination that it was not until 25 November that the last organised resistance was overcome. The capture of the airfield, however, in the first few days, achieved the object of the operation by removing the threat to the flank of the advance to Leyte. Meanwhile Ulithi Atoll had been occupied without opposition to provide a magnificent anchorage and forward base for the whole Pacific Fleet.

The Leyte operation opened on 10 October when the first of MacArthur's transports sailed from Manus in the Admiralty Islands and Task Force 38, which had sailed from Ulithi on the 6th, began a sweeping series of strikes against air bases to the northward from which interference and reinforcement might be expected. On the 10th, Okinawa was pounded; two carrier task groups struck Aparri in northern Luzon during the 11th; from the 12th to the 14th the Formosan airfields were the targets, more than 200 Japanese aircraft being destroyed. The Japanese reacted by sending out large numbers of twin-engined 'Betty' torpedo-planes to make twilight and night attacks on the carriers. They succeeded only in torpedoing the cruisers U.S.S. *Canberra* and *Houston*,[10] but at a heavy cost to themselves, more than 40 of them being shot down. Nevertheless they claimed to have wreaked havoc in Task Force 38 as a result of which Admiral Toyoda, though he can hardly have accepted the figure of 11 carriers, two battleships and three cruisers sunk, besides eight more carriers, two battleships, four cruisers and 13 unidentified ships damaged, put out by Tokyo Radio, believed that a heavy defeat had been inflicted. Despatching the partially trained carrier air groups from Japan to Formosa and instructing Admiral Fukudome,

---

[10] Not to be confused with H.M.A.S. *Canberra* and U.S.S. *Houston* sunk in 1942.

commanding the shore-based naval air forces, to annihilate the remnants of the retreating 3rd Fleet, he ordered out from the Inland Sea a force comprising three cruisers and five destroyers to mop up the cripples. Taking a leaf out of the Japanese book, Halsey offered the damaged cruisers, being towed back to harbour, as a decoy. When the Japanese, discovering that Task Force 38 was still very much intact, refused the bait and turned for home, Halsey gleefully made his famous signal that the sunken ships of the 3rd Fleet had been salvaged and were 'retiring at high speed towards the enemy'. The massed air attacks which Fukudome launched in response to Toyoda's call, and others made against Task Group 38.4 which had been striking Luzon airfields, were uniformly disastrous for the Japanese. Between 10-16 October, at the cost of two cruisers badly damaged, minor damage to three carriers and 90 planes lost with 64 pilots and air-crew, the 3rd Fleet had reduced the air strength in Formosa and the Philippines to something under 200 planes, and had largely destroyed the carrier air groups sent to reinforce the shore-based air force. A vital element of the forces on which the Japanese relied for the last desperate, decisive battle about to begin had been largely eliminated.

For the next three days the carrier task groups kept up their assault on northern Philippine airfields while South-West Pacific shore-based air forces pounded those in Mindanao. All the while, MacArthur's great armada was steering for Leyte. On 17 October, in the early dawn, Japanese look-outs on the island of Suluan at the mouth of the Gulf of Leyte saw a flotilla of destroyer transports approaching, preceded by minesweepers clearing a channel and followed by two light cruisers and four destroyers. Within the hour Toyoda, at his headquarters in Japan, received the warning message which gave him the vital information for which he had been waiting — the point at which the Americans were next to strike. As the guns of the cruiser *Denver* opened fire on Suluan, the message 'Prepare to carry out Operation SHO-1' went out from Tokyo to the various units of the Mobile Fleet.

Since the Battle of the Philippine Sea this had been divided into two main portions. In Japanese home waters were the four surviving operational aircraft carriers, *Zuikaku*, *Zuiho*, *Chitose* and *Chiyoda* and the battleships *Ise* and *Hyuga*, which had had their after gun turrets removed and replaced by a small flight deck. All had been waiting to embark the fresh air groups as they emerged from the training schools. Besides a numerous screening force of light cruisers and destroyers, there were also three heavy cruisers. For the purposes of Operation SHO-1, which called for an intricate pattern of movements by a number of separate units to fall simultaneously on the American invasion fleet, this home-based force was divided into two. Two cruisers, *Nachi* and *Ashigara*, screened by the light cruiser *Abukuma* and four destroyers were grouped together under Vice-Admiral Kiyohide Shima and designated and Striking Force. (The third cruiser, *Aoba*, was diverted to escort a troop transport operation in the Philippines and took no part in the SHO-1 operation.) The remainder of the fleet in home waters under Ozawa, formed the Main Body.

In the Lingga Roads, near Singapore, was the 1st Striking Force under Vice-Admiral Kurita, containing all the surviving Japanese battleships and all the heavy cruisers except for the three in Shima's squadron. This force was also divided into two main portions each with a separate mission in SHO-1. Force A under Kurita himself, flying his flag in the cruiser *Atago*, comprised five battleships, ten heavy cruisers, besides a screen of light cruisers and destroyers.[11] The remainder, known as

Force C, comprised two battleships and one cruiser with a screen of four destroyers under Vice-Admiral Shoji Nishimura.

Waiting only to make sure that Leyte was indeed the American objective, Toyoda signalled the executive order for SHO-1 on the morning of 18 October, setting the early hours of the 25th for the simultaneous arrival on the scene of these four forces by their various routes. Kurita's mission was to take his whole battle fleet first to Brunei Bay to refuel whence Force A would proceed by the Palawan Passage, the Mindoro Strait, the Sibuan Sea and the San Bernadino Strait, rounding Samar to approach Leyte from the north. Force C would make its way through the Mindanao Sea and the Surigao Strait to attack from the south. It would be supported by Shima's 2nd Striking Force, coming south from Japan. Finally, Ozawa's Carrier Force would take the direct route from Japan to the Philippine Sea. The original intention had been that its air groups would be thrown into the battle to engage Task Force 38. But they had been expended, half-trained as they were, in the great air battles off Formosa in the previous week. Now, with only 100 planes aboard his four carriers (none on board the *Ise* and *Hyuga*) manned by pilots insufficiently adept to alight back on deck once they had taken off, Ozawa was condemned to offer himself in the classic Japanese role of sacrificial bait whose purpose was to lure Halsey's carrier force away.

At dawn on 20 October 1944, the Allied assault on Leyte began with the crump of bombs from aircraft from the 14 escort carriers of Rear-Admiral Thomas L. Sprague's Task Group 77.4 and the thunder of heavy guns from battleships and cruisers of the support and bombardment groups of Vice-Admiral T. C. Kinkaid's 7th Fleet. Bombers of Task Force 38

---

[11] For details see Appendix II.

roared in from seaward to add their quota. By 0945, when the waves of landing craft from the transports swept forward to the beaches, the opposition had been driven inland and by noon a beachhead had been established. Then came the moving, dramatic moment when General MacArthur, accompanied by President Osmena of the Philippines, waded ashore and broadcast his famous speech opening with the ringing announcement 'People of the Philippines, I have returned'.

Until the invasion forces were able to advance inland, however, and establish air bases, their essential air support had to come from the decks of aircraft carriers. Though the local airfields at Leyte were quickly captured, much time was needed to make them operational. Furthermore, other Japanese airfields in the Philippines were too numerous, too close and too well linked to the home islands of Japan, whence could come reinforcements, for them to be quickly subdued, and air supremacy established. Until then the whole safety of MacArthur's troops was dependent upon the freedom of Kinkaid's and Halsey's aircraft carriers to operate in the offing. It was to strike at these and at the swarm of transports anchored in the Gulf, laden with essential supplies for the troops ashore, that on the 20th, Toyoda set his fleet in motion. On that day Kurita's 1st Striking Force arrived in Brunei Bay and set about refuelling. From Amami-O-Shima, the most northerly of the Ryukus, Shima's 2nd Striking Force sailed for the Pescadores en route for a refuelling rendezvous at Koron in the Calamian Islands, while Ozawa grimly setting out on his sacrificial task, led his Carrier Force out from the Inland Sea through the Bungo Strait. Early on the 22nd, Kurita led Force A to sea and steered northwards for the Palawan Passage between Palawan Island and the wide area of dangerous shoals to the westward. He was followed that evening by Nishimura's Force C, making for the Balabak Strait entrance to the Sulu Sea.

The first intimation that anything was afoot came to Admirals Halsey and Kinkaid at 0620 on the 23rd in a message from the U.S. submarine *Darter*. In company with the *Dace*, she had been on patrol off the southern end of the Palawan Passage when, at 0116 that morning a radar contact had been made which, as they closed at high speed, revealed itself as a large force of heavy ships in two columns with a destroyer screen. Kurita, strangely unwary, and despite a warning from his radio office that an enemy submarine had been heard transmitting close by, was advancing on a steady course at 16 knots with his heavy ships formed in two columns, 2.2 miles apart, destroyers on either beam but none screening ahead. The two submarines had little difficulty in reaching perfect firing positions. The *Darter* took the port column led by Kurita's flagship, *Atago*, with the cruiser *Takao* next astern. At the point-blank range of 980 yards she fired her six bow tubes at the *Atago*, then swung round to loose four torpedoes from her stern tubes at the *Takao*. Both cruisers were hit, the *Atago* sinking in 18 minutes; the *Takao*, heavily damaged, crawled away for Singapore with a destroyer escort. While Kurita and his staff were swimming from the sinking flagship to the destroyer *Kishinami*, the *Dace* had been squaring up to attack the starboard column. Selecting the third ship in the line, the cruiser *Maya*, she launched four torpedoes. In one tremendous explosion, the cruiser disintegrated and vanished in a cloud of spray and smoke. The remainder of the Japanese force, increasing to 24 knots, raced on to clear so unhealthy an area. Later in the day Kurita hoisted his flag in the battleship *Yamato*.

For the rest of that day, 23 October, no further contacts were made with any of the Japanese forces. Force C was crossing the Sulu Sea and by the next morning would be approaching the Mindanao Sea. Admiral Shima's force was at Koron, his destroyers topping up their fuel tanks from the cruisers in the absence of the expected tanker which had, instead, gone out to fuel Kurita's destroyers. Far to the north, Ozawa's carriers were steering south, keeping outside the range of American planes from Saipan. The time was not yet ripe for him to make his presence known. Meanwhile Halsey had sent away one of his carrier groups, Vice-Admiral John McCain's Group 1, to Ulithi to replenish. The other three groups operating some 260 miles north-west of Samar, having achieved nothing with their searches, were brought westward during the night, so as to be in a better position to reconnoitre in the morning. Group 4, close east of Leyte Gulf at daybreak on the 24th, launched a search mission which discovered Nishimura's Force C at 0905 and attacked it, slightly damaging the *Fuso* and a destroyer. Searches from Group 3, operating to the eastward of Polillo Islands found nothing to the west of Luzon and Mindoro. It was aircraft from Group 2, launched from a position east of San Bernadino Strait, that gave the all-important news of Kurita's Striking Force, skirting the southern end of Mindoro at 0812, and got the first view by any American aviator of the almost mythical monsters, *Yamato* and *Musashi*.

Kurita's impressive battle fleet was obviously the main objective for Halsey and he at once ordered his three carrier groups to concentrate on Group 2 and prepare to launch their air groups to the attack. At the same time he recalled Group 1, by this time well on its way to Ulithi. He had hardly given the order, however, when Rear-Admiral Sherman's Group 3 found themselves fully engaged beating off a series of massive raids. Dawn searches from Luzon airfields had discovered them and Admiral Fukudome had lost no time in launching his bombers and torpedo-planes with a numerous fighter escort. Sherman's Group was caught thoroughly off balance with a striking force of bombers and torpedo-planes being ranged on deck, some of his fighters away on a strafing mission against the Manila airfields and only 12 Hellcats aloft on patrol. Torpedo-planes and bombers were hastily struck below and every available fighter launched, to a total of about 50. They had 200 enemy aircraft in three groups to drive off. These were formidable odds; but the Japanese airmen, recently arrived replacements from Japan, were being thrown into battle half-trained and, though many of their bombers were engaged only by ships' gunfire as they swooped to the attack, while the fighters battled overhead, they failed to cause any damage — all, that is, except one solitary 'Judy' dive-bomber. The pilot of this plane, with consummate skill or beginner's luck, had succeeded in remaining undetected amongst the rolling overcast and rain squalls until the raid was over. Then, as the carriers were recovering fighters and refuelling them at 0938, out of a low cloud the 'Judy' dived on the *Princeton* and with deadly accuracy dropped her 550-lb. bomb squarely on the carrier's flight-deck. The pilot had little time to appreciate his handiwork, being quickly chopped out of the sky by a Hellcat from the *Langley*. But he had set in train a sequence of events of horror. Plunging down through three decks, the exploding bomb found the carrier's dreaded Achilles Heel, aviation petrol. The hangar was quickly ablaze. The flames engulfed six Avengers, their torpedoes slung beneath their bellies. At 1002 they began to explode with devastating effect, one of the eruptions hurling the after lift platform high into the air to crash back in the elevator pit. All but a nucleus of the crew to fight the raging fires were ordered to abandon ship. Destroyers stood by to pick them up, coming alongside to allow men to jump down on to their forecastles. Then the cruiser *Birmingham* came to the rescue and Captain Inglis decided to lay her alongside to windward and bring his fire-fighting equipment into play, sending volunteer fire-parties across to the stricken carrier. The cruiser *Reno* followed the *Birmingham*'s lead and remained alongside for an hour until she had to cast off to help repel a renewed air attack. The *Birmingham* also got under way when a submarine alarm was sounded. Hour after hour the fight with the flames went on and fires were, one by one, subdued. But one defied all efforts. This was near the stern and threatening a store of bombs. Nevertheless Captain Inglis steered once again to take the *Birmingham* alongside to help fight the fire and to prepare to take the *Princeton* in tow. His upper deck was packed with men as he drew alongside; and at that moment the bomb store exploded. The carrier's stern was blown off; the cruiser was little damaged, but it was aboard her that the worst horror struck as blast and steel splinters swept the crowded decks. In all 233 of her crew were killed outright, and more than 400 wounded, many of them severely. The *Princeton* was now finally abandoned, two torpedoes from the *Reno* sending her to the bottom.

While this long fight to save the *Princeton* had been going on, much had been taking place elsewhere. Further air raids, of which Sherman's Group 3 bore the brunt, had been successfully beaten off. One of them, 76 strong, had come 210 miles from Ozawa's carriers, the survivors heading afterwards for airfields ashore. Ozawa by this time was getting impatient at his enemy's failure to locate him. During the afternoon he detached the *Ise* and *Hyuga* with a screen of light forces to probe southward and at last, at 1540 this force was sighted and reported, followed an hour later by a sighting of Ozawa's carriers. The bait had been proffered and seen. How eagerly it would be taken will be seen later.

First must be told the story of what has been called the Battle of the Sibuyan Sea, one of the four major encounters which together make up the Battle of Leyte. Admiral Kurita, who would have had to be superhuman not to be shaken by the simultaneous loss of three cruisers, including his own flagship, from which he had had to swim to safety, had nevertheless pressed on. The U.S. submarine *Guitarro* shadowed his force as it steered southwards along the Mindoro coast in the early hours of the 24th, but it was not until a search plane from the carrier *Intrepid* of Group 2, as mentioned above, sighted it rounding the southern tip of Mindoro that Task Force 38 was ordered to concentrate on Group 2 and launch its striking forces. Group 3 was too busy defending itself to comply until the afternoon: Group 4 was occupied recovering the armed reconnaissance groups which had discovered and attacked Nishimura as well as a destroyer-transport unit to the west of Panay. It fell to Bogan's Group 2, therefore, to open the Battle of the Sibuyan Sea with a striking force of 12 dive-bombers, 12 torpedo-planes and an escort of 21 fighters from the *Intrepid* and *Cabot* which took off at 0910. Another strike of the same size from Group 2 took off at 1045 and a smaller one from Sherman's group 3 at 1050 during a lull between enemy raids. By the afternoon, Rear-Admiral Davison's Group 4 was able to join in with a large strike of 39 dive-bombers and torpedo-planes and 26 fighters launched at 1313, and at 1350 Group 2 returned to the attack yet again with 12 dive-bombers and three torpedo-planes.

Flying over the tranquil blue sea studded with lush, emerald islands under an almost cloudless sky, they had no difficulty in locating their target an hour's flight away. But the perfect flying weather deprived them of any cover from gunfire and at an early stage in their approach they found themselves flying through a daunting and spectacular curtain of shell-bursts. As their air strength seeped away, the Japanese had had to turn to anti-aircraft gunfire to provide defence. Not only had they crowded their ships with light machine-guns, 120 in each battleship, 90 in cruisers and 30 or more in destroyers, but they had adapted their control systems so that even the huge battleship turret guns could be brought to bear on aircraft. The shells they fired burst in pink, purple and white, ejecting phosphorus or silver balls. They proved to be more spectacular than effective, however, and, as a result of the meagreness of the fighter defence provided from the airfields of Luzon, American air losses were to be very light during the long day of battle ahead, a total of 18 being lost.

The huge battleships, *Yamato* and *Musashi*, details of which the Japanese had managed to keep secret, attracted the chief attention, the latter receiving one bomb and one torpedo from the first wave of attackers. *Yamato* and *Nagato* were both hit by bombs but their armoured bulk was little affected. Only to torpedoes, striking at their underbellies, were battleships really vulnerable and when Group 2's second strike and Group 3's merged to concentrate on the *Musashi*, around noon, putting no less than eight in her hull as well as four bombs, her fate was sealed. Power failing, she dropped astern, with the cruiser *Yone* in attendance, and turned to try to struggle back to base. So stoutly built was she that even now she might have survived had not planes from *Intrepid*, *Cabot*, *Franklin*, *Essex* and *Enterprise* concentrated on her at 1520 to hit with ten torpedoes and a number of bombs. She lay, an immobilised hulk, settling slowly deeper and listing ever more steeply until at 1935 she capsized and sank, five minutes after the order to abandon ship. In her brief career, the monstrous man-of-war had never been within sight of an enemy ship.

By this time, in the absence of the fighter protection he had expected from shore bases and which Admiral Fukudome had been expending on mainly profitless assaults on Sherman's carrier group, it had been borne in on Kurita that to continue his advance across the Sibuyan Sea in daylight was suicidal. Reporting to Toyoda that he 'considered it advisable to retire temporarily from the zone of enemy air attacks' until Fukudome's efforts had borne fruit, he turned back on to a westerly course at 1500. Already the intricate time-table of SHO-1 was going awry. Toyoda, who had steeled himself to the possible loss of the whole fleet in this last desperate effort to halt the invasion of the Philippines, was in no mood for such a cautious move. At 1925, Kurita received a message from him, 'Trusting in Divine aid, the entire force will attack'. Half an hour later he was explicitly ordered to proceed according to plan. He had, in fact, already reversed course once again at 1910 and was steering for the San Bernadino Strait. He could no longer reach Leyte Gulf at dawn as planned and as Nishimura was still steering to do. He gave Force C a rendezvous for 0900 the following morning ten miles north-east of Suluan Island.

As darkness closed down over the Philippines on 24 October, with Kurita hurrying forward at 20 knots in single line ahead to thread the intricate channels through the islands, Nishimura crossing the Mindanao Sea *en route* for the Surigao Strait between Leyte and Dinagat Island, with Shima following some 40 miles astern, the centre of interest moved to Halsey's flagship, the battleship *New Jersey* attached to Carrier Group 2. Through the long, hot hours while the Battle of the Sibuyan Sea was raging, details of its progress being extracted from the excited radio chatter of the attacking airmen, Halsey had waited impatiently for news of location of the final piece on the widespread chess board — the enemy's carrier force. Given the experience of the past three years of war during which battleships had been relegated to the auxiliary tasks of bombardment and escort, it was perhaps inevitable that the carrier force should be looked on as the enemy's king. That it had instead become a mere pawn to be sacrificed was not imagined. Halsey's instructions from Nimitz, his Commander-in-Chief, were 'to cover and support forces of the South-West Pacific', that is to say Kinkaid's 7th Fleet, comprising the amphibious fleet in the Gulf of Leyte and its naval support, the battleships and cruisers of the fire support units and above all the Escort Carrier Group under Rear-Admiral Thomas L. Sprague. For MacArthur, risking his army without air cover of its own, had been guaranteed naval air support. Halsey was also told, however, that 'in case opportunity for destruction of major portion of the enemy fleet offer or can be created, such destruction becomes the primary task'. Here were all the makings of confusion.

While Kurita's 1st Striking Force was the only major portion of the enemy fleet located, Halsey had no difficulty in construing his instructions. All efforts were concentrated on destroying it. In case it should become convenient to concentrate his battleships and cruisers to fight a surface action, Halsey signalled, at 1512, an organisational instruction that these ships would comprise Task Force 34, under Vice-Admiral Lee. This purely preparative instruction was intercepted by his fellow Fleet Commander, Kinkaid, who misconstrued it with unfortunate consequences as will appear later. By mid-afternoon, from his airmen's reports, Halsey estimated that Kurita's force had been so damaged that it was no longer a serious menace; furthermore it was apparently retreating. Thus when Ozawa's force, with the potential strength of air groups from four carriers, was finally located less than 200 miles to the northward during the afternoon, it was at once classified as the primary objective. While his own carriers were gathering in their aircraft at sundown and launching a few night-flying reconnaissance planes, Halsey pondered his next move. The alternatives of leaving Task Force 34 to guard the exit from the San Bernadino Strait either alone or with one carrier group to give it air cover were considered and rejected, the former as being too risky, the latter because Halsey wanted to take his full carrier force in annihilating strength against Ozawa. Even when a night-flying scout reported Kurita heading once again eastward at 1935, Halsey was not swayed, believing, as he said in his action report, that the 1st Striking Force had suffered 'at least four and probably five battleships torpedoed and bombed, one probably sunk; a minimum of three heavy cruisers torpedoed and others bombed; one light cruiser sunk; one destroyer probably sunk and four damaged'. The proclivity of airmen of all nations to exaggerate, in all honesty, their achievements in battle can rarely have had more baleful consequences. At 2000 Halsey gave the order to the three carrier groups with him to head northwards to attack Ozawa at dawn. Admiral McCain was ordered to bring his Group 1 back to rejoin at his best speed. At the same time he signalled to Kinkaid: 'Am proceeding north with three groups to attack enemy carrier force at dawn.'

Kinkaid, who had organised the six old battleships, four heavy and four light cruisers and 21 destroyers of his bombardment and fire support groups into a battle force under Rear-Admiral J. B. Oldendorf to block the exit of the Surigao Strait against the approach of Nishimura's and Shima's forces, presumed that this message meant that Halsey was going north with his three carrier groups, leaving the battleships of Task Force 34 on guard off the San Bernadino Strait. The situation seemed well in hand, therefore. The outcome of the night was awaited with quiet confidence. Soon after midnight, from patrolling motor torpedo boats, came the expected report of Force C approaching the southern entrance to Surigao Strait. At that moment, unknown to any on the Allied side, Kurita was leading through the San Bernadino Strait. While he was pressing on, out into the Philippine Sea to turn south down the east coast of Samar, the second of the four separate actions which make up the Battle of Leyte was taking place in the Surigao Strait.

Nishimura had no illusions as to the daunting odds facing him in Leyte Gulf. A scout seaplane launched from the cruiser *Mogami* had reported at noon on the 24th that six battleships as well as numerous cruisers and destroyers were guarding the invasion force. Worse odds, however, had been faced and overcome in night battles in the past and there seemed no reason to suppose it could not happen again. But the situation was hardly comparable to those which had arisen in the Solomon Sea. Rear-Admiral Oldendorf was able to draw up his ships in battle array to bring the whole of his immense radar-controlled gunpower to bear on the head of any enemy force threading the Surigao Strait. Manoeuvring would be minimal and opportunities would hardly arise for the Japanese to bring their torpedoes into play. No doubt such matters were given due consideration by Nishimura and by Shima following him; but at that moment of final decision on the fate of the Empire and with Toyoda's order in front of him for 'all forces to attack', doubts could only be brushed aside.

So it was that, at 2250 on 24 October, a section of three motor torpedo boats operating off the island of Bohol, following up a radar contact, sighted the dark bulk of Nishimura's battleships against the faint glimmer of the night sky. A brief melee ensued during which the ambition of the motor torpedo boats to strike a blow by delivering a torpedo attack overrode the more vital task of getting away an enemy report. The attack failed, but one of the motor torpedo boats, pierced by a shell which knocked out her radio set but failed to explode, managed to contact a neighbouring section through which the alarm reached Oldendorf half-an-hour after midnight. As Nishimura pressed steadily on, section after section of motor torpedo boats attacked but were uniformly unsuccessful. By 0215 his squadron had brushed past the last one and was in the Surigao Strait. In the lead were the destroyers *Michishio*, *Asagumo*, *Shigure* and *Yamagumo*. Two miles astern came the flagship *Yamashiro* with the *Fuso* and *Mogami* following at half-mile intervals. Through water glassy calm in the darkness which seemed all the more dense on account of the humid, tropical heat and the intermittent flashes of lightning, they drove forward at 20 knots. It was now the turn of Oldendorf's destroyer flotillas to go into action.

The first to do so was Destroyer Squadron 54, commanded by Captain Coward, five ships of which had been thrown forward as pickets. Coward's plan was to lead three of them — *Remey*, *McGowan* and *Melvin* — down the east side of the strait while Commander Philips with the *McDermut* and *Monssen* advanced down the opposite side to deliver simultaneous

257

attacks from either bow. From reports coming in from the motor torpedo boats, Coward plotted the enemy's progress and at 0230 set his two divisions in motion. A few minutes later radar contact was made at 18 miles range. Racing forward at 30 knots, laying a smoke-screen behind which to retire, Coward's division reached the firing position first at 0300 and turning to port in succession in the glare of searchlights, launched 27 torpedoes before retiring independently on zig-zag courses behind the smoke. Star shells blazed overhead and a heavy volume of gunfire followed them; but night gunnery was not the *forte* of the Japanese with their still primitive radar, and not a ship was hit. Nishimura took no evasive action and never knew that the *Fuso* astern of him had been torpedoed and so seriously damaged that she dropped out of line and came to a halt to survive for only 30 minutes more, after which she broke into two burning halves and finally sank.

Meanwhile the *McDermut* and *Monssen* had also fired 20 torpedoes at 0310. Nishimura swerved briefly away but this did him little good. His flagship was hit, though not stopped, by one torpedo. His destroyers suffered worst, the *Yamagumo* blowing up in a spectacular explosion seen 20 miles away in the *Louisville*, Oldendorf's flagship; the *Michishio* was brought to a stop in a sinking condition; the *Asagumo*, with her bow blown off, retired painfully from the fray. Roles had, indeed, been exchanged since those desperate nights off Savo Island. Nishimura, ignorant of the disaster which had befallen the *Fuso*, reported to Kurita and Shima the presence of enemy destroyers and the loss of two of his own with minor damage to the *Yamashiro*, and pressed blindly on.

Loosed on him by Oldendorf, the six destroyers of Captain McManes' Squadron 24, which had been screening the cruisers of the right flank, were already approaching. Advancing in two sections, McManes with the *Hutchins*, *Daly* and *Bache*, hugging the eastern shore of the strait, overshot the best torpedo-firing position and the 15 torpedoes they launched in their first salvoes achieved nothing. The other division, comprising the Australian Tribal Class destroyer *Arunta* and the U.S. destroyers *Killen* and *Beale*, led by Commander Buchanan, R.A.N., in the *Arunta*, reached a good position on the enemy's port bow and at 0325 launched 14 torpedoes one of which hit the *Yamashiro*, slowing her temporarily to five knots. The Japanese squadron was beginning to break up in confusion. And now the nine destroyers of the left flank, Captain Smoot's Squadron 56, were streaking forward to get in an attack before the gun battle, now imminent, should begin. They advanced in three sections, of which two duly launched their torpedoes from either bow of the enemy and sheered away unharmed by the Japanese gunfire or that of the Allied cruisers whose shells began to roar overhead at 0352. As they fired, however, the enemy ships, flinching from the appalling hail of shells now raising an impenetrable barrier of water spouts ahead of them, sheered away, turning for a while on to a westerly course before retreating southwards. Captain Smoot's own section. *Albert W. Grant*, *Richard P. Leary* and *Newcomb*, coming down the centre of the strait from right ahead of the enemy, waited to estimate the *Yamashiro*'s new course, and turned parallel to it before firing. In doing so they closed to 6,200 yards and ensured achieving two torpedo hits on the battleship. But it also brought them under heavy gunfire both from the enemy and from the gun batteries of some of Oldendorf's cruisers. The *Leary* and *Newcomb* bore a charmed life as they zig-zagged away northwards; but the *Grant* took no less than 18 hits, the majority by six-inch shells from the American light cruisers and within a few minutes was a shattered, stationary wreck, with more than 120 casualties. She was rescued, however, by the *Newcomb* which came alongside and towed her clear.

The 'friendly' gunfire which smothered the *Grant* had opened at 0351. Admiral Oldendorf had ranged his forces across the exit from the Surigao Strait in three squadrons. His battleships were arrayed in single line ahead — *Mississippi* (flagship of Rear-Admiral Weyler), *California, Tennessee, Pennsylvania, West Virginia* and *Maryland*. Some four miles further into the strait were the cruisers divided into a Right Flank squadron — *Phoenix* (flag of Rear-Admiral Berkey), *Boise* and the Australian cruiser *Shropshire* — and a Left Flank squadron — *Louisville* (flag of Rear-Admiral Oldendorf), *Portland, Minneapolis, Denver* and *Columbia*. At 0351 both squadrons of cruisers opened fire at ranges between 15,800 yards and 16,600 yards — 30 six-inch in continuous rapid fire and eight eight-inch guns from the Right Flank, 60 eight-inch from the Left Flank. They were joined two minutes later by three of the battleships which, equipped with up-to-date radar equipment, were able to identify a target. A fantastic stream of tracer projectiles began roaring through the air to converge on the head of the Japanese formation. It is not to be wondered at that Nishimura's ships at once sheered away from this daunting display as the forest of splashes rose ahead and around them. Both *Yamashiro* and *Mogami* were hit again and again and set on fire. Only the destroyer *Shigure*, which turned away to starboard ran out of the danger zone and escaped after suffering a single hit which passed through her without exploding. It was now that the *Yamashiro* received the two torpedoes from Smoot's squadron. They sealed her fate and at 0419 her fires were extinguished as she capsized and sank, taking with her Admiral Nishimura and all but a handful of her crew. The *Mogami*, having fired torpedoes at the retiring American destroyers as she turned, limped away southwards, burning fiercely, to be further hit by shells from McManes' destroyer division as they ran past on a retirement course.

At 0409 the flash and thunder of gunfire died away at Oldendorf's order to cease fire to allow his own destroyers to get clear. By the time the order to resume firing was given at 0419, the *Mogami* and *Shigure* were out of range. Meanwhile, coming up from the south was Admiral Shima's 2nd Striking Force. Shima had made no attempt to get in touch with Nishimura or to join forces with him. The flicker of gun flashes reflected from the northern sky with an intermittent ominous glare from burning ships sent him hurrying forward at full speed. He had been able to follow the fortunes of Force C to some extent from intercepted radio messages, but the last had been at 0330 when the *Yamashiro* was still in action and no mention had been made of the catastrophe to the *Fuso*. Motor torpedo boats had attacked as his force was entering the strait and *PT-137* had scored the only success by these craft by torpedoing the light cruiser *Abukuma*. Severely damaged she was left to limp away.[12] Pressing on up the Surigao Strait, his four destroyers scouting ahead of his two heavy cruisers, the *Nachi* leading the *Ashigara*, Shima hurried past the two burning halves of the *Fuso*. A few minutes later the burning *Mogami* was identified and the *Shigure*, away to starboard, but no details of what had happened to the remainder of Force C were passed to the *Nachi*. That this could only have been catastrophic was by now clear to Shima, however, and when his primitive radar registered two contacts on the starboard bow beyond the pall of smoke left by the retiring enemy destroyers, he ordered the two cruisers to turn to starboard and fire eight torpedoes each

---

[12] The *Abukuma* reached Dapitan Harbour, Mindanao, only to be sunk by air attack two days later.

261

at this target, which may have been the Hibuson Islands. He then recalled his destroyers and turned south on a retiring course. As he ran past the *Mogami*, she suddenly picked up speed and steered to form up with Shima's cruisers, only to collide heavily with the *Nachi*, damaging her aft and causing her to reduce to 18 knots. At this speed the whole force steered south for a while. It may be that this unexpected access of strength reinspired the understandably faint heart of the Japanese Admiral, for he now reversed course and once again stood north up the strait. Discretion soon reasserted itself, however, and as the first streaks of dawn were lighting the sky, he gave up and led away in flight.

It was as well for him that he did so. By this time Oldendorf had started in pursuit and at 0520 was able to make out the Japanese ships in the early light. *Louisville*, *Portland* and *Denver* engaged them scoring further hits on the shattered *Mogami*, which continued, incredibly, to make good 18 knots though she was ablaze from bow to stern. Oldendorf now called off the chase, leaving the Japanese ships to the attention of the motor torpedo boats waiting for them. They escaped without further damage, however, and hit back fiercely at the motor boats to damage one and drive off the remainder. One last flare up was to bring the Battle of the Surigao Strait to an end when, after sunrise, the wreck of the destroyer *Asagumo* was discovered and brought under fire by two American destroyers. She fought back gallantly with her after gun until the cruisers *Denver* and *Columbia* arrived to smother her with six-inch gunfire and send her to the bottom. It was left to naval aircraft from the escort carriers off Leyte Gulf to take up the chase. They finally brought the seemingly indestructible *Mogami* to a halt. Her crew was taken off by the destroyer *Akebono* which sank her with a torpedo. The *Nachi* and *Ashigara* with Shima's destroyers and the *Shigure* escaped.

12. LEYTE: SAMAR AND CAPE ENGAÑO

Kinkaid's 7th Fleet had successfully destroyed one arm of the pincers designed by the SHO plan to crush the Allied Expeditionary Force off Leyte. There was a feeling of much satisfaction abroad, as the sun climbed up into a blue sky on the morning of 25 October. The consternation was all the greater when at 0700 an anguished emergency message in plain language was received from Rear-Admiral Clifton Sprague, commanding the northern group of escort carriers supporting the landings on Leyte, reporting himself under fire from enemy battleships and beseeching assistance.

The 16 carriers forming Task Group 77.4 were of the type variously nicknamed 'Woolworth' or 'Jeep' carriers, the earlier examples being converted merchantmen, though later ships were specially constructed. Devised originally by the British to provide air escort for Atlantic convoys, in which capacity the first, H.M.S. *Audacity*, had a brief but most successful career in the latter part of 1941, they had soon proved themselves invaluable in providing air support for landing operations until airfields ashore became available. For this purpose each of the American escort carriers operated up to 18 Wildcat fighters and a dozen Avengers, normally armed with bombs, though torpedoes for them were also available. It was in the role of air-support for the Leyte landings that Task Force 77.4 was deployed in three self-contained task units.

Unit 1, southernmost of the three off northern Mindanao, commanded by the group commander, Rear-Admiral Thomas Sprague, comprised four escort carriers with a screen of three destroyers and four destroyer escorts, the latter being little ships primarily equipped and trained for anti-submarine duties though mounting three torpedo tubes as well as three five-inch guns. Unit 2, commanded by Rear-Admiral Stump, with five carriers and escort, was stationed off the entrance to Leyte Gulf. Finally, off Samar, to the northward, was Unit 3, from which Rear-Admiral Clifton Sprague had sounded the alarm. It comprised the carriers *Fanshaw Bay* (flagship), *St Lo*, *White Plains*, *Kalinin Bay*, *Kitkun Bay* and *Gambier Bay* with the destroyers *Hoel*, *Heerman* and *Johnston* and the destroyer escorts *Dennis*, *Butler*, *Raymond* and *Roberts*.

Aboard the escort carriers the night of 24-25 October had passed quietly. From Kinkaid had come down the order to fly dawn searches which would cover the San Bernadino Strait and its approaches, eastern and western. This was simply a precaution in support of Lee's battle force — Task Force 34 — which he assumed was in station off the eastern exit. The *Ommaney Bay* of Unit 2 was selected to provide the searches, but for some reason the last of the ten Avengers did not get off until almost 0700. By that time their mission had been made redundant by the startling sight from Clifton Sprague's flagship of battleship mastheads on the horizon. At 0646 the *Fanshaw Bay* had radar and radio evidence of the approach of an enemy unit. A minute later it was dramatically confirmed by Ensign Jansen, pilot of a plane on anti-submarine patrol, who gave the startling news that he was looking down on a force of four Japanese battleships, eight cruisers and a number of destroyers only 20 miles north of Unit 3.

Hardly able to credit the report, Clifton Sprague was quickly convinced by the sight of the pagoda-like top hamper of Japanese battleships on the northern horizon. He at once ordered his unit to turn easterly and work up to their full speed of 1½ knots. On that course, though not fully into the wind, which was blowing from east-northeast, strike aircraft could be launched. Frenzied efforts to get them armed and ranged were made. Before any could be flown off, Kurita's huge guns had opened fire from beyond the horizon and at 0659 the first tall splashes, coloured with identifying dye, were leaping from the water astern of the *Fanshaw Bay* and the *White Plains*.

Surprise was complete. The thin-skinned and lightly armed escort carriers had been caught by four fast and powerful battleships and six heavy cruisers. Many of their strike aircraft were airborne, engaged on support missions armed with general purpose bombs or on antisubmarine patrols carrying depth charges. To launch others, they had to steam almost at right angles to the direction of the enemy. Nevertheless their aircraft must be launched at all costs. Except for the doubtful ability of their few, widely-spread destroyers to hold off the enemy with torpedo attacks, the aircraft were their only defence. The battleships and cruisers of the 7th Fleet were all of three hours' steaming away in the Surigao Strait. Halsey's mighty Task Force 38, still in company with Lee's Task Force 34, was some 300 miles to the northward, its air groups at that very moment swarming to attack Ozawa's decoys.

Until Clifton Sprague's appeal for assistance, Admiral Kinkaid had been quietly confident that Task Force 34 was on guard off the San Bernadino Strait. So confident had he been that Halsey was taking care of Kurita that only the most meagre night air reconnaissance had been ordered, which in the event never came within detection range of the Japanese force. But now, in quick succession, signal after urgent signal was made to Halsey, starting with a plain language message at 0707, giving him the startling news of enemy battleships and cruisers off Samar. The information that the 7th Fleet battleships were short of ammunition was quickly followed by a request for Lee to proceed at top speed to the rescue. Clifton Sprague added to the shower of alarming signals falling on Halsey's chart table and, at 0829 Kinkaid reported the 'situation critical'. From Pearl Harbour came a tart demand to know the whereabouts of Task Force 34. It was all to no avail. Lee could not reach the scene in time to affect the issue. Halsey ordered Admiral McCain's Group 1 to assist, but it was still hundreds of miles to the eastward and the earliest time at which his planes could intervene would be 1300. Task Group 77.4 was left to protect itself as best it might. The situation in which it found itself, if staged on the tactical table of a War Game, would have spelt annihilation. What actually occurred illustrates the imponderable effect of the personal touch upon theoretical odds.

Strangely enough, Kurita was far from elated at the sight that had greeted him. The long, previous day, spent cowering under the swoop of carrier planes, during which the splendid *Musashi* had been destroyed for the price of a mere handful of planes shot down, was affecting his nerve. And now the horizon to the south east was broken by the shape of aircraft carriers launching planes. That they were little auxiliary carriers never occurred to him. Nevertheless he gave the order for General Chase. His fleet had been in the act of changing from its night cruising formation in columns to the usual circular anti-aircraft formation. His ships now surged ahead, therefore, at their best speed, acting for the most part independently and in some confusion, except for two light cruisers and 12 destroyers which were ordered to the rear.

Clifton Sprague's Unit 3, running easterly at its top speed of 17½ knots, launching planes, was formed in a rough circle with the *Fanshaw Bay* and *White Plains* nearest to the enemy and receiving the brunt of the enemy's fire. The salvoes were creeping steadily closer. The *White Plains* was thrice straddled by 14-inch salvoes and savagely shaken and, as Sprague was to recall later, 'At this point it did not appear that any of our ships could survive another five minutes'. No hits had been suffered, however, when the carriers ran out of the sunlight and the all too clear visibility into the cover of a rain squall at 0706. All ships were adding to the smother with black funnel smoke. The accuracy of the enemy's fire deteriorated for the time being. Nevertheless, desperate measures were called for, and at 0716, as the carriers were beginning to emerge from the rain, Sprague gave the order for his destroyers to attack. Three destroyers against Kurita's powerful fleet spelt fearful odds. One of them, the *Johnston*, nearest to the enemy and laying down a smoke-screen, had already opened gunfire on the cruiser *Kumano* scoring a number of hits but calling down a concentrated fire from several ships in return. At the order to attack, her captain, Commander Ernest Evans, steered at once for the cruiser and at 10,000 yards range launched ten torpedoes. As the *Johnston* regained the shelter of her smoke-screen, her crew felt the thump of underwater explosions as one or more torpedoes hit. Emerging a minute later from the smoke, her crew had the satisfaction of seeing the bow of the *Kumano* burning furiously and, in fact, the cruiser had been crippled and knocked out of the fight. So far the destroyer had escaped scot-free; but now came fearful retribution, as two salvoes of shells struck. Heavily damaged, with many of her crew killed in the after boiler-room and engine-room, which were knocked out, and three of her officers killed on the bridge, where Evans had his clothes above the waist blown off and lost two fingers, the stout little ship survived for the time being. Gaining a respite as rain and smoke shrouded her again, her injuries were sufficiently patched to allow her to pick up a speed of 17 knots and get three of her five-inch guns back into action.

At about the time the *Johnston* was launching her torpedoes, her divisional leader, the *Hoel*, was also racing into action with the battleship *Kongo*. As she steered for her mighty opponent, all guns blazing, she was hit on the bridge but was able to close to 9,000 yards to launch half of her outfit of ten torpedoes. The battleship avoided them by a sharp turn away and the *Hoel*, turning to escape, was hit by several shells which slowed her down and, jamming her steering engine with the rudder hard-over to starboard, set her back on a course for the enemy before steering control was regained. Commander Kintberger, in spite of having three of his five guns knocked out and one engine wrecked, now headed back into the fight, being joined by the *Heermann*. Selecting the cruiser *Haguro* for target launched the remainder of his torpedoes at her. He was rewarded by the sight of columns of water leaping up the cruiser's side apparently indicating torpedo hits. From Japanese records these torpedoes missed; they were not wasted, nevertheless. Beyond the cruisers were the battleships, and at 0754 from Kurita's flagship *Yamato* their tracks were sighted. The battleship turned away to port to parallel them, and, finding herself sandwiched between tracks on either side, was forced to continue to steer away for nearly ten minutes. By the time she could turn back she had run far out of the battle, taking the Commander-in-Chief out of touch with events.

The *Heermann*, whose captain, Commander Amos Hathaway, had brought her from her screening position on the far side of the carrier formation, also took the *Haguro* for her target and fired seven torpedoes which were avoided. As she was doing so, out of the smoke to the northward appeared the battleship

Kongo with the *Haruna* astern of her and Hathaway launched his last three torpedoes at the latter. At about the same time the little destroyer escorts joined in the melee, having sought permission from Clifton Sprague. The *Roberts* trailed along 3,000 yards behind *Hoel* and *Heermann*, where she was joined by the *Johnston* which, with no torpedoes left, decided to give gunfire support. Taking advantage of the smoke screen laid by the destroyers, the *Roberts* pressed her attack close and fired her three torpedoes at the enemy cruisers. None of these torpedoes hit, but like those which fortuitously drove the *Yamato* out of the fight, they were having their effect, forcing the enemy ships to sheer away and the destroyers themselves were drawing fire that would otherwise have been falling on the carriers. All four ships had now shot their bolt and turned to retire. The *Heermann*, *Roberts* and *Johnston*, guns blazing, jinking through the splashes, escaped scatheless — for the time being. The crippled *Hoel*, however, had not the speed to escape. Concentrated on by several enemy ships, she was slowly, remorselessly beaten to a wreck. At 0835 she was abandoned and 20 minutes later went to the bottom.

While the *Roberts* was attacking in company with the larger ships, her sister ships, *Raymond* and *Dennis*, raced in individually to launch their torpedoes at the Japanese cruisers. Forced to divide their fire amongst so many targets and to swerve back and forth to avoid the torpedoes, the cruisers failed to hit either of the destroyer escorts before they retired, the *Raymond* by herself, the *Dennis* joining the *Heermann*, *Johnston* and *Roberts*.

All these intricate high-speed manoeuvres in and out of smoke clouds and rain squalls, which defy any clear pictorial display and during which hair-breadth escapes from collision occurred, had taken less than 45 minutes. With all torpedoes expended, except for three in the *John C. Butler* which had not yet got into action, the escort force was now heading back towards the carriers, laying smoke to screen them and harassing the advancing enemy ships with five-inch gunfire. The doomed *Hoel*, trailing far behind, was near her heroic end.

Only one torpedo hit had been achieved, that which put the *Kumano* out of the fight. But the Japanese heavy ships, in avoiding others aimed at them and in turning their guns on to the destroyers as they dashed in and out of smoke and rain to snap like terriers at their powerful opponents, had given the carriers a breathing space. It was taken advantage of to launch planes as fast as possible as Sprague's ships ran to the eastward under cover of the rain storm, and then swung southerly as soon as they emerged at about 0739. By this time nearly all operational planes had taken off. Without hesitation they flew straight for the enemy to deliver individual attacks, bombing and strafing to distract their attention from the defenceless carriers. A bomb hit the heavy cruiser *Suzuya* reducing her speed to 20 knots, leaving her lagging behind the running fight. As the carriers, in their roughly circular formation, fled southwards at their meagre top speed of 17½ knots, belching black smoke from their funnels and white chemical smoke from their sterns which gave the ships in the van some intermittent cover, the heavy cruisers *Haguro, Tone, Chokai* and *Chikuma* were coming up on the port quarter. Astern were the battleships and the remainder of the cruisers, while on the starboard quarter were the Japanese flotillas waiting for an opportunity to move in to attack with torpedoes.

The range was remorselessly closing and, in spite of the distraction offered by the American destroyers and aircraft, the Japanese gunfire was increasing in accuracy and volume. The two rear carriers, *Kalinin Bay* and *Gambier Bay* bore the brunt of it. The former was the first to be hit, at 0750, while the destroyer attacks were at their height. During the next hour she suffered no less than 13 hits by eight-inch shells, but heroic work by damage repair parties kept her in action. The *Fanshaw Bay* and the *White Plains* were also hit but not seriously damaged, while the *St Lo*, on the starboard quarter, getting the benefit of the destroyers' smoke-screens and the *Kitkun Bay*, the most southerly of the circular formation, escaped unharmed. It was the *Gambier Bay* nearest to the Japanese advanced heavy cruisers, which was to play the part of scapegoat. For a while she successfully dodged the slow, deliberate, long-range fire of the cruisers. But by 0810 the range had fallen to 10,000 yards and the eight-inch shells began to strike home with increasing regularity and cumulative damage. With a boiler-room and engine-room holed and flooded, her speed fell away and she was left behind, listing and burning, to suffer the full fury of the cruisers' gunfire.

To the *Gambier Bay*'s aid came the destroyers *Johnston* and *Heermann* to add selfless gallantry to the zestful dash with which they had gone earlier into the attack. With only three of her guns in action, in local control, the *Johnston* steered for the *Chikuma*, which was concentrating on the crippled carrier, closing to 6,000 yards and scoring five hits on her. The *Chikuma* refused to be diverted, however, and ignored the *Johnston*'s efforts. When the *Heermann*, up to now undamaged, also opened fire on the *Chikuma*, however, the cruiser was forced to transfer some of her armament on to her tormentors.

Further help was on its way, too. Clifton Sprague had ordered the destroyer escorts on his starboard side to join in the desperate defence of the carriers. The *Roberts* and *Raymond* were already in action and the *Butler* and *Dennis* now joined them to challenge the *Chikuma* and the other cruisers following her, *Haguro*, *Chokai* and *Tone*. Black smoke streaming from their funnels to screen the fleeing carriers as best they could, they brought their puny, individual gun armaments into concentrated play to draw off the enemy's fire. They inevitably paid the price. The *Dennis* was first to suffer with her guns knocked out by direct hits which forced her to retire. At almost the same moment the *Roberts* was smothered by a hail of eight-inch shells and then staggered under the devastating explosion of one of the few 14-inch salvoes from the battleships to score. Shattered and burning she came to a halt to be abandoned a few minutes before she rolled over on to her beam ends and sank.

But for all the little ships' gallant efforts, the *Gambier Bay* could not be saved. As the enemy cruisers came on into point-blank range, she was hammered to a wreck. At 0850 she was abandoned and 17 minutes later she capsized and sank. The situation of Clifton Sprague's carrier force now seemed more than ever desperate, with the Japanese cruisers and battleships closing in for the kill; and now four enemy destroyers led by the light cruiser *Yahagi* came racing forward for a torpedo attack. There seemed nothing to stop them. The *Hoel* was sinking, the *Roberts* was finished. The remainder of the escorts were engaging the cruisers. But from one of them the new threat was sighted. This was the *Johnston*. Commander Evans at once steered his battered ship to intercept, engaging first the *Yahagi*, scoring a number of hits. The light cruiser turned sharply away and the *Johnston*'s guns were shifted on to the leading destroyer. To Evans' astonished triumph the enemy destroyers now sheered away also and the whole squadron fired their torpedoes at long range. By the time these torpedoes caught up with the fleeing carriers they were near the end of their run and were slowing down, and coming to the surface. An Avenger dived on one threatening the *Kalinin Bay* and exploded it with machine-gun fire. Another, in the carrier's wake, was diverted by a shot from her single five-inch gun. The remainder ran harmlessly on a parallel course. The *Johnston*'s gallant defiance had now to be paid for, however. The Japanese, browbeaten into a premature attack, concentrated their gunfire on to the lone destroyer. Sandwiched between the frustrated destroyer squadron on one side and the Japanese cruisers on the other, the *Johnston* 'desperately traded shots with one group and then the other' as her First Lieutenant was later to record. Hits multiplied and damage accumulated. Until the one remaining engine-room was finally wrecked and the ship came to a stop, Evans continued to con her from the quarter deck, passing his orders down to where the rudder was being worked by hand. The Japanese destroyers now closed in and circled, pouring in a heavy fire at close range. As the *Johnston* sank, the captain of the Japanese destroyer which had delivered the last fatal salvo stood at the salute in honour of a very gallant foe. The casualties were grievous, indeed, with only 141 saved out of a complement of 328. Commander Evans was not amongst the rescued.

While this tragic but heroic epic was being enacted, the battle off Samar was approaching its amazing climax. During the two hours that the escorts had been so desperately defending the carriers against seemingly overwhelming odds, the aircraft of the two northern carrier units had been harassing the enemy with equal gallantry and persistence. Their chief problem had been to get themselves refuelled and re-armed during the battle, those from Sprague's Unit 3 being unable to land on their own carriers which were fleeing down wind, while many of the aircraft from Admiral Stump's Unit 2 were away on support missions and unsuitably armed when the alarm was sounded.

What occurred was a miracle of improvisation with Sprague's planes landing on Unit 2 carriers to pick up bombs and torpedoes or going to the newly prepared Tacloban airfield ashore, while Stump's planes were hastily gathered in to be re-armed for shipping strikes. The results achieved by airmen only partially trained for such tasks were remarkable. So long as bombs and torpedoes were available the Avengers returned again and again to the attack and Wildcats swooped to strafe and harass. From Stump's Unit 2, torpedo-planes flew to launch no less than 49 torpedoes, fighters dropped hundreds of bombs — from 500 pounds downwards — and sent salvoes of rockets into bridges and control positions. When there was nothing more to throw at the enemy, the Avengers returned to make dummy attacks, while the Wildcats distracted attention with machine-gun fire. Time was what Sprague needed — time to retire under the cover of Oldendorf's big guns which he hoped were coming to the rescue, time for McCain's massive air-power to enter the battle. Time was what the destroyers' 'forlorn hopes' and the Avengers' attacks, real as well as feint, were gaining by distracting the enemy's fire and diverting him from the chase. They made impressive claims of actual hits, indeed; but, as so often, these have to be much reduced when analysed.

Even so, between them, escorts and aircraft inflicted much solid damage. The *Kumano* had been stopped by a destroyer's torpedo, the *Suzuya* by a bomb, and judging by her ultimate fate, must have been further damaged by later air attacks. And towards 0900 two more of the Japanese cruisers, *Chikuma* and *Chokai*, began to succumb to the repeated damage they had suffered, perhaps from destroyers' torpedoes or guns, perhaps from aerial torpedoes and bombs, or a combination of them all. It has been impossible to disentangle the records to gain a clear picture, but Japanese reports mention the *Chokai*, hit repeatedly by shells and her engines knocked out at 0815. Fifteen minutes later four Avengers led by Commander Fowler of the *Kitkun Bay* swooped from cloud cover to plaster her with bombs. Under the triumphant airmen's eyes she blew up and sank. At about the same time the *Chikuma*, already much battered by the destroyers' gunfire, was torpedoed by Avengers, probably from Stump's Unit 2, and she, too, went to the bottom.

Nevertheless it seemed at this time, that for all their gallant defence, a massacre of the carriers of Unit 3 was about to take place. The two remaining heavy cruisers, *Haguro* and *Tone*, had closed to a killing range of 10,000 yards and, racing ahead on the carrier squadron's port side were in a position to herd them back into the jaws of Kurita's battleships which were still firing from astern. It seemed a miracle that Sprague's carriers, other than the unlucky *Gambier Bay* had survived so long. *Fanshaw Bay*, *White Plains* and *Kalinin Bay* had all been hit. No vital spot had yet been found; but such luck could not go on. Then, suddenly at 0915, to the astonishment of the hard-pressed, almost despairing Americans, the surviving Japanese cruisers were seen to swing away, abandoning their now easy prey and retire. Kurita, still far astern of the running fight as a result of the *Yamato*'s long flight from the American destroyers' torpedoes, and unaware of the true position, had called his scattered forces to rejoin him. Still believing that Sprague's little ships and those of Stump's unit which had been sighted, hull down, on the south-eastern horizon from the *Yamato*'s mast-head, were fleet carriers of Halsey's 3rd Fleet, he had decided to concentrate his fleet while he considered what next to do. For the next three hours he hesitated, steering for a time towards Leyte Gulf while trying to estimate from the flood of intercepted American signals the opposition he could expect, and setting this alongside the grim news of the fate of Nishimura's force and the absence of any word from Ozawa. At 1236 he threw in the sponge, turning north for the San Bernadino Strait, though expecting to have to fight his way past an enemy force which had been wrongly reported in that direction.

Clifton Sprague's ordeal was not over, nevertheless. Giving thanks for what he was to describe as 'the definite partiality of Almighty God', he had led his force south and by 1050 had been able to turn into the north-easterly wind to recover planes when his new-found peace was shattered as, apparently from nowhere, Zeros were suddenly plummeting down. One of them, choosing the *Kitkun Bay* for its target, dived at the bridge firing its machine-guns and, making no effort to pull out of its dive, crashed the port side of the flight deck and bounced into the sea. As it did so, the bomb it carried exploded. At the same time two dived on the *Fanshaw Bay* and two on the *White Plains*. Caught in a concentrated cross-fire of 40-mm. machine-guns, three fell flaming into the sea. The fourth sheered away and dived on the *St Lo*, plunging squarely on to her flight deck through which it broke to burst in flames in the hangar. As bombs and torpedoes on the hangar deck exploded, the ship was rent asunder with huge sections together with entire planes being hurled high in the air. Within 30 minutes the *St Lo*, burning fiercely, had sunk.

Clifton Sprague's squadron had added its first experience of a 'Kamikaze' suicide attack to the events of this action-packed day. Away to the south, Thomas Sprague's Unit 1 had already received the very first of these desperate Japanese efforts to compensate for the lack of skill of their surviving airmen who had to be thrown into battle half-trained. Arriving overhead undetected while Unit 1 was launching planes to go to the assistance of Unit 3, four Zeros had screamed down in vertical dives. The first, enjoying maximum surprise, before any guns could be brought to bear on it, crashed through the flight deck to the *Santee*, the explosion of its bomb causing 43 casualties, blowing a huge hole and setting off the deadly fires to which all carriers were so fearfully vulnerable. But good damage control and fearless fire-fighting amidst flames threatening bombs and depth-charges in the hangar, saved her. Within ten minutes the fire was out. Then, as though the *Santee* had not had her full share of calamity, she was shaken by an underwater explosion. The Japanese submarine *I-56*, taking advantage of the preoccupation with air attack, had hit her with a torpedo. The *Santee*, however, a converted tanker, was saved by the multiple subdivision of her hull and was not seriously damaged. Meanwhile two other Kamikaze had been shot down, but a fourth crashed on the flight deck of the *Suwannee*. In spite of large holes torn out of her flight and hangar decks, however, the carrier's crew were able to repair her sufficiently to resume flight operations within two hours.

The Kamikazes now turned their attentions to Unit 3 with the initial calamitous results described earlier. At 1110 came a second attack in which the *Kalinin Bay* took two Kamikazes, one on her flight deck and one on her superstructure, but survived with extensive damage. The ordeal of the escort-carriers was now, at last, over for the day. Not only was the enemy's air effort for the time being spent, but air-strikes from Admiral McCain's Task Group 1, flown off from the carriers *Hancock*, *Hornet* and *Wasp* 340 miles away at 1030, were approaching to occupy Kurita's attention and speed him on his retirement course. Kurita, now reformed, was still under attack by the indomitable airmen of Clifton Sprague's unit, who, flying through a daunting concentration of gunfire, managed to hit the battleship *Nagato* and the cruiser *Tone*, when the 52 bombers and 48 escorting Hellcats from Task Group 1 arrived at 1316. A second strike was made during the afternoon and, though little damage was achieved by either, they confirmed Kurita in his determination to retire. Three of his cruisers had been lost during the day (the *Suzuya* succumbed to her bomb damage at 1322). His experiences of the previous day convinced him that annihilation would be his fate if he were to remain within striking distance of the 3rd Fleet carriers. By nightfall he was entering the San Bernadino Strait.

Meanwhile, during the night of 24-25 October, which saw the destruction of Nishimura's force in the Surigao Strait, and while Kurita was threading his way through the San Bernadino Strait, Halsey with three carrier Task Groups, 38.2, 38.3 and 38.4 (which incorporated within them Vice-Admiral Lee's battleship Task Force 34 until such time as it should be detached), was driving northwards, bent on launching strike forces at first light. Ozawa's carrier force had been at last located during the previous afternoon, much to the satisfaction of the Japanese admiral who had intercepted the American scout plane's report. During the night he recalled the detachment sent south to attract the enemy's attention and himself steered south-east for a rendezvous with it at dawn.

At midnight, Halsey, who up to this time had kept the tactical command of Task Force 38 in his own hand, delegated it to Marc Mitscher. An hour later radar-equipped Avengers took off from the *Independence* to regain contact with the enemy, lost since the previous afternoon. By 0235 on the 25th they were in touch with both sections of the Japanese force. The position they gave was considerably in error making it appear that the enemy was only 90 miles ahead, instead of the true distance of 210 miles, and that if Ozawa maintained his south-easterly course, contact would occur before daylight. Task Force 34, which had been organised for just such a contingency, was now detached therefore, and with his six battleships, including Halsey's flagship, seven cruisers and 17 destroyers, Admiral Lee moved out ten miles ahead of the carriers.

The error was discovered when Mitscher's first strike of 120 planes with strong fighter escort found nothing at the expected position and they were kept orbiting until, at 0710, a fresh contact reported the enemy 145 miles ahead. Ozawa had duly made rendezvous with his detached squadron under Rear-Admiral Matsuda and was steering into the fresh north-easterly breeze under a clear blue sky, calmly waiting for the nemesis he had deliberately courted. In all his carriers only 19 Zero fighters remained since the strike sent against Sherman's carrier group the day before. They were flown off when the swarm of executioners was detected approaching, to put up their pitiful resistance until shot down or their fuel ran out. After that the ships' guns remained the only defence. These put up the same impressive but strangely ineffective display as had Kurita's ships in the Sibuyan Sea, and in the battle to come, only ten of Mitscher's planes were to be lost.

At 0830 the first wave came in, directed to their target by a coordinator, Commander McCampbell of the *Essex*, dive-bombers and strafing fighters drawing the first fire away from the torpedo-planes following them in. The carrier *Chitose* was the first to be smothered in this way, the dive-bombers devastating her and leaving her blazing to go down an hour later. The remainder of the huge force of attackers achieved surprisingly little, sinking one destroyer, crippling the light cruiser *Ta ma* with a torpedo and putting a single bomb into the *Zuiho* which did no vital damage. Ozawa's flagship, the veteran *Zuikaku*, was hit by one torpedo, however, which reduced her speed to 18 knots and wrecked her steering system so that she could only be awkwardly steered manually. By the time a second strike arrived around 1000 the Japanese force was in confusion. This time it was the carrier *Chiyoda* which bore the brunt and, hit by a number of bombs, was stopped and set on fire. The carrier-battleship *Hyuga* stood by her, attempting to take her in tow.

A lull now followed during which Ozawa shifted his flag from the *Zuikaku* to the light cruiser *Oyodo*. Aboard the *New Jersey*, flagship of his opponent, Halsey, that indomitable fighter, had the bit between his teeth and visions in his mind's eye of the Japanese fleet going down before the fire of the 16-inch guns of his battleships. In fact, had he responded at once to Kinkaid's appeal for help at 0822, by taking his battleships at top speed for the entrance to the San Bernadino Strait, it is probable that he would have intercepted Kurita during the night with incalculable consequences. Instead, messages of alarm and the appeals for help put before him in quick succession between 0822 and 1000 only strengthened his determination to press on; but then came Nimitz's intervention, demanding to know the whereabouts of Task Force 34. At last he yielded to the mounting pressure and at 1115, at his orders, Task Group 38.2 plus the other four battleships of Task Force 34, turned away south and steered to the help of the 7th Fleet. It was too late. At 1700 after a delay caused by the necessity to fuel his destroyers, he sent a detachment composed of the battleships *Iowa* and *New Jersey*, three light cruisers and eight destroyers to press ahead at 28 knots. It arrived off the Strait just three hours after Kurita escaped through it.

The enemy force from which Halsey so reluctantly turned away, had become strung out with the *Zuikaku* and *Zuiho* making 18 knots, in the lead, guarded by the carrier-battleship *Ise* and destroyers, the crippled *Tama* trailing in their wake 20 miles astern. Further south were the immobilised *Chiyoda* and the *Hyuga*. The biggest strike of the day, 200 strong, which came in soon after 1300 caused the *Hyuga* to abandon the *Chiyoda* and her crew to their fate; but the majority of the planes flew on to concentrate on the main group, drawn by the magnet of the last surviving big carrier and villain of Pearl Harbour. She and the other veteran of carrier battles, the *Zuiho*, had nearly run their course. The *Zuikaku* took three torpedo hits from aircraft of the *Lexington* which finally doomed her. At 1410 she rolled over and sank. The *Zuiho* was allocated by the target co-ordinator to the *Essex*'s air group which set her ablaze with bombs; but fires were quickly extinguished and the carrier steamed on at high speed. The air group from Task Group 38.4 was now directed on to her; nevertheless it was not until 1526 that, hit again and again, she finally succumbed to her many wounds and sank. Of Ozawa's carriers only the *Chiyoda* now remained afloat, immobilised and awaiting execution, to come at about 1700 at the hands of cruisers of Task Force 38. The pursuit went on through the night but only the destroyer *Hatsuzuki* was added to the toll, caught and sunk by gunfire.

This brought to a close the action which was to be called the 'Battle off Cape Engaño' (the north-eastern corner of Luzon). Remaining to Ozawa at the end of it were the *Ise* and *Hyaga*, both of which survived countless bomb attacks with only minor damage, the light cruiser *Oyodo* and five destroyers.[13]

---

[13] The *Tama*, crawling painfully away from the battle was ambushed

The sacrificial offering of his empty carriers had nobly achieved its strategic purpose, though Kurita had failed to take advantage of it. There remains only to tell of the final efforts to destroy Kurita's force during 26 October. Two carrier task groups, McCain's Group 1 and Bogan's Group 2 combined to send massive strikes after it as it ran south between Mindoro and Tablas and on into the Sulu Sea. They succeeded only in sinking the light cruiser *Noshiro* and scoring a single bomb hit on the crippled *Kumano* which nevertheless escaped to Manila. Forty-seven Liberators of the U.S. Army Air Force attacked the battleships to the west of Panay but achieved nothing. Kurita led the *Yamato*, *Kongo* and *Nagato* and the survivors of his cruisers to Brunei Bay and thence to Japan for repairs. Only the *Yamato* was ever to go into action again when she sortied in April 1945, for a last one-way death ride to meet her end at the hands of carrier aircraft.

The Battle for Leyte, the biggest sea-fight in history, had been, from its inception, a final suicidal attempt to delay Allied victory, a monstrous 'Kamikaze' operation. Toyoda had accepted the almost certain destruction of the whole Mobile Fleet to prevent the loss of the Philippines which would cut Japan off from her southern conquests, and her only source of oil. Failure would make useless hulks of the Japanese ships, immobilised for lack of fuel. It would be better to go down fighting in the true Samurai tradition. Ozawa and Nishimura played their parts faithfully, but Kurita allowed himself to be ignominiously repulsed by the high-hearted courage of the destroyer crews and airmen of the escort carrier force. Yet perhaps 'ignominiously' is an unfair judgment. Was it incompetence or moral courage in refusing to order a profitless

---

on the following day by the submarine *Jallao* and sunk by three torpedoes.

sacrifice in lives that turned him back from Leyte Gulf? Interrogated after the war, the old Admiral did not commit himself on this point.

The other controversial figure is, of course, Bill Halsey, whose acceptance of Ozawa's bait seemed to many a nearly disastrous folly. Halsey never admitted this and S. E. Morison, author of the Official History of the *U.S. Naval Operations in World War II*, quotes the Admiral as saying that the only move in the Battle for Leyte Gulf that he regretted was calling Task Force 34 off the chase of Ozawa to go to Kinkaid's assistance. The Commander-in-Chief Pacific, Admiral Nimitz, on the other hand, in his book, *The Great Sea War*, says: 'Yet elements of both the Northern and Centre Japanese forces were able to escape because Halsey carried the main American surface strength fruitlessly north and then south through the most crucial hours of the battle, leaving inferior forces to deal with the enemy in two areas.' Thus he condemns both Halsey's failure to leave Task Force 34 behind when he ordered the carrier groups north, and the eleventh-hour reversal of his decision to keep them to complete Ozawa's annihilation. It is difficult to disagree with this indictment or to deny Ozawa great credit for successfully decoying Halsey away.

The Battle of Leyte was a decisive victory for the U.S. 3rd and 7th Fleets, encompassing the end of the Japanese Navy as a fighting force. Against a loss to the Americans of one light fleet carrier, two escort carriers, two destroyers and one destroyer escort can be set the Japanese loss of three battleships, one large carrier, three light carriers, six heavy cruisers, four light cruisers and nine destroyers. It can be argued that the battle had, in fact, been already won by the massacre of Japanese naval air power at the Battle of the Philippine Sea and during the great air battles brought on by the 3rd Fleet's raids on Luzon, Formosa and Okinawa between 10-12 October. Nevertheless the Japanese Navy had never previously suffered clear-cut defeat in surface action as occurred in the Surigao Strait even before the superior strength of Oldendorf's battleships and cruisers joined in to turn defeat into massacre, and as occurred off Samar when a handful of destroyers held off Kurita's powerful fleet long enough for air power to intervene. These defeats were necessary to temper the overweening contempt of Japanese sailors for their opponents which might otherwise have survived to foster a dangerous legend of invincibility.

From now on the U.S. Fleet roamed at will, joined soon by the British Pacific Fleet, striking ever closer to the heart of Japan, opposed only by a dwindling shore-based force of ill-trained airmen which could only hit back by means of desperate Kamikaze attacks. There were still, it is true, many months of hard fighting ahead, on land and in the air, and it would be necessary eventually to use the appalling mass destruction of the atomic bomb in order to break down the Japanese inability to contemplate surrender. Yet the Allied victory had been assured from the time the Japanese Fleet was eliminated.

APPENDIX I: OPPOSING FLEETS AT THE RATTLE OF THE PHILIPPINE SEA

19-20 June, 1944

United States Navy — Fifth Fleet
Commander-in-Chief, Admiral Raymond A. Spruance,
Indianapolis

TASK FORCE 58

Commander, Vice-Admiral M. A. Mitscher, *Lexington*

TANK GROUP 58.1 Rear-Admiral J. J. Clark

Fleet carriers: *Hornet, Yorktown*

Light fleet carriers: *Belleau Wood, Bataan*

Cruisers: *Boston, Baltimore, Canberra*

Light cruisers (AA): *San Juan, Oakland*

14 destroyers

TASK GROUP 58.2 Rear-Admiral A. E. Montgomery

Fleet carriers: *Bunker Hill, Wasp*

Light fleet carriers: *Monterey, Cabot*

Light cruisers: *Santa Fe, Mobile, Biloxi*

12 destroyers

TASK GROUP 58.3 Rear-Admiral J. W. Reeves

Fleet carriers: *Enterprise, Lexington*

Light fleet carriers: *San Jacinto, Princeton*

Cruiser: *Indianapolis*

Light cruisers (AA): *Reno, Montpelier, Cleveland, Birmingham*

13 destroyers

TASK GROUP 58.4 Rear-Admiral W. K. Harrill
Fleet carrier: *Essex*
Light fleet carriers: *Langley, Cowpens*
Light cruiser (AA): *San Diego*
Light cruisers: *Vincennes, Houston, Miami*
14 destroyers

TANK GROUP 58.7 Vice-Admiral W. A. Lee
Battleships: *Washington, North Carolina, Iowa, New Jersey, South Dakota, Alabama, Indiana*
Cruisers: *Wichita, Minneapolis, New Orleans, San Francisco*

Imperial Japanese Navy — First Mobile Fleet
Commander-in-Chief, Vice-Admiral Jisaburo Ozawa, *Taiho*
VAN FORCE Vice-Admiral Kurita, *Atago*
Light fleet carriers: *Chitose, Chiyado, Zuiho*
Battleships: *Yamato, Musashi, Haruna, Kongo*
Cruisers: *Atago, Takao, Maya, Chokai*
9 destroyers

FORCE A Vice-Admiral Ozawa, *Taiho*
Fleet carriers: *Taiho, Shokaku, Zuikaku*
Cruisers: *Myoko, Haguro*
Light cruiser: *Yahagi*
9 destroyers

FORCE B Rear-Admiral Joshima
Fleet carriers: *Junyo, Hiyo*
Light fleet carrier: *Ryuho*
Battleship: *Nagato*
Cruiser: *Mogami*
10 destroyers

APPENDIX II: OPPOSING FLEETS AT THE BATTLE OF LEYTE GULF

23-26 October, 1944

United States Navy — Third Fleet Commander-in-Chief,
Admiral W. F. Halsey, Jr.
New Jersey

TASK FORCE 38
First Carrier Task Force Pacific Fleet
Commander, Vice-Admiral M. A. Mitscher, *Lexington*

TASK GROUP 38.1 Vice-Admiral J. S. McCain
Carriers: *Wasp, Hornet, Hancock*
Light carriers: *Monterey, Cowpens*
Cruisers: *Chester, Salt Lake City, Pensacola*
Light cruisers (AA): *Oakland, San Diego*
13 destroyers

TASK GROUP 38.2 Rear-Admiral G. F. Bogan
Carrier: *Intrepid*
Light carriers: *Cabot, Independence*
Battleships: *Iowa, New Jersey*
Light cruisers: *Vincennes, Biloxi, Miami*
16 destroyers

TASK GROUP 38.3 Rear-Admiral F. C. Sherman
Carriers: *Essex, Lexington*
Light carriers: *Langley, Princeton*
Battleships: *Massachusetts, South Dakota*

Light cruisers: *Santa Fe, Mobile, Birmingham*
Light cruiser (AA): *Reno*
15 destroyers

TASK GROUP 38.4 Rear-Admiral R. E. Davison
Carriers: *Franklin, Enterprise*
Light carriers: *San Jacinto, Belleau Wood*
Cruisers: *New Orleans, Wichita*
13 destroyers

TASK FORCE 34
Heavy Striking Force: Formed 0430 25 October
Commander, Vice-Admiral W. A. Lee, Jr, *Washington*
TASK GROUP 34.1 Battle Line: Vice-Admiral W. A. Lee
Task Unit 34.1.1 (Bat. Div. 7): *Iowa, New Jersey*
Task Unit 34.1.2 (Bat. Div. 8): *Massachusetts, Washington*
Task Unit 34.1.3 (Bat. Div. 9): *South Dakota, Alabama*

TASK GROUP 34.2: Right Flank; Rear-Admiral F. E. M. Whiting
Task Unit 34.2.2. (Cru. Div. 14): *Vincennes* (flagship), *Miami, Biloxi*
Task Units 34.2.3, 34.2.4: 8 destroyers

TASK GROUP 34.3: Centre; Rear-Admiral C. T. Joy
Task Unit 34.3.1 (Cru. Div. 6): (flagship), *New Orleans*
Task Unit 34.3.3: 4 destroyers

TASK GROUP 34.4: Left Flank; Rear-Admiral L. T. Du Bose
Task Unit 34.4.2 (Cru. Div. 13): *Santa Fe* (flagship), *Mobile*
Task Unit 34.4.3: 6 destroyers

United States Navy — Seventh Fleet
Commander-in-Chief, Vice-Admiral T. C. Kincaid
Wasatch

TASK FORCE 77
Covering Force
Commander, Vice-Admiral T. C. Kincaid

TASK GROUP 77.2: Fire Support and Bombardment Group, Rear-Admiral J. B. Oldendorf, *Louisville*

Battle Line: Rear-Admiral G. L. Weyler

Battleships: *Mississippi* (flagship), *Maryland*, *West Virginia*, *Tennessee*, *California*, *Pennsylvania*

Destroyers: *Aulick, Cony, Sigourney, Claxton, Thorn, Welles*

Left Flank Force: Rear-Admiral J. B. Oldendorf

Heavy cruisers: *Louisville* (flagship), *Portland*, *Minneapolis*

Light cruisers: *Denver* (flagship), *Columbia*

Destroyers: *Newcomb, Leutze, Bennion, Heywood L. Edwards, Richard P. Leary, Robinson, Albert W. Grant, Bryant, Halford*

TANK GROUP 77.3: Close Covering Group, Rear-Admiral R. S. Berkey, *Phoenix*

Right Flank Force

Light cruisers: *Phoenix* (flagship), *Boise*

Heavy cruiser: H.M.A.S. *Shropshire*

Destroyers: *Hutchins, Bache, Daly, Beale, Killen,* H.M.A.S. *Arunta*

SPECIAL ATTACK GROUP 79.11
Eastern Attack Group —
Destroyers: *Remey, McGowan, Melvin*

Western Attack Group —
Destroyers: *Monssen, McDermut*
Patrol — Destroyers: *McNair, Mertz*

PANAON CARRIER -GROUP 77.4.1

77.4.11 Escort Carriers: *Sangamon* (flagship), *Suwannee, Santee, Chenango*

77.4.12: *Saginaw Bay* (flagship of Rear-Admiral G. R. Henderson), *Petrof Bay*

77.4.13 Screen —

Destroyers: *McCord, Trathen, Hazelwood*

Destroyer escorts: *Richard S. Bull, Richard M. Rowell, Eversole*

SOUTHERN CARRIER GROUP 77.4.2: Rear-Admiral F. B. Stump

77.4.21 Escort Carriers: *Natona Bay* (flagship of Rear-Admiral F. B. Stump), *Manila Bay*

77.4.22: *Marcus Island* (flagship of Rear-Admiral W. T. Sample), *Kadashan Bay, Savo Island, Omnamey Bay*

77.4.23 Screen —

Destroyers: *Haggard, Franks, Hailey*

Destroyer Escorts: *Richard W. Suesens, Abercrombie, Leray Wilson, Walter C. Wann*

NORTHERN CARRIER GROUP 77.4.3: Rear-Admiral C. A. F. Sprague

77.4.31 Escort carriers: *Fanshaw Bay* (flagship of Rear-Admiral C.A.F. Sprague), *St Lo, White Plains, Kalinin Bay*

77.4.32: *Kitkum Bay* (flagship of Rear-Admiral R. A. Oftsie), *Gambier Bay*

77.4.33 Screen —

Destroyers: *Hoel, Heerman, Johnston*

Destroyer escorts: *Dennis, John C. Butler, Raymond, Samuel B. Roberts*

Imperial Japanese Navy Commander-in-Chief, Vice-Admiral S. Toyoda

CARRIER FORCE Vice-Admiral J. Ozawa

Aircraft carrier: *Zuikaku* (Fighters: 52, Fighter-bombers: 28)

Light carriers: *Chitose* (Torpedo-bombers: 25), *Chiyoda* (Bombers: 7), *Zuiho* (Attack torpedo-aircraft: 4, Float reconnaissance aircraft: 2)

Battleship-carriers: *Hyuga, Ise*

Light cruisers: *Tama, Oyoda, Isuzu*

Destroyers: *Hatsuyuki, Wakatsuki, Akitsuki, Shimotsuki, Kuwa, Maki, Sugi, Kiri*

FORCE A: Vice-Admiral T. Kurita

Battleships: *Yamato, Musashi, Nagato, Kongo, Haruna*

Cruisers: *Atago, Takao, Maya, Chokai, Myoka, Haguro, Kumano, Suzuya, Chikuma, Tone*

Light cruisers: *Noshiro, Yahagi*

Destroyers: *Hayashimo, Akishimo, Asashimo, Kishinami, Okinami, Naganami, Hamanami, Fujinami, Shimakaze, Isokaze, Urakaze, Hamakaze, Yukikaze, Kiyoshimo, Nowake*

FORCE C: Vice-Admiral S. Nishimura

Battleships: *Yamishiro, Fuso*

Cruisers: *Mogami*

Destroyers: *Michishio, Yamaguro, Asagumo, Shigure*

2nd STRIKING FORCE Vice-Admiral K. Shima

Cruisers: *Nachi, Ashigara*

Light cruiser: *Abukuma*

Destroyers: *Shiranuhi, Kasumi, Usho, Akebono*

APPENDIX III: AMERICAN AND JAPANESE CARRIER AIRCRAFT

AMERICAN

Douglas TBD-1 — Standard U.S. Torpedo-Plane.
Code Name: 'Devastator'
Engine: Air-cooled Radial — 850 h.p.
Speed: 206 m.p.h.
Range: 455 miles (with torpedo)
Load: 1,000-lb. bombs or 1 torpedo
Crew: 3

Grumman TBF — Standard U.S. Torpedo-Plane (Replaced Devastator)
Code Name: 'Avenger'
Engine: Air-cooled Radial — 1,700 h.p.
Speed: 271 m.p.h.
Range: 1,215 miles with torpedo, 1,450 miles as scout
Load: 2,000-lb. bombs or 1 torpedo
Crew: 3

Douglas SBD — Carrier Scout/Dive-Bomber
Code Name: 'Dauntless'
Engine: Air-cooled Radial — 1,000 or 1,200 h.p.
Speed: 250 or 252 m.p.h.
Load: 1,345 miles, or 1,115 miles with 1,000-lb. bombs
Crew: 2

Grumman F4F — Naval Fighter
Code Name: 'Wildcat'

Engine: Air-cooled Radial — 1,200 h.p.
Speed: 330 m.p.h.
Range: 845 miles normal — 1,690 miles maximum
Climb: 3,650 feet in 1 minute
Crew: 1

Grumman F6F — *Naval Fighter* (*Replaced 'Wildcat'*)
Code Name: 'Hellcat'
Engine: Air-cooled Radial — 2,000 h.p.
Speed: m.p.h.
Range: 1,090 miles normal, 1,590 miles maximum
Climb: 3,500 feet in 1 minute
Crew: 1

JAPANESE

Nakajima Type 97 — *Carrier-Based Attack Plane*
Code Name: 'Kate'
Engine: Air-cooled Radial — 770 or 1,000 h.p.
Speed: 217 or 235 m.p.h.
Range: 683 miles
Load: 1,764-lb. bombs or 1 torpedo
Crew: 3

Aichi Type 99 — *Carrier-Borne Dive-Bomber*
Code Name: 'Val'
Engine: Air-Cooled Radial — 1,000 or 1,300 h.p.
Speed: 240 or 267 m.p.h.
Range: 572 or 839 miles
Load: 882-lb. bombs

Yokosuka Naval Air Depot D4Y — *Carrier-Borne Dive-Bomber*
Code Name: 'Judy' (Replaced 'Val')

Engine: Air-cooled Radial or water-cooled in line (Mk. 2) 1,400 h.p.

Speed: 360 m.p.h.

Range: 943 miles

Load: 1,102-lb. bombs

Crew: 2

Mitsubishi Type 'o' — Naval Fighter (Zero)

Code Name: 'Zeke'

Engine: Air-cooled Radial — 1,130 h.p.

Speed: 351 m.p.h.

Range: 1,500 miles

Climb: 19,685 feet in 7 minutes

Crew: 1

APPENDIX IV: TORPEDOES

The most important single weapon in the naval battles of the Pacific War was undoubtedly the torpedo in its several varieties. Torpedoes wreaked the greatest havoc amongst the U.S. battleships at Pearl Harbour, they sank the *Prince of Wales* and *Repulse*, as well as the Dutch cruisers at the Battle of the Java Sea. Although it was bombs which won the Battle of Midway, on almost every other occasion when the Japanese and American Fleets met in battle it was torpedoes which struck the decisive blows. Torpedoes sank the two most powerful battleships in the world, *Yamato* and *Musashi*. American seamen and naval aviators complained, not without justification, until a late stage of the war, that their torpedoes were unreliable and ineffective.

A torpedo's effectiveness depends upon three main factors:

(a) reliability of its propelling machinery and guiding mechanisms;

(b) performance, i.e. speed and range;

(c) effectiveness of its warhead.

Though the type of American torpedo supplied for use by surface ships, submarines or aircraft in each case differed in many respects, the basic principle on which its propelling machinery operated was the same — turbines for which the steam was generated by forcing a spray of water through an alcohol torch. Direction was controlled by a gyroscope, depth by a hydrostatic valve, level running by a pendulum connected to horizontal rudders. Detonation of the warhead in every type could be effected either by impact with the target or by magnetic influence when passing under it.

The type issued to U.S. surface ships was the Mark 15, a rugged and relatively reliable performer with a warhead containing 500 lb. of T.N.T. and with three alternative speed and range settings — 28 knots to 15,000 yards, 34 knots to 10,000 yards, 46 knots to 6,000 yards. This performance, compared to that of the Japanese 'Long Lances', might have been expected to evoke complaints had their existence been known. These remarkable weapons, which utilised liquid oxygen as their propellant, had been under development since 1922, and by 1938 all Japanese destroyers and cruisers were fitted with them and carried reloads up to half the number of available tubes. Twenty-four inches in circumference, as compared to the 21 inches of all other navies, they carried a warhead twice the size of that on American torpedoes, at 36 knots for 22 miles (44,000 yards) or at 49 knots for 11 miles (22,000 yards).

It was difficult to gauge the effectiveness of torpedoes fired in surface actions, especially by night, and it was not until post-war analysis could be made that the failure of many of those fired from American destroyers could be deduced. The causes of failure were then ascribed to the same defects as had been discovered in the torpedoes issued to submarines, where the faulty runs and detonation failures were immediately evident. These defects were numerous and various, with one masking another so that it was not until one type of failure was rectified that the other revealed itself. The torpedoes ran as much as ten feet deeper than their settings; the magnetic exploder was unreliable, either failing altogether or actuating prematurely; the contact exploder failed; the distance run before the warhead 'armed' itself was too long; if the warhead was correctly detonated, it appeared to lack punch. These defects were still being ironed out when electric torpedoes, copied from German models, began to supersede the steam Mark 14 torpedo in submarines.

The American airborne torpedo, the Mark 13, with which the U.S. Navy entered the war, apart from the fact it could not be dropped from a height greater than 60 feet or at a speed greater than 115 knots, went through a cycle of troubles similar to the Mark 14; and, when efforts were made to adapt it for higher launching speed and height, the problem of achieving stabilisation during its flight through the air proved for a long time insoluble. Analysis of 105 drops at more than 150 knots in mid-1943 revealed that 36 per cent ran cold, 20 per cent sank, 20 per cent had faulty deflection, 18 per cent unsatisfactory depth, while only 31 per cent ran satisfactorily. It was not until the autumn of 1944 that modifications to the Mark 13, in the shape of a 'drag-ring' attached to the torpedo head to provide air stabilisation and a 'shroud-ring' round the rudders to improve underwater steadiness, at last produced a torpedo of proven reliability.

SELECT BIBLIOGRAPHY

Fuchida, Matsuo and Okumiya, Masatake, *Midway*, Hutchinson & Co. Ltd.

Ito, Masanori, *The End of the Imperial Japanese Navy*, Weidenfeld & Nicolson

Lord, Walter, *Day of Infamy*, Longmans, Green & Co. Ltd.

MacArthur, Douglas (General of the Army), *Reminiscences*, William Heinemann Ltd.

Morison, S. E., *History of U.S. Naval Operations in World War II*, Little, Brown & Co.

Newcomb, Richard F., *Savo*, Holt, Rinehart and Winston

Nimitz, Chester W. (Fleet Admiral) and Potter, E. B., *The Great Sea War*, George G. Harrap & Co. Ltd.

Okumiya, Masatake and Horikoshi, Jiro, *Zero!*, Cassell & Co. Ltd.

Sakai, Saburo, *Samurai*, Ballantyne Books

Wohlsetter, Roberta, *Pearl Harbor*, Stanford University Press

Woodward, C. V., *The Battle for Leyte Gulf*, MacMillan Co., N.Y.

Potter, E. B. and Nimitz, Chester W., *The Great Sea War*, U.S. Naval Institute, Annapolis, Md. 1960

Hara, Tameichi, *Japanese Destroyer Captain*, translated by F. Saito and R. Pineau, New York 1961

Humble, Richard, *Japanese High Seas Fleet*, Ballantine Books 1973

Macintyre, Donald, *Leyte Gulf*, Ballantine Books 1970

Inoguchi, R, Nakajima, T, and Pineau, R, *The Divine Wind*, U.S. Naval Institute, Annapolis

Field, James A., Jnr., *The Japanese at Leyte*, Princeton University Press

Coox, Alvin D., *The Fall of Japan*, Ballantine Books
Macintyre, Donald, *Aircraft Carrier*, Ballantine Books
Caidin, Martin, *Zero*, Ballantine Books

ACKNOWLEDGMENT

Acknowledgment is due to the authors and publishers of the following books for permission to quote from them: *Samurai* by Saluro Sakai (Ballantyne Books Inc.) and *Zero!* by Masatake Okumiya and Jiro Horikoshi (Cassell & Co. Ltd. and E. P. Dutton and Co. Inc.).

A NOTE TO THE READER

If you have enjoyed this book enough to leave a review on **Amazon** and **Goodreads**, then we would be truly grateful.
Sapere Books

Sapere Books is an exciting new publisher of brilliant fiction and popular history.

To find out more about our latest releases and our monthly bargain books visit our website:
saperebooks.com

Printed in Dunstable, United Kingdom